LEADERSHIP

WHAT THE BIBLE SAYS SERIES

WHAT THE BIBLE SAYS ABOUT

LEADERSHIP

Arthur Harrington

College Press Publishing Company, Joplin, Missouri

Printed and bound in the
United States of America

Library of Congress Catalog Card Number: 85-072670
International Standard Book Number: 0-89900-250-1

DEDICATED

to the memory of my father,

Horace E. Harrington

who exemplified church leadership.

Table of Contents

PREFACE

The longer I serve as a consultant to churches in the area of church leadership development, the more aware I become of the magnitude of the crisis confronting us in the majority of our churches today. As I have worked with church leaders and have studied the problems we are experiencing in the accomplishment of our mission, I have become increasingly convinced that the answers to our dilemma lie within the Scriptures. We have tried just about everything except God's plan for the church. Tragically, most of our churches do not even realize that their leadership concepts are not biblical. There has never been a more urgent necessity than exists today for rediscovering and restoring that divine plan for the church.

Consequently, the efforts expended in writing this volume are intended to accomplish far more than merely satisfying the curiosity of readers about what the Bible has to say on the subject of leadership. It is my fervent hope and prayer that the Biblical exegesis and historical perspective reflected in this book may in some way serve as catalysts to help ignite a new fervor to restore New Testament faith and practice in all things—especially in the area of church leadership.

I am deeply indebted to the many church leaders who have shared with me their experience and insights. They have been most helpful. I am also grateful to the California Graduate School of Theology for their permission to use material included in my doctoral dissertation, *The Historical Development of the Concept of Leadership in the Restoration Movement*. Finally, I am most appreciative of the support and encouragement of the leadership of the United Christian Youth Camp in this project. They are solidly committed to the concept of making the primary ministry of the camp one of developing leadership for the churches.

I do not begin to have all of the answers. I am still studying and learning. I would urge you to cast off any preconceptions and traditions you may have concerning church leadership, and to join me in taking a fresh new look at this subject which is so vital to the accomplishment of our God-given mission as Christians.

—Art Harrington

1

A CRISIS IN THE CHURCH

Understanding the Crisis

John was everyone's choice to succeed. Bright, multi-talented, personable and good-looking, he was brought up in the church, made his own commitment to Christ at a young age, and soon became the spark plug which ignited his church youth group. He was active in everything at church, in addition to his many extra-curricular involvements at school. Challenged during high school to consider the ministry as his calling in life, he made his decision one summer at a Christian camp to enter a Bible college and to prepare for the pastoral ministry. Camp and church leaders encouraged him, and Bible college recruiters began pursuing him.

Bible college proved to be an exciting, challenging and growing time for John. He was thrilled by his daily discoveries in God's Word and was gripped with a sense of urgency about the need to fulfil the church's mission in a world which desperately needed Christ. He could hardly wait until the day when he would finish his course of study and be able to devote his fulltime energies to leading a church in the accomplishment of that mission. In the meantime, he served part-time as a youth minister for a nearby church, wrote for the school newspaper and was elected student body president. Church, camp and college leaders increasingly nodded with approval and pride. This boy would do all right! There was no doubt about it. He was the cream of the crop.

Commencement finally came for John. With two degrees now under his belt, he was aware that he did not know everything; but he was more than ready to tackle his first fulltime church leadership responsibility. The church was delighted to have called such an obvious prize, and John and his family were welcomed with open arms. Enthusiasm abounded over the personable new minister, and attendance grew in the services as members invited friends and relatives to come and hear this fine young minister.

All appeared to be going well until the honeymoon suddenly ended. John seemed to be serious about some changes which would have to be made if the church were to keep growing. He was becoming frustrated over the constant delays, bottlenecks and outright resistance he encountered whenever he attempted to launch a new program for more effective ministry or outreach. His popularity began to wear thin. Criticism began to rise about the length of his sermons, the use of his time, the conduct of his family, the amount of time he spent with the youth, the lack of his calls on members and his apparent preference for the "new people" over the old. John's wife was growing increasingly sensitive to the criticisms and disenchanted with life in the fishbowl, particularly since she was so acutely aware of the long hours John worked and the erratic schedule he kept in attempting to conscientiously minister to everyone. She knew his commitment to serve the Lord and to lead the church.

It was becoming more obvious to John every day, though, that the church had not intended to call a leader. They wanted a performer. As long as his performance could draw a crowd, bring in enough in offerings to pay the bills and keep everyone happy, he was welcome to stay. Any significant changes in the church's program or personnel, however, would never be tolerated. They could be stalled in committee indefinitely. The harder John tried to press ahead, the more resolute the entrenched leadership became. Dissention in the church began to grow. Attendance began to decline, and the offerings gradually dwindled. Subtle hints turned into outright declarations: it was time to get a new preacher!

John's spirits sagged. He had tried so hard! He had approached this ministry with such high hopes. He had been so sure that God wanted him in the ministry and that God had called him to this church. What had gone wrong? Maybe he had misunderstood God's call to the ministry in the first place? He seriously considered moving to another church, but if he could not succeed where he was, how could he expect to do any better elsewhere? God knew that he had given this work his best! Finally, beaten and burned-out, John submitted his resignation with a sense of complete defeat, and he left the ministry. Today John is a successful insurance executive. The church is still swapping preachers every year or two, and its membership has declined.

George is a 30-year veteran in the ministry. Although he is a man of moderate talents, he does everything in the church—and the church lets him. The congregation is not lacking for officers, though. Almost every member with any seniority has at least one title and a couple of committee memberships. In fact, there are so many titular "chiefs" that there are few left in the church to be "Indians." That is why they hired George. He could spend fulltime taking care of things. So they leave it all to George to do. George sort of likes it that way, even though he complains about being over-worked and underpaid. George leads the worship, does the preaching, teaches the adults and the youth (if any happen to come), types up the worship bulletin and the church newsletter, tidies up the buildings and grounds, calls on the sick and visits in the homes whenever he can. George's wife plays the piano for the services, teaches the children and runs the women's society.

Not long ago George celebrated his 30th anniversary in the ministry. Of course he and his wife had to plan the affair and invite the other churches. George naturally served as the master of ceremonies for the occasion and recounted the highlights of his sixteen ministries. The chairman of the church board was on hand to present the commemorative plaque at the appropriate moment, and George's wife served refreshments afterwards to all who had gathered. George just recently moved on to his 17th ministry in another part of the country, and the church is still looking for another George.

Harold is the super-gifted senior minister of one of the largest and fastest-growing churches in the country. He is known internationally, and his calendar is booked years in advance with speaking dates. His success story is documented in his best-selling book. His opinion is sought by the leading journals and by all of the church growth specialists, and the annual clinic he and his staff host at First Church is designed to teach anyone who comes the secrets of his successful formula for building a church.

At First Church Harold is recognized as the empire builder. He rules the roost. His decisions are final. He hires and fires the staff, as well as setting their salaries. They work for him and answer to him. Harold believes himself to be God's man for the time, called to provide leadership and to set a course for the church. He does have an advisory board in the church, but they serve mainly to ratify and to help implement Harold's recommendations.

Numbers and buildings dominate Harold's agenda and goals for his church. He is an excellent motivator, a gifted organizer and a superb administrator. His staff is one of the best in the country, all hand-picked. Both they and the members at First Church are proud to have a man of Harold's reputation and ability in the driver's seat. There is no doubt that the church will continue to grow under Harold's leadership. Some may disagree with him from time to time, but they are welcome to leave.

The stories of John, George and Harold are each representative of leadership styles evidenced in the church today. Most church members and leaders can personally identify with one or more of these stories from their own experience. Sadly, each of these leadership styles represents a departure from the picture painted of church leadership in the New Testament, and each is contributing in part to the aggregate crisis facing the church today.

Consider the story of John. Here was a man who honestly believed that God had specially gifted him and had called him to the ministry and church leadership. He responded to that perceived call with a commitment which included years of his life and thousands of dollars to educationally equip himself for that ministry. But John, like so many other bright, talented and committed young leaders encountered, after that brief "honeymoon" period, a concept of leadership by committee. In this system, church leadership is equated with representative government. Leaders are elected to offices, given terms and tenure, and are expected to reflect the preferences of those who have elected them whenever they meet together to make decisions for the church. Meeting as "Church Boards" or "Official Boards," these officers generally conceive leadership to consist almost entirely of an advice and consent function of attending meetings and voting on issues. These decisions rendered by the board are then expected to be carried out by the minister or some other church employee. Directives from the Scriptures are generally subordinated to provisions in the By-Laws or the Articles of Incorporation, or to the prevailing mood of the congregation and its elected representatives. Whatever knowledge of the Bible, insights, experience or expertise the pastor may have are generally ignored by the leaders in such a system, particularly if they call for change.

Someone has humorously observed that a camel is really a horse which had the misfortune of being designed by a committee. Another has pointed out that there is probably no quicker way to frustrate or to kill any idea or venture than to appoint a committee to study it. These observations unfortunately reflect the sad plight of any church which must find its leadership and direction solely through the operation of a committee. It also accounts for the frustrations and premature "burn-out" experienced by an alarming percentage of young ministers, which leads to their early exodus from the ministry. Few Bible college graduates who have been out of school at least ten years can now find even half of their classmates still engaged in fulltime ministry. The drop-out rate has reached epidemic proportions, and the loss and waste is an enormous tragedy for the church.

George, though, has learned to cope in the ministry. He realizes that most small churches simply want a short-term performer. They leave it all to George, and George puts up with it until it is time to move on to greener pastures. When it comes to changing things or trying to challenge and equip a scriptural leadership within the church, George gave up on that a long time ago. When conflict and disenchantment eventually arise, George recognizes them as signals to move along. Of course, George moves a lot; and the churches are no better off after he leaves than they were before he came.

There are a lot of Georges in the ministry today. Estimates of the average length of ministry range between 18 and 24 months. Of course, the grass is seldom greener over the next hill, and churches left behind rarely benefit in any significant way from the experience of their brief relationship. Nothing lasting is ever built, and almost everyone loses in a short ministry.

Harold, on the other hand, intends to be around for a long time. He is convinced of his call and his ability to lead, and there is no way he intends to allow any committee or individual to derail him from his chosen track. Let others fall by the wayside; he will both survive and succeed. If he must, Harold will even go "independent" of everyone else with his church in order to escape all ties that bind and any perceived challenges to his leadership. Rapid growth and super-size make for influence and security of position. Critics and challengers beware!!

Not every pastor or preacher is a gifted super-star like Harold, though. And what happens when Harold makes a mistake, or when Harold is wrong? Might does not always make for right. Is any man that good? Where are the divinely-designed checks and balances to protect the church and Harold from himself? Can anyone raise a warning or a criticism without being cast out and run over by Harold's express?

Of such as the Johns, the Georges and the Harolds is made the crisis and the plight of the church today. Having lost sight of New Testament leadership, the church is beset with countless counterfeit models. As a result, almost every major Christian denomination is declining in both membership and influence, and the Christian Churches have fallen into some of the same traps.

The Roots of a Movement

Many within the Christian Churches today regard the developments within their Restoration Movement to be somehow exclusive and unique. Nothing could be further from the truth. In fact, such a movement to restore the church of the New Testament in faith and practice cannot be understood or fully appreciated apart from at least a cursory examination of the developments in church leadership prior to its inception.

The Development of a Hierarchy. Up until the last half of the second century there is no evidence of any church hierarchy. Each congregation was autonomous and selected its own leadership. Gunnar Westin says:

> This polity was prominent among the local Christian assemblies long into the second century. Bishops and elders . . . made up the leadership, and there was no clear mark of distinction between them. The suggestion is not valid that the elders and the bishops in the local congregations obtained

> a sacramental position similar to priests and mystagogues within Judaism and the heathen religions. It is natural that elders and bishops exercised leadership in matters of doctrine and also in the baptismal ceremony and the observance of the Lord's Supper. This was, however, a matter of organization within the local churches. These leaders did not have the designation which was common to the priesthood, nor at this period is it possible to find the use of the altar or any direct influence of Temple worship.[1]

Even though locally autonomous and independent, the churches enjoyed a close association and relationship to one another. The writings of the era, including the First Epistle of Clement of Rome (95 or 96), Polycarp's letter to the Philippians, and the Ignatian epistles to the churches of Asia Minor (during the first part of the second century), all followed Paul's example of directing letters to the local assemblies, rather than to any bishop or superintendent.[2] Justin Martyr in his *Apology* gives the following interesting account (around 150) of congregational function within this period:

> On the day called Sunday, all who live in cities or in the country gather together in one place, and the memoirs of the apostles or the writings of the prophets are read for so long as time permits. Then, when the reader has ceased, the overseer instructs us by word of mouth, exhorting us to put these good things into practice. Then we all rise together and pray.[3]

---

1. Gunnar Westin, *The Free Church Through the Ages,* trans. by Virgil A. Olson (Nashville: Broadman Press, 1958), p. 3.
2. Westin, p. 4.
3. Westin, p. 6.

From his writings and others we learn that the observance of the Lord's Supper followed that part of the services each Sunday. While the primary meeting of the church was on Sunday, in commemoration of Jesus' resurrection, the church did meet also at other times to minister to the various needs of the members and to preach the gospel.

By the end of the second century, however, the concept of leadership within the churches had begun to evolve and find expression in different forms. Whereas the presbyter (elder) or bishop had been initially regarded as a position of leadership within each church, an office of bishop began to emerge, with the bishop being regarded as superior to the elder. At first he was only the bishop of a single church. With the growth of influence of the large city churches, as they sent out preachers and organized churches in adjacent areas, the bishops came to exercise a regional authority on the basis of their office in the maternal city of that territory. Rome, for example, was regarded as the mother church of the churches of Italy. With its position grew the perception of certain rights and privileges. Irenaeus (about 130-190) regarded the church as an organic unity whose doctrine had been handed through a succession of bishops. McGiffert writes:

> Irenaeus was the first so far as we know to appeal to it in support of episcopal infallibility. According it his theory the bishops were not ordinary officials chosen by the people and responsible to them; they owed their appointment to the Apostles, by regular succession from the original appointees, and possessed an authority quite independent of the churches over which they ruled. They were bishops by divine right and were subject to no control except that of the collective episcopate speaking in synods and councils.[4]

4. Arthur Cushman McGiffert, *A History of Christian Thought,* Vol. 1 (New York: Charles Scribner's Sons, 1954), p. 161.

Bishops of the larger cities exercised the power to convene and preside over these synods or councils as chief bishops. The councils of bishops then claimed the authority to rule in matters of faith and practice, to determine the extent of the canon of the Scripture, and to form a creed which would be binding on the churches. With the acceptance of the principles espoused by Irenaeus, those who disagreed with the councils could be branded as heretics and excluded from the churches. Upon this principle the Roman Catholic Church was built.

The chief bishop was empowered to enforce the decrees of these councils. Six of these high dignitaries evolved—one each in Rome, Antioch, Jerusalem, Alexandria, Ephesus and Corinth. These became known as metropolitan bishops. As early as the latter part of the second century the *Clementine Homilies* advanced the idea of Peter as the bishop of Rome. This became the foundation used to support the recognition of the primacy of the Roman church and its chief pastor.[5] Westin adds:

> It was during this period that the bishop at Rome began to issue statements implying that he was the head of the churches. With the development of this centralized authority there was pressure on the congregations and the various church groups to accept a standard of orthodoxy in matters of doctrine as well as polity. The so-called ancient Catholic Church arose from this situation, and it was supplemented by the Judaistic ideas of officials and offerings, the Roman juridical concepts, and the practical needs for church authority.[6]

---

5. John F. Rowe, *History of Reformatory Movements* (Cincinnati: G. W. Rice, Publisher, 1884), p. 14.
6. Westin, p. 6.

Consequently, the Roman episcopate did dominate the church by the beginning of the third century, although its authority was not universally accepted by any means.

Up until the fourth century Christianity existed as an illegal religion in the Roman Empire. From the days of Nero in 64 to the time of Constantine in 306 waves of persecution lapped against the church, one after another. No one knows the actual number of disciples whose lives were taken by being burned at the stake, crucified, beheaded, buried alive, fed to the lions, or having their bodies torn apart. It is safe to estimate, however, that well over one hundred thousand paid for their faith with their lives during this period of history. With Constantine's succession as the Roman Emperor, and his dramatic conversion to Christianity in 312, a new era dawned for the church. His Edict of Milan in 313 was an edict of official toleration, making Christianity for the first time one of the legal religions of the empire. Had he stopped at that point, the church might have flourished. In 323, however, he proceeded to make it the state religion.[7]

Historians will long debate whether Constantine's marriage of the church and the state was a matter of principle or simply an expedient political decision, attempting to win Christian support and to use the vehicle of the church and its growing structure and power to advance his own career. In fact, this unholy marriage ushered in the period of history known as the Dark Ages. E. H. Broadbent explains why:

> The Roman world had reached its greatest power and glory. Civilization had attained to the utmost of which it was capable apart from the knowledge of God. Yet the misery

7. Albert Henry Newman, *A Manual of Church History,* Vol. 1 (Philadelphia: The American Baptist Publishing Society, 1933), p. 252.

> of the world was extreme. The luxury and vice of the rich were boundless; a vast proportion of the people were slaves. The public exhibitions, where the sight of every kind of wickedness and cruelty amused the population, deepened the degradation. There was still vigour at the extremities of the Empire, in conflict with surrounding enemies, but disease at the heart threatened the life of the whole body, and Rome was helplessly corrupt and vicious.
>
> As long as the Church had remained separate it had been a powerful witness for Christ in the world, and was constantly drawing converts into its holy fellowship. When, however, already weakened by the adoption of human rule in the place of the guidance of the Spirit, it was suddenly brought into partnership with the State, it became itself defiled and debased. Very soon the clergy were competing for lucrative positions and for power as shamelessly as the court officials, while, in congregations where a godless element predominated, the material advantages of a profession of Christianity changed the purity of the persecuted churches into worldliness. The church was thus powerless to stem the downward course of the civilized world into corruption.[8]

Development of the hierarchy continued. M. M. Davis notes that the patriarchate, an office higher than the metropolitan, was created, with these patriarchs given the power to consecrate all bishops and to have general supervision of all spiritual matters, including being the final court of appeal.[9] In fact, the church's hierarchy became the counterpart of civil government. As Constantine divided the empire into four praetorian prefectures, so the decree of the Council of Nicaea, enforced by imperial power, gave the bishops of

---

8. E. H. Broadbent, *The Pilgrim Church* (London: Pickering and Englis, Ltd., 1931), p. 23.

9. M. M. Davis, *The Restoration Movement of the Nineteenth Century* (Cincinnati: The Standard Publishing Company, 1913), p. 24.

Rome, Alexandria, Antioch, Ephesus and Jerusalem the highest authority over all the bishops of their respective provinces. As that council gave the bishop of Rome authority over all of the bishops in the West, this further encouraged the Roman bishops to assert supremacy over all the churches.[10]

Space does not permit the further tracing of the developments of asceticism and monasticism, the formulation of the doctrine that salvation could only be dispensed by the church, the papal evolution and the declaration of his infallibility, or the theological developments which led to the terrible persecution of any person or group who dared to challenge the conclusions or the decisions of the hierarchy. Through such vehicles as the Inquisition, organized by papal decree in 1232, the church was given a weapon by which it could systematically eradicate all who were deemed heretics.[11] Suffice it to say that the atrocities committed under the guise of protecting and propagating the faith will forever remain among the blackest marks against Christianity ever achieved by Satan. Ironically, he accomplished it all under the cloak of church leadership! Ever-increasing corruption in the hierarchy, including the papacy, ushered in an era spanning several centuries which has become known in history as the Pornocracy. The papacy became a vicious and corrupt power struggle between immoral men and women. One murdered another to gain the position, power and wealth of the Roman Catholic empire. Pope John XII, for example, who became the head of both civil and church government at the age of 18, is described by Newman as follows:

10. Newman, Vol. 1, pp. 314-315.
11. Westin, p. 26.

> He was charged by his contemporaries with the violation of almost every principle of morality and religion: sacrilege, adultery, violation of widows, living with his father's mistress, invocation of Jupiter and Venus, and turning the papal palace into a brothel. He was driven from the city at the request of the people by the aid of the German emperor Otho before whom he had been tried. After a time he was restored through the intervention of harlots, but was soon afterward killed by the injured husband of a paramour.[12]

One might well ask what all of this relatively ancient history has to do with the issues of church leadership facing us today. In the rise of the Roman Catholic hierarchy we have been given fair warning through history of the consequences of creating congregational or supra-congregational offices of authority and power. Indeed, no argument of apostolic succession, edict of any emperor, declaration of any man or decree of any council can create any such position for the church or declare its occupant's infallibility. Yet, we have seen this tragic cycle repeated again and again in history as hierarchy after hierarchy has risen to power within the church. Before men ever began tampering with the pattern or building their ecclesiastical castles of sand, the apostle Paul declared in Romans 3:23, "All have sinned and fall short of the glory of God" (RSV). Sinful, corruptible men placed in untouchable offices of church leadership will eventually corrupt those offices, and the church will follow in their footsteps.

The Free Church Heritage. From the earliest days of the rise of the hierarchy there was resistance to it. Nor were these weak, lone voices which could easily be silenced by

---

12. Newman, Vol. 1, p. 450.

those in power. They often separated themselves in great numbers from the apostate body, seeking to restore the church of the New Testament in its purity and mission. E. H. Broadbent says of these:

> There has been a continuous succession of churches composed of believers who have made it their aim to act upon the teachings of the New Testament. This succession is not necessarily to be found in any one place; often such churches have been dispersed or have degenerated, but similar ones have appeared in other places. The pattern is so clearly delineated in the Scriptures as to have made it possible for churches of this character to spring up in fresh places and among believers who did not know that disciples before them had taken the same path, or that there were some in their own time in other parts of the world.[13]

While these movements had many things in common, it is impossible to link them together in such a manner as to imply that one resulted from the other in some kind of unbroken chain of apostolic succession. They did, however, share similar goals; and some were directly related to others in one way or another. Each movement can be said, also, to have had its blind spots, even as we do yet today. In spite of this, all have been determined to restore the New Testament pattern as they understood it.

Historians have differed over what to call this movement as it has existed in its various forms down through the ages. Gunnar Westin,[14] James DeForest Murch,[15] and others have chosen to call it "The Free Church." E. H. Broadbent[16] prefers

13. Broadbent, p. 33.
14. Westin, *ibid.*
15. James DeForest Murch, *The Free Church* (n.c.: Restoration Press, 1966).
16. Broadbent, *ibid.*

to term it "The Pilgrim Church." Donald F. Durnbaugh[17] opts for the designation, "The Believers' Church," and Ross Bender[18] uses "The People of God." Neither have they shared a consensus concerning those who should be included in that list.

The movements led by Marcion and Montanus in the 2nd century are generally cited, along with the Novatians of the 3rd century. The Donatists and the movements of Priscillian and Vigilantius are noted in the 4th century. The reformer Pelagius of the 5th century and the British Christians of the 6th century are cited, along with the Paulicians of the 7th and 8th centuries. The related Bogomiles and Phundagiagitae of the 10th century were followed by the Cathari of the 11th and 12th centuries. The Waldensians and the Albigenses also arose during the 11th and 12th centuries, followed by the Lollards of the 13th and 14th centuries, along with the United Brethren in the 15th century. The 16th century brought the Anabaptists, often called the Radical Reformation, from which the present-day Mennonites, Amish and Hutterites (and indirectly, the Baptists) all claim their ancestry. The 16th century was also the era of the well-known Protestant Reformation, led by men like Martin Luther, Ulrich Zwingli, Philip Melanchthon, John Calvin, Harry Bullinger, John Knox and John Wesley. Lutherans, Presbyterians, Baptists, Methodists and Episcopalians all stem from this period of reformative action. Each of these movements named is a fascinating study in itself, and one would be well-advised to review their sagas and to learn from their experiences.

---

17. Donald F. Durnbaugh, *The Believers' Church*, (New York: The Macmillan Company, 1968), p. 28.

18. Ross Thomas Bender, *The People of God* (Scottsdale: Herald Press, 1971).

America eventually became a haven and a land of new opportunity for many within the often-persecuted Free Church Movement. This interest in America as a land of opportunity for religious factions was at first suppressed and frustrated by both royalty and the Anglican clergy. It did not take England long, however, to see the economic advantages of encouraging this movement to help settle her new colonies. Charles and Mary Beard note:

> Instead of banishing merchants and artisans to enrich other countries, English statesmen opened the gates of their American colonies to every kind of religious faith that the stirring life of the Old World could furnish—to Catholics, Separatists, Puritans, Quakers, Presbyterians, and Baptists from the British Isles; to Lutherans, Dunkards, Moravians, Mennonites, Huguenots, and Salzburgers from the Continent. They looked with favor upon the German Lutherans who crowded into Pennsylvania, subdued the wilderness, and produced wheat, corn, bacon and lumber to exchange for English manufactures. They even winked at news of Jews settling here and there in the colonies, especially after Oliver Cromwell's example of toleration at home. When the plantations were once started and their significance to trade and empire disclosed, it was impossible to bring them into any scheme of religious uniformity. On the contrary clerical authority waned with the growth of business enterprise.[19]

As during the reformation in Europe, however, minority groups who now found themselves in majority positions in regions established their own brand of religion as the State Church of their colony and gained thereby tax support, as well as civil law to enforce conformity to their views. By the

---

19. Charles A. and Mary R. Beard, *The Rise of American Civilization*, rev. ed. (New York: The Macmillan Company, 1934), p. 30.

time of the American Revolution, nine of the thirteen colonies had established state churches. The land which had held such promise as a haven of religious freedom had become a land of intolerance. Any deviation from the viewpoints and practices of those who held the local religious monopoly brought certain persecution, deprivation of rights and property, loss of vote, and—in some cases—even death. While the atrocities committed in America by these groups did not approach in severity or scope those sanctioned earlier in other parts of the world by the Roman Catholic hierarchy or the hierarchies of the "Free Churches" who had come into the majority in an area, they did indeed add further black marks against Christianity, give rise to further reformative movements, and demonstrate the cyclical nature of human behavior in history. As the wise Solomon indicated in Ecclesiastes, there is really nothing new under the sun—even in church leadership!

As America emerged a free and independent nation following the Revolutionary War, both political and religious life underwent major changes. In some places the established churches were able to maintain some degree of control for a time, but in most places the monopolies on religion had been broken. The period known as "The Great Awakening," under the influence of men such as Jonathan Edwards and Cotton Mather, had run over New England "like wildfire, spread to the other colonies, and finally expired in a spasm of exhaustion."[20] In its wake the country lapsed into a period of secularization, with a growing preoccupation with politics, business and the expansion of the new frontiers. English Deism and French skepticism had begun to heavily influence

---

20. Beard and Beard, p. 148.

the academic community and had made major inroads into the popular philosophy of the people. B. B. Tyler says of this period:

> The moral and religious life of our fathers at the close of the eighteenth and the beginning of the nineteenth centuries was very low. Unbelief in Jesus as the Son of God, and in the Bible as a book of supernatural origin and divine character, and in what are esteemed by evangelical believers generally as the fundamental facts and truths of the Christian religion, abounded. The greatest immoralities were permitted to exist almost without rebuke. The Lord's house was disregarded. The message of divine love was scorned. The Bible was treated with contempt.[21]

The churches of America had, for all purposes, lost their influence and relevance. There was a far greater concern over the preservation of the institution and its forms than with the decline of public morality and the need for evangelism. (Does that sound familiar?) M. M. Davis lists eight characteristics of American religion of that period:

1. Human creeds had become rigid tests of fellowship.
2. The clergy claimed exclusive rights to interpret the Scripture, administer the ordinances, and to teach and preach.
3. There was no intelligent grasp of the Bible.
4. The doctrine of total depravity was almost universally accepted.
5. Conversion was expected to be accompanied by extraordinary manifestations.
6. The Bible was a "dead letter"—powerless to accomplish conversion.

---

21. B. B. Tyler, *A History of the Disciples of Christ* (Louisville: Guide Printing and Publishing Company, 1895), pp. 2-3.

7. Divisions were numerous.
8. These divisions were at war with each other.[22]

With the churches in such a state, with the growing problem of immorality and drunkenness among the general population, it was inevitable that a great revival should come in response to the need. The Restoration Movement came as a part of that Great Revival in America at the turn of the century. Twenty-three New England ministers had joined together in concerted prayer to pray for such a revival, and they urged churches of every denomination to join them on the first Tuesday of each quarter, beginning in January, 1795, in united petition to God to raise up a force which would convert and change America.[23] Their prayers were indeed heard and answered.

The Restoration Movement. Garrison and DeGroot note that there were two basic convictions in the minds of the fathers of the Restoration Movement:

1. That the church ought to be one, without sectarian divisions.
2. That the reasons for its divisions were the additions of "human opinions" to the simple requirements of Christ and His apostles as tests of fitness for admission to the one church, and the usurpation of rule over the church by clergy and ecclesiastical courts unknown in the days of its primitive unity and purity.[24]

---

22. M. M. Davis, *The Restoration Movement of the Nineteenth Century* (Cincinnati: The Standard Publishing Company, 1913), pp. 59-64.
23. James DeForest Murch, *Christians Only* (Cincinnati: The Standard Publishing Company, 1962), p. 23.
24. W. E. Garrison and A. T. DeGroot, *The Disciples of Christ - A History* (St. Louis: The Christian Board of Publication, 1948), p. 11.

From among the Methodist denomination came James O'Kelly and Rice Haggard and the Republican Methodists of Virginia. From within the Baptist denomination came Abner Jones and Elias Smith and the New England Christians of Vermont and New Hampshire. From the Presbyterians of Kentucky came Barton Warren Stone and others with the Kentucky Christians. From the Baptists of Indiana emerged John Wright and the Blue River Christians. The fifth stream of the Restoration Movement involved the Scotch Baptists of New York, Pennsylvania, Maryland and Connecticut, and was led by men like Henry Errett and Walter Scott. These were, in fact, the heirs to an earlier movement in Scotland led by the Haldane brothers, Robert Sandeman and John Glas. That movement had spread to England, Ireland, South Africa, New Zealand and America.[25] The sixth and final stream of the Restoration, which was identified most notably with Thomas and Alexander Campbell of Pennsylvania, can be traced initially to Ireland and the Independency, which had been led by John Gibson, George Hamilton and Alexander Carson. It, in turn, was related to the Scotch Baptist movement of the Haldanes, Glas and Sandeman.[26] Influenced by their contact with the Independents in Ireland, the Campbells' movement in America resulted from conflict within their Presbyterian denomination.

As each of these six streams discovered one another and their common quest for a restoration of the New Testament faith and practice, there was a natural rejoicing, and the six tributaries joined to become a united, mighty river. Now

---

25. Harold W. Ford, *A History of the Restoration Plea* (Joliet: Mission Services, 1956), p. 11.

26. Harold L. Lunger, *The Political Ethics of Alexander Campbell* (St. Louis: The Bethany Press, 1954), pp. 20-21.

together, even as they had separately, these elements of the Restoration appealed to the Christians in all denominations to find a common ground for unity based on the Scriptures alone, discarding all divisive names, creeds and other impediments to the union of all Christians and the consequent accomplishment of the mission Christ had given His church. It was James A. Garfield, President of the United States and a minister among the Christian Churches of this Restoration Movement who, in response to a lady's inquiry, gave one of the simplest summaries of the Christians' positions in his statement, "Where We Stand":

1. We call ourselves Christians or Disciples.
2. We believe in God the Father.
3. We believe that Jesus is the Christ, the Son of the living God and our Savior. We regard the divinity of Christ as the fundamental truth of the Christian System.
4. We believe in the Holy Spirit both as to its agency in conversion and as in-dweller in the heart of the Christian.
5. We accept both the Old and New Testament Scriptures as the inspired Word of God.
6. We believe in the future reward of the righteous and the future punishment of the wicked.
7. We believe that Deity is a prayer-hearing and prayer-answering God.
8. We observe the institution of the Lord's Supper on every Lord's day. To this table we neither invite nor debar. We say it is the Lord's supper for the Lord's children.
9. We plead for the unity of all of God's people on the Bible and the Bible alone.
10. The Bible is our only creed.
11. We maintain that all the ordinances should be observed as they were in the days of the apostles.[27]

27. President James A. Garfield, "Where We Stand," *Webster City Christian*, February, 1893, p. 4.

The Evolution of an Ideal

It has been the continuing conviction of the Restoration Movement that the New Testament church must be restored. "A return to apostolic practices and views was held as prerequisite to achieving the spiritual results of apostolic times."[28] As we have seen, this has been the theme of the entire Free Church Movement down through the ages. It has always been a noble quest, but a difficult one to achieve. Each Free Church has had to wrestle with its own biased perspectives in first discovering what pattern may exist in the New Testament, and then has had to struggle with the religious establishments of their time to gain sufficient freedom to be able to restore the New Testament church as they perceive it. These struggles have been written on some of the bloodiest pages in history, and out of these struggles has usually risen an over-reaction to the religious monopoly in power. Once the pendulum has swung to one extreme, it will inevitably swing back to the other for some period of time until its reactionary momentum has run down. Such was the case with the Restoration Movement and the development of its concept of leadership.

As has been noted, the movement's streams originated in reaction to the abuses of the clerical hierarchies of the Presbyterian, Methodist and Baptist denominations. Had these groups at that time allowed for more freedom and reformation from within, it is doubtful that the Restoration Movement would have ever come into existence. The Restoration fathers had no desire to be separatists or to create another denomination. But when thwarted, maligned

28. H. Eugene Johnson, *Duly and Scripturally Qualified* (Cincinnati: The Standard Publishing Company, 1975), p. 149.

and excommunicated by the hierarchies of their denominations for their efforts toward restoring the apostolic doctrine and methods, they had no choice but to initiate a Free Church fellowship in which these aims could be pursued. With them they carried much that was familiar, either consciously or unconsciously, along with their common reaction to the clergy with whom they had just recently done frustrating battle. They shared a common resolve to prevent any such clerical power structure from ever arising in their fellowship. But they went one step further, initially eliminating the pastoral position entirely from any recognized leadership of the church. Alexander Campbell wrote in 1835 in *The Christian System:*

> The standing and immutable ministry of the Christian community is composed of Bishops, Deacons and Evangelists. Of each of these there is but one order, though possessing great diversities of gifts. There have been bishops, deacons and evangelists, with both ordinary and extraordinary gifts. Still the office is now, and ever was, the same. . . . *Bishops,* whose office is to preside over, to instruct, and to edify the community—to feed the church of the Lord with knowledge and understanding—and to watch for their souls as those that must give account to the Lord at his appearing and his kingdom, compose the first class. *Deacons,* or servants—whether called treasurers, almoners, stewards, doorkeepers, or messengers—constitute the second. . . . *Evangelists,* however, though a class of public functionaries created by the church, do not serve it directly; but are by it sent out into the world, and constitute the third class of functionaries belonging to the Christian system.[29]

29. Alexander Campbell, *The Christian System* (1835; rpt. Nashville: Gospel Advocate Company, 1956), pp. 60-61.

More noteworthy than what he said in this instance, perhaps, is that which he did not say. By naming these three positions only, he locked out the position of pastor or minister. He did concede the necessity of having preachers, but he limited them to either being evangelists or one of the elders.

The Role of the Minister. While the position of preacher did exist in the early stages of the movement, the anti-clerical reaction also brought a great aversion to calling him anything more than "preacher," "minister," or perhaps "elder," for fear that even the name itself would somehow create a hierarchy. Lunger says:

> This fear was almost a "phobia" in Campbell's case, as it is seen from his almost neurotic fear of the Presbyterian clergy. It will be noted that he became less nervous on the subject as the years passed, and his own energies became more fully absorbed in the tasks of constructive churchmanship and responsible citizenship.[30]

Particularly odious among the Restoration leaders was the term "pastor," due to its use among the denominations to describe their clergy. This is evidenced by McGarvey's comments in 1865:

> But as the case now stands we are being constantly seduced into violations of our great law, that Bible things must be called by Bible names. The most unceasing vigilance and the most unrestrained criticism of one another will be necessary to preserve this law in practical operation. We cannot think of allowing it to become a dead law, for its observance is necessary to the final triumph of truth, and it is really a law of God (I Pet. 4:11; II Tim. 1:13). The term "pastor" furnishes a striking example of the power with which sectarian

30. Lunger, p. 52.

> usage forces itself upon us. Now it has gained a currency among us almost as universal as among the Presbyterians and Baptists, and in quite the same sense. . . . To style a preacher "the pastor" is still more unscriptural, for it robs the eldership of this title, and makes it appear that there is but one pastor to the congregation, whereas the apostolic churches all had a plurality of them.[31]

Such an argument from one of McGarvey's scholastic stature can only be accounted for as a typical reaction of the Restoration to the clerical hierarchy from which they had emerged as a movement. The argument of exclusion as applied by McGarvey could have equally applied to the terms "preacher," "minister," "evangelist," or "elder" which he preferred. All such terms had wider application in the Christian community in apostolic times, as he well knew. In fact, McGarvey did write his approval of a "preaching elder" who would devote his entire labor to that work, taking "the lead part in teaching."[32] Even this designation, however, was contested by a number. An 1868 article in the *Christian Standard* by Philaleethes (pseud.) argues: "Where there is a New Testament eldership there are preachers or pastors: for elders or pastors are preachers. The New Testament knows of no elders who are not apt to teach."[33]

There was obviously a reluctance on the part of many to give the preacher even equal position with the elders. In a 1910 *Christian Standard* editorial Isaac Errett questions calling the preacher "pastor" unless he has been chosen as an elder by the congregation. He also objected to the

31. J. W. McGarvey, "Pastors," *Lard's Quarterly*, April, 1865, pp. 311-312, 316.

32. J. W. McGarvey, *A Treatise on the Eldership* (1870; rpt. Murfreesboro DeHoff Publications, 1962), p. 66.

use of the term "the Pastor" because he felt, like McGarvey, that it implied the exclusion of the elders as pastors. He admits that "minister" is probably not any better, since all disciples are ministers. He concludes that "the Australian brethren solve the problem by terming the located preacher an evangelist."[34] One might further wonder how that solves anything, since all Christians are also called to evangelize. Errett had written several years earlier:

> If they (the congregation) desire him (the preacher) to be one of the elders, they can so appoint. That is something for the church to decide. In deciding it there may be wisdom in looking at the man called, his age and fitness for the place. In some cases it might be well not to burden a young preacher with a position among the elders.[35]

Particularly offensive was the title "Reverend," since " 'reverend' is never applied to man, not even to an apostle, bishop, elder, or minister, but to God only, and used but once in the Bible, 'Holy and reverend is His name.' Therefore what right has any man to assume this title?"[36]

Stripped of any distinguishable name, for fear of excluding others who might share the described function by using its name, and relegated to a position generally below the eldership in leadership of the church, it is little wonder that it was said in an 1869 article:

---

33. Philaleethes (pseud.), "Church Organization," *Christian Standard*, October 3, 1868, p. 313.

34. Isaac Errett, "Church Polity," *Christian Standard*, February 19, 1910, p. 315.

35. Isaac Errett, "Eldership, Presbytery, or Church Board, or Elders and Deacons," *Christian Standard*, February 9, 1895, p. 132.

36. Thomas W. Phillips, *The Church of Christ* (Cincinnati: The Standard Publishing Company, 1948), p. 268.

> It strikes me that our people are extremely fickle about their pastors, if it can be said that they have any fixed ideas of a pastorate. Scarcely do they call one, and he has hardly time to reconnoiter the field, when they desire a change. A year is the general rule, and many, when they begin a year are uncertain they will be satisfied enough to justify a continuance through it.[37]

Bruce Brown, writing in 1901 from years of experience in the ministry in various parts of the country, penned the following observation:

> It is . . . true that churches get the reputation of being preacher killers. Preachers who have been successful everywhere go down in regular order in some churches. These congregations come to be avoided by preachers who value their good names and reputations. . . . No vigorous, progressive preacher will entrust his good name and reputation into the care of a preacher-killing church.[38]

Times have continued to change in the Christian Churches, but they have changed slowly for the minister. The words of Errett in 1869 and of Brown in 1901 could be written of many of the churches through the years and up until the present. The black cloud of suspicion about a paid ministry created by Alexander Campbell's reactionary writings has kept the preacher's role subservient at best in the vast majority of churches in the Restoration Movement. Periodically there are those who excitedly rediscover Campbell's early writings and who once again launch crusades to eliminate the paid

---

37. Johnson, p. 57, quoting an article by Isaac Errett, *Christian Standard*, May 8, 1869, p. 169.

38. Bruce Brown, "Church Character," *The Christian Messenger*, May 3, 1901, p. 2.

ministry. They would do well to read on and to learn from the experience of the movement. McGarvey wrote in 1870 about the unworkable experiment of having a church led only by elders:

> If we estimate the results of these methods, we must confess that hitherto they have proved quite meagre. The efforts of the majority of our Elders are so little instructive and edifying, that not even the members of the church will attend, in good numbers, when it is expected that one of them will occupy the hour. Hence, there is a constant complaint that the members will not come out to church except when the preacher is present. . . . Indeed, it is a rare thing to find a preacher, who is capable of speaking to edification in the same congregation for a series of years. This accounts, in great measure, for the frequent removals of preachers from place to place. A congregation will rarely consent to the loss of a preacher who uniformly instructs and edifies them in public, and whose deportment is at all reputable.[39]

The Roles of Elders and Deacons. Alexander Campbell wrote in The Christian System, "Every well-organized church has its eldership."[40] A congregation might exist for a time without elders, but not for long. It was expected that they would soon grow sufficiently in numbers and spirit to enable them to select elders and deacons, at which time the evangelist's work would be complete, and he would move along to begin another church. These three positions, it will be recalled, formed the exclusive threefold leadership for the church, according to Campbell's early writings. The plurality of the eldership was repeatedly emphasized. McGarvey

39. McGarvey, *A Treatise on the Eldership*, p. 47.
40. Campbell, *The Christian System*, p. 70.

went so far as to say, "Indeed, there must be none until they can have more than one who is qualified."[41] It became the recognized sign of maturity of a congregation, then, if they had elders.

Much debate has been generated throughout the history of the movement concerning the qualifications for elders, with a seeming majority of it centering around perhaps the least significant qualification, that of being "the husband of only one wife." In general, there seems to have always been far more concern about the circumstances of a man's life than about the weightier qualifications of character and Christian maturity, or about a man's record of function as an elder. More will be said on this subject when we examine the scriptural qualifications for the eldership in the next chapter.

It has also been generally held that, as overseers, authority is vested in these elders by the congregation. Moses Lard wrote, "The overseers did not become such in virtue of their age, but in virtue of their special appointment to the office."[42] He further explains:

> Before the ordination the man is an elder, and after it an elder; but before the ordination he is an elder without authority, after it an elder with authority. It is the act of ordination that gives office, that gives authority.[43]

W. R. Walker wrote: "The selection of the men who fill it is a congregational prerogative. Christ authorizes the office. Men fill it by a process of election." He further notes,

---

41. McGarvey, *A Treatise on the Eldership*, p. 89.
42. Moses E. Lard, "Ordination of Church Officers," *Lard's Quarterly*, July, 1865, p. 351.
43. Lard, p. 360.

however, "A congregation not only has the right, but it is its duty, to remove a dictatorial, trouble-making elder from office. The authority to create postulates the authority to control or remove."[44]

W. L. Hayden recounted in 1895 a test of church polity in the civil court regarding the Christian Church of Howard, Pennsylvania. "The elders held to life tenure of office" and that "the elders are the church governmentally." They also held "that each church is absolutely independent of every other, and hence that there is no possibility of holding them to account for their official acts." He reported that two-thirds of the congregation protested and asked for a hearing with them of grievances. When denied, they appealed to a tribunal from a neighboring church to decide the questions raised. The tribunal "rendered a decision sustaining the complaints against the elders, and recommended a congregational meeting . . . to give practical effect to their decision." The elders forbade such a meeting and bolted the doors, whereupon the meeting was held outside the church on the front of the property under the trees. At this time the Elders were unanimously deposed. Conflict followed, with an eventual lawsuit being filed, after all other measures failed (including the intervention by an evangelist, whom the elders promptly had thrown in jail for his interference). The case went all the way to the Supreme Court. The congregation was ruled to be within its rights in its actions, both to appeal to a tribunal of a neighboring church and to depose the elders.[45]

---

44. W. R. Walker, *A Functioning Eldership* (Cincinnati: The Standard Publishing Foundation, 1940), p. 29.

45. W. L. Hayden, "Church Polity in the Civil Court," *Christian Standard*, June 8, 1895, p. 555.

Such a case of a congregation dismissing its elders was extremely rare, of course. It can be said that the elders were generally regarded to possess the vested authority of the church and were allowed to exercise that authority within just about any reasonable bounds. There were, however, a few voices raised to question the origin and right of such authority being placed in the hands of the elders. M. M. Parker, writing in 1895 in the *Christian Standard* pointed out that: (1) There is no reference in the New Testament to anyone in authority, (2) Neither the elders nor anyone "is in authority in matters of church government or discipline," and (3) elders, when mentioned, "are addressed as to their behavior and how they may teach and be an example to the church and watch the flock." He contended, "No one can lawfully exercise authority in the church. Here the great distinction between civil polity and church polity is stated."[46] His point was good and valid. Sadly, his was a minority voice, and no one seemed to be listening or wanted to hear. Tradition had already become strongly established. Elders in the Christian Churches were an authority over all the church as long as they held their positions as elders. That was the way it was and has basically remained.

In the evolution of the concept of the elders it must be noted that, as the authority over congregation and preacher became entrenched, a "supreme control in ruling" mentioned by McGarvey[47] and others became a kind of established judiciary and legislature for the church. Elders claimed the right to interpret the Bible for both congregation and preacher. If the Bible contained no applicable "thus saith the Lord,"

46. M. M. Parker, "The Apostolic Church Polity," *Christian Standard*, August 10, 1895, p. 757.

47. McGarvey, p. 66.

in many churches the elders felt compelled to speak and to pass a law on the subject. If the practice or doctrine in question differed from their interpretation or decree, they took action to correct the "error" and to keep all "in line." One recalls the councils which also evolved from the early churches in the rise of the Roman Catholic hierarchy, which also appropriated unto themselves such legislative and judicial rights.

Aside from the few Bible School classes sometimes taught by elders, and the group meetings of the elders to sit in judgment upon the orthodoxy of preacher and people, the other visible function which evolved for the elders in the Restoration Movement was the task of praying and presiding at the Lord's Table over the communion each Sunday. J. H. Garrison, in 1892 queried:

> Is the only difference between elders and deacons that the elders preside at the Lord's Table and the deacons distribute the elements and take up the collection? This seems to be the way that many congregations understand it.[48]

Garrison's comment was all too true concerning a great number of churches in the movement. Few congregations understood the New Testament role of the elder, and few elders knew much about their duties when elected, except that they would be expected to preside at the Table, to "sit on the Board," and to keep the preacher in line. Isaac Errett lamented in 1920 about the "difficulty of selecting elders who in any considerable measure conform to the Scriptural ideal." He said:

---

48. J. H. Garrison, "A Rambling Talk About Church Officers," *The Christian-Evangelist*, January 2, 1892, p. 34.

> We have all felt this. . . . What is the church doing to meet this crying need for competent leadership? What can she do? Would it be possible to train our young men for service with the eldership and deaconate in view?[49]

No serious attempt has been made in the Restoration Movement to define the role of the deacon. Most congregations provided for their election, and many specified in their by-laws, articles of incorporation or church constitutions the number of deacons to be elected. Besides the general expectation that they would serve on Sundays to distribute the communion and receive the offering, it was expected that they would also serve on the Official Board of the church. Most congregations did not go beyond this definition of the deacon's role, even though it was often implied that the deacons were "understudies" to the elders. This was almost always regarded as the beginning point for one who was to "move through the chairs" toward the ultimate office of the eldership.

Further attention will be given in another chapter to the evolution of the Official Board in the Christian Churches. It is probably the most curious creature to be evolved by the Restoration Movement in its developing concept of church leadership. In an endeavor committed to the restoration of New Testament faith and practice, its development is a particular enigma and something of a theological embarrassment to the movement.

The Role of the Evangelist. When a correspondent to his *Millennial Harbinger* in 1858 wrote: "I regard our 'Evangelist' as a new edition of the clergy—nothing worse—perhaps no

49. Isaac Errett, "Church Polity," *Christian Standard*, February 19, 1910, p. 315.

better—would like to know their parentage, genealogy, etc.," Alexander Campbell responded:

> Evangelists—or preachers of the Gospel—are needful; indeed essential, to the mission and influence of the Christian Church. . . . They were indeed to discharge all duties incumbent upon missionaries sent out to heathen islands, as times and circumstances might indicate and demand. . . . After churches or communities had been organized and set in order, with their Bishops and Deacons, their proper work as Evangelists ceased. They had no official authority over them. . . . A church set in order by an Evangelist is not under him as an official. After organization it has its own Bishops who watch for their souls as those who give account to the Lord.[50]

Campbell, then, was so anti-clergy that he would not even allow the evangelist to exist as a position within the church once it had bishops or elders. He only had authority over those he baptized until that point in their maturity when they could manage for themselves. Then he was to move on.

The concept of the evangelist's role in leadership did, however, evolve. Men became area evangelists, such as Walter Scott, who served the Mahoning Baptist Association. Johnson cites a further development:

> In October, 1835, messengers for churches in four counties of Kentucky met to choose evangelists, at a salary of "not less than $500.00" per year. John Smith, Jacob Creath, Jr., B. F. Hall, and J. P. Lancaster were chosen. "It was agreed that the most successful method of operating was for each Evangelist to take a small district of country for the field of his operation, say one or two counties, and cultivate it well."

---

50. Alexander Campbell, "Office of an Evangelist," *Millennial Harbinger*, June, 1858, pp. 328, 330.

> These evangelists assumed many prerogatives that are customarily associated with the role of such as a Methodist bishop.[51]

Beyond being simply itinerant preachers in their districts, they assumed, based on their identification with Timothy and Titus, a kind of superintendency of the congregations begun there. While Campbell at first protested this, neither he nor these others could sit idly by and allow total congregational autonomy to exist if a problem in a church went uncorrected by its elders and threatened the scriptural function of the church. Speaking of Campbell's relationship to the churches, Johnson describes the personal evolution which took place:

> Campbell performed more as an evangelist than a congregation's elder in much of his ministry. He toured, debated, held "protracted meetings," influenced the movement as author and editor. He assumed the role of an evangelist when he journeyed to Nashville, and from the pulpit of the church denounced its minister, J. B. Ferguson, for three consecutive nights. He returned to Bethany and carried his victory into print under "The Fall of Mr. J. B. Ferguson."[52]

The article was carried in the September 6, 1824, issue of the *Christian Baptist,* which Campbell edited. Robert Milligan, in his *Scheme of Redemption* also corroborates this kind of intervention. Johnson says of him:

> Milligan was more frank about the authority exercised by the founding fathers of the movement than they themselves usually were. These men "interfered" in congregations with elected elders, acting as counselors and judges of

51. Johnson, p. 45.
52. Johnson, p. 37.

factions. They assumed for themselves, often without multi-congregational approval, a position similar to that occupied in the 1940's and 1950's by the State Secretaries of the Disciples of Christ.[53]

Peter Vogel, in his four-part series on "Church Organization" in the early 1877 issues of the *Christian Standard* also espoused this concept of evangelists over districts. In the February 17, 1877, issue he says: "The Evangelists were the proper court of appeal, on the part of the private members, from the decision of the elders. . . . The Apostles, Prophets and Evangelists had authority over the local churches and their officers."[54] Their intervention was not, however, always welcome. As we have seen already, one early group of elders had the evangelist thrown in jail when he sought to intervene on behalf of the church's members. Nor were the evangelists always welcomed by the preachers who served the churches. H. C. Patterson, in 1872, wrote in defense of the evangelist's role in *The Christian-Evangelist:*

> I feel myself called upon to write a few lines in justification of the class of God's laborers to which I belong. Not infrequently have I heard it said that the evangelist is an injury to any church and especially to any pastor. . . . We call upon any intelligent and earnest pastor whom we have assisted to say he was not strengthened with his congregation.[55]

He continues by citing his practice of trying to build up both the church and pastor through his meetings. It was

53. Johnson, p. 47.

54. Peter Vogel, "Church Organization," *Christian Standard*, February 17, 1877, p. 49.

55. H. C. Patterson, "That Awful Evangelist," *The Christian-Evangelist*, July 12, 1892, p. 452.

held important that an evangelist be commissioned by a church or group of churches. Indeed, not all that went on under the name of "evangelism" could be condoned. The April, 1894, issue of the *Webster City Christian* carried the following unusual news item headed, "A New Style":

> A new style of evangelizing has been started in Kentucky. A man by the name of W. C. Spratt was discharged from the lunatic asylum as cured. He went home and seemed all right in mind and body. He got fired up on religious matters, and he had a "call to preach." If a man refused to listen to him, he "pulled a gun" and held respectful attention to the close of his sermon. He determined to "spread the gospel" in the town of Stanford, and knowing something of the job before him, he armed himself with a Bible, two guns, a pistol and an orthodox bowie-knife. He went into the store of Vandever and Severance, and both the proprietors were in. He drew his Bible and made ready his gun, and took his text; and although the two merchants were not noted for piety, it is said no two men ever paid more attention to a sermon or gave more respectful regard to a preacher than they did on that occasion. Since then, Bro. Spratt has been arrested and put back into the asylum, and his ministry has ceased. There is no question that his "plan of work" would hold an audience. The only difficulty would be to get the same audience a second time.[56]

By 1887 the first evangelistic teams were touring the country, holding revivals in the churches.

The most famous such evangelist was Charles Reign Scoville. He joined the Church of Christ in Angola, Indiana, in 1891, and began to preach almost immediately. Scoville

56. Bruce Brown, ed., "A New Style," *Webster City Christian*, April, 1894, p. 1.

was better educated than most leaders of the "sawdust trail," having received his AB and MA degrees from Hiram College. More than any other Disciples preacher of his time he held union meetings with denominations. . . . In Jefferson City, Missouri . . . he closed a seven week meeting in which four thousand "hit the glory trail." Scoville developed the team approach, using eleven to twelve assistants. Advance agents preceded him to his revival areas preparing the community. It is reported he would preach for an hour to an hour and a half, then exhort for another thirty minutes if he felt the necessity. He was instrumental in forming the National Evangelistic Association, and led in the efforts to create the "Department of Evangelism" of the United Christian Missionary Society (UCMS).[57]

Problems Within the Movement

Within the early years of the Restoration Movement unprecedented growth took place. It appeared that it would sweep the nation almost overnight. But the new movement was not without its problems. Finding and restoring a New Testament pattern for the church proved to be, as we have already seen, far easier declared than accomplished. W. Carl Ketcherside somewhat critically describes some of the tendencies, fallacies and pitfalls of the would-be restorers:

> Since God did not provide us a pattern we set in to provide Him one. That is where we went astray. We took the apostolic love letters and warped them into a code of jurisprudence and immediately started judging our brothers and measuring them by ourselves. What we call "the pattern" is not really derived from God's revelation at all. We created the pattern and then searched the scriptures to find justification for what we already had.

57. Johnson, pp. 44-45.

> Most of our patterns consist of a combination of elements derived from three sources: (1) Cultural and environmental factors; (2) Reactions to other religious groups whom we consider as apostates or compromisers; (3) Misconception and misapplication of scriptural passages lifted from their contextual setting and used to establish our preconceptions and presuppositions.[58]

While most would find Ketcherside's assessment to be at least a slight overstatement of the facts, the substantial element of truth remains undeniable. Disagreements over interpretations of the scriptural pattern arose early in the movement and eventually led to the division of the movement into three segments, now identified as the Christian Churches (Disciples of Christ), the Churches of Christ (non-instrumental) and the Christian Churches and Churches of Christ (independent). In its divided state, the movement has continued to grow until recently, but at a greatly reduced pace. B. L. Smith, writing in 1901, offered the following perspective at the turn of the century:

> As to the success of this plea for a return to the teachings of the apostles and a surrender of human creeds, we give the following figures as representing the numerical growth of the people identified with this movement and who are known as Disciples of Christ, Churches of Christ, or Christian Churches:

1830	12,000	1880	475,000
1840	40,000	1890	641,000
1850	118,000	1895	889,019
1860	225,000	1900	1,151,000
1870	350,000		

58. W. Carl Ketcherside, "Sources of Our Patterns," *Mission Messenger*, June, 1970, pp. 81-82.

> We began the 19th century with a Christianized population of 200,000,000; we go into the 20th with 500,000,000. Thus in a single century Christianity has gained more upon paganism than in its 18 predecessors. Is it not possible that the 20th century may see all the nations of the earth Christianized?[59]

The Movement Slows. Sadly, we have not come near realizing Smith's dream. The 1979 edition of the *Directory of the Ministry* of the Christian Churches reflects the most positive picture presented in years, showing net gains in every category over the 1978 statistics: 9,023 new members, 65 new churches, 89 new agencies, 385 increase in personnel, and 19 new foreign missionaries.[60] That edition listed the total membership of the Christian Churches in the United States and Canada (not counting the Disciples of Christ or the non-instrumental Churches of Christ) at 1,059,410. It also lists a total of 5,062 churches, 809 agencies, and 10,978 personnel, including 693 foreign missionaries.[61] A check of the two following editions of that annual directory was much less encouraging. Then the 1982 directory brought the bad news reflecting a decline in membership of 63,561 from the 1981 totals and a loss of 280 churches and fifteen agencies. A net gain of one new foreign missionary was recorded.[62] The 1983 directory discreetly omits any membership total or comparison with previous years.

---

59. B. L. Smith, "The Christian Church and the 20th Century," *The Christian Messenger,* February 15, 1901, p. 1.

60. Ralph McLean, *Directory of the Ministry,* (Springfield: Directory of the Ministry, 1979), p. F-13.

61. McLean, p. F-54.

62. McLean, (1982), p. F-54.

Dr. Jameso Fuzzell, Executive Director of the Arizona Evangelistic Association, located in one of our fastest-growing "sunbelt" states, recently rang the following warning bell:

> According to the 1984 Arizona Christian Convention booklet statistics, our total membership in the state has *decreased* by 90 in 1983! Total additions have *decreased* by 153 and baptisms by 94! The effect of these decreases is compounded by the fact that we are a state with a rapidly growing population. God is, indeed, in His heaven, but all is not right in Arizona.[63]

The Fervor Cools. It has been accurately observed by many that one of the key reasons for the slowed growth and present decline of the Restoration Movement has been the fact that it has largely ceased to be a movement. As time has passed, the initial fervor to restore the ancient order of things in the church has cooled. The churches have gradually and increasingly become encrusted with layer upon layer of traditions. These have become the accepted and comfortable standards for "the way it is done in our churches." A perpetual pride of accomplishment in "being right" in certain areas of faith and practice has dulled both the conscience and awareness of many church leaders concerning the frontiers yet untouched, and has supplanted the earlier sense of urgency about moving toward a restoration of all things. Satisfaction with, and acceptance of, the status quo have become major impediments to further re-evaluation and restoration. Such moves are, in fact, viewed by many with alarm as a threat to the "brotherhood" and as troublesome rabble-rousing and rocking of the boat. The arthritic

---

63. Jameso Fuzzell, "A Bell For Arizona," *Arizona Christian*, April, 1984, p. 1.

symptoms of institutionalism within the movement are readily apparent, however, to the diagnosticians; and the pains from any sudden movements are keenly felt throughout the body.

Back to the Basics

Somewhere along in the evolution of the movement the ideal of restoring New Testament leadership forms within the church ceased to be a driving compulsion. Compromises and cultural adaptations were made. Those New Testament leadership styles which were discovered were largely abandoned for representative government and legislative forms of leadership. Servant-leaders became officers instead, and officers formed boards. The debates over titles, methods and forms took precedence over concern about the accomplishment of the movement's objectives. This evolution did not happen overnight; and as Ketcherside has noted, it has been affected by many outside influences. While these influences are not readily recognized or admitted by many in the movement, who prefer to see themselves as the primary representatives of "The New Testament Church,"[64] these factors must be honestly acknowledged and recognized before anyone can fully understand the present leadership crisis facing the Restoration Movement, or before possible solutions can be discovered.

The scriptures dealing with the subject of church leadership are, in fact, perceived through the lens of evolved traditions to such an extent that it is almost inconceivable to most congregational leaders within the Christian Churches

---

64. P. H. Welshimer, *Facts Concerning the New Testament Church* (Cincinnati: The Standard Publishing Company, n.d.), pp. 1-19.

today that their present practices may not have scriptural precedents or authority. Having "arrived" in some matters is, in too many cases, tragically assumed to extend to all matters—including the restoration of scriptural church leadership. The resultant blindness in this area has proven to be exceptionally costly to this great movement. Rather than evolving a workable substitute for New Testament leadership for the local church, the current largely-stereotyped patterns which have emerged are neither New Testament nor successful. As such, they represent perhaps the movement's most serious handicap.

There is an urgent need for the church in this time of crisis both to see itself in the perspective of history, as it has evolved through an oft-repeated cycle, and to once again return to the basics. This necessarily involves a re-examination of the Biblical blueprint for the church. What does the Bible actually say about church leadership? What guidelines has the Lord given to direct this, His Body? These are the vital questions which must be raised and answered if the church is to emerge successfully from its current crisis and again become a Restoration Movement. It is time to strip away pride and pretense. The plain hard truth of the matter is that the movement has evolved, for all practical purposes, into its own denominational model of congregational government. The truth is that very little real grass roots concern exists, or has existed for years, in a revival of the goals to restore New Testament faith and practice in the church. This is particularly true wherever that restoration would require us to give up forms and practices we hold dear. It is especially true in the area of church leadership.

In spite of our reluctance, we must either return to the basics and revive restorationism, or we must face the inevitable consequences of a further repetition of history—the eventual demise of a once-great and promising movement. We have seen the handwriting on the wall.

In Summary

The church is in crisis! It is being sabotaged by its leadership styles. Believing them to be New Testament in origin, the church has in fact evolved them primarily through historical reactions and assimilation of its culture. The Restoration Movement began with the noble goals of restoring New Testament faith and practice as a means of uniting all Christians in the task of fulfilling the Lord's purpose for His church, as reflected in His prayer in John 17. That which began with such promise has sadly followed the repetitive cycle of other reformative movements in history, and has gradually evolved into the practical status of another declining denomination. Only a return to the New Testament basics and a revival of restoration fervor is seen as the answer for the church in its time of crisis.

2

THE BIBLICAL BLUEPRINT

Principles vs Patternism

Much has already been said about the restoration of the church of the New Testament. We have seen how this has been the stated intention of both the Free Church Movement and the Restoration Movement. More than one person has inquired, however, "Which church in the New Testament would you restore?" To be certain, no two churches mentioned there were identical, just as no one can find any two people who are really identical. It must be admitted that each of the churches mentioned in the New Testament had its separate character and that it also had both strengths and weaknesses. Due to their human composition, none of the churches of that or any era has been perfect.

But is there not some fixed standard—some pattern—by which all churches were measured, and to which all sought to conform? In particular, is there not a New Testament blueprint for leadership which may have existed in the mind of God and was revealed through His apostles—even though the blueprint was never fully evidenced by any actual church?

The search for such a pattern for church leadership has some definite pitfalls which must first be considered, and which we must attempt to avoid. It is vitally important that we begin at the right point in this matter, or we will almost certainly wind up with the wrong conclusions. Michael Harper is right on target when he says:

> What may be . . . a more important task is to discover the meaning of the Church in its contemporary setting, for the ministry exists for the Church, not the Church for the ministry. If we do not get our understanding of the Church right, there is no hope that we shall get the ministry right.[1]

Harper is reminding us that everything in our understanding of the church's ministry and leadership is dependent upon a correct understanding of the basic nature of the church. Robert Fife is in agreement with this point and speaks to it with a definition:

> The church is persons in relationship to the person of the Son of God. Theirs is a shared relationship in mission, and it is in this relationship the essential order of the church exists. . . . Within this life-relationship created and exhibited in "one Lord, one faith, one baptism, one God and Father," and continually renewed in the "one bread," there is room for growth in grace and in knowledge of the truth. The fellowship is not defined by a stage of growth, but it is rather marked

1. Michael Harper, "Duplicating the New Testament Church," *Eternity*, April, 1978, p. 25.

> by a constant process of growth, until the whole body shall have attained the "measure of the stature of the fulness of Christ."[2]

We shall return later to a discussion of the church's essence and purpose. The primary point these men are making is that there is a grave danger of misunderstanding the nature of the church, and viewing it as a static structure. It is by divine design a dynamic organism, ever requiring flexibility, change and adaptation in order to successfully exist in each culture and historical setting it encounters. The church was designed with the necessary adaptability, but our failure to perceive that will keep us from understanding our roles in church leadership. Even worse, too rigid an interpretation of the organizational indicators given in the New Testament can petrify the church in its past context and prevent it from being a vital, ministering fellowship in its contemporary setting. Harper very vividly points out a prevalent tendency to force the Scriptures by reading into them our own ideas and viewpoints. Speaking of the Scriptures, he says:

> We also put them into cold storage. We try to "freeze" them in the first century and re-create "New Testament" churches. It's like a rich American who sees an old house in England and loves it so much that he has it moved, stone by stone, to his own country and re-created there, totally out of context. The Holy Spirit won't let us do this. We cannot freeze the Church at the first century or any other century, however much it may appeal to us.[3]

Considering the many legalistic attempts to set in concrete an inflexible, perceived pattern for church leadership, such

---

2. Robert O. Fife, "Is There a Pattern for the Church?" Part 1, *Christian Standard*, November 4, 1967, p. 698.

3. Harper, p. 25.

a warning can be appreciated. Fife concludes that there is an order revealed in the New Testament, but that its reproduction should not be pursued as an end in itself:

> But what is it in the order discerned in the New Testament which makes it worthy of imitation? We believe that the order was created by the Holy Spirit as a fit body for the continuing ministry of the risen Christ. And we believe that our primary motive for "restoration of the ancient order" should be to present to Him a body suited to His ministry in this generation.[4]

It becomes evident that our search for a New Testament blueprint for leadership needs to concentrate on the discovery of dynamic principles which can be applied to the church's leadership in every generation, rather than attempting to find and reproduce a standardized mold into which all church leadership must always be forced. The pattern and principles must be tied directly to the nature of the church and the fulfillment of its divine mission, or they are irrelevant at best. At worst, they may paralyze the church.

The Church in Essence

As we seek to understand the nature of the church, we discover that the primary word used in the original Greek of the New Testament to designate the church is *ekklesia*. It is a noun derived from a similar Greek verb which meant "to summon forth." As a noun it applies to those who had been summoned or gathered together. The word was commonly used in Greek and Roman days to describe a regularly assembled political body. We still today commonly refer to

4. Robert O. Fife, "Is There a Pattern for the Church?" Part 2, *Christian Standard*, November 11, 1967, p. 713.

many of our legislatures as "assemblies." The term had wider usage still in describing any assemblage, gathering or meeting of people. In the Greek translation of the Hebrew Old Testament, this is the term used for the "congregation" of the Israelites, especially when they were gathered for religious purposes (Deut 4:10; 9:10; 18:16; 31:30; Judg 20:2; Ps 22:22). The concept is carried over into the New Testament as applied to Israel in Acts 7:28 and Hebrews 2:12 (quoting Ps 22:22), utilizing the same Greek word. It then rather naturally began to be applied in the Christian context to the gathering of Christians. I Corinthians 11:18 is translated, "when you come together as a church," for example. A study of I Corinthians 14:4, 5, 19, 28, 34, 35 reveals Paul's same use of the word in this context.[5]

In the bulk of the New Testament references, *ekklesia* is utilized to describe a church or congregation consisting of the total number of Christians who were living in one geographic location. This would seem to be the sense of the word when used by Jesus in Matthew 18:17, as well as when it is used in Acts 5:11; 8:3; 14:23; I Corinthians 4:17; Philippians 4:15; I Timothy 5:16, 17. It is most certainly the case when it is used to specifically describe the churches at Jerusalem (Acts 8:1; 11:22), Cenchrea (Rom 16:1), Corinth (I Cor 1:2; II Cor 1:1), Thessalonica (I Thess 1:1; II Thess 1:1), and the churches cited in Revelation 2:1, 8, 12, 18; 3:1, 7, 14. The term is also used in the plural to identify several such groups of Christians (Acts 15:41; 16:5; Rom 16:16; I Cor 7:17; II Cor 8:18, 19).

It is highly significant to note that this Greek word for "church" is never used in the singular to describe the Christians

---

5. William F. Arndt and F. Wilbur Gingrich, *A Greek-English Lexicon of the New Testament and Other Early Christian Literature* (Chicago: The University of Chicago Press, 1952), p. 240.

of a geographic region, state or country. In other words, the New Testament never speaks of "the church of Judea" or "the church of Greece." Instead, it uniformly speaks of the churches (plural) of Judea (Gal 1:22; I Thess 2:14), Galatia (Gal 1:2; I Cor 16:1), Asia (I Cor 16:19; Rev 1:14) and Macedonia (II Cor 8:1). The "church" in every one of these references consisted of living, identifiable people in a particular place who were bonded together by their common allegiance to Christ. The word is never used, either, to describe a hierarchy of leadership, a state or national organization, a piece of property or a building. Its total focus is upon an autonomous group of people and their relationship to Christ.

We would, however, do an injustice to the subject if we did not also note the additional application of the term to the church in the universal sense. *Ekklesia* is also used a number of times in this way to represent all of the believers through the ages who belong to Christ and are, consequently, a part of the church which He came to establish (Matt 16:18; Acts 9:31; I Cor 6:4; 12:28; Eph 1:22; 3:10, 21; 5:23-32; Col 1:18, 24; Phil 3:6). In Romans 16:4 it is linked in the plural with the Gentiles. In I Thessalonians 1:1 it is associated with the Thessalonians, God the Father and the Lord Jesus Christ. In Romans 16:16 it is linked in the plural with Christ. It is further related to God elsewhere in Acts 20:28; I Corinthians 1:2; 10:32; 11:16, 22; 15:9; II Corinthians 1:1; Galatians 1:13; I Thessalonians 2:14; II Thessalonians 1:4; I Timothy 3:5, 15.

In every case noted above, it seems that the emphasis of the word "church" in its Christian context is upon the relationship of people to each other, due to their common relationship to God through Christ. This is a key concept to be grasped by anyone who would seek to comprehend the New Testament's blueprint for leadership.

This also brings us to our second word which is used to describe the church in its essence. The Greek word is another familiar one, *koinonia,* which we have generally translated as "fellowship" in the English. It could also be legitimately translated as "association," "communion," or "close relationship." It is first and foremost a word of relationship.[6] Note its usage in I Corinthians 1:9, describing our "fellowship with His Son." In II Corinthians 13:13 we have the "fellowship with the Holy Spirit," and again the same in Philippians 2:1. But especially take note concerning what the inspired apostle has to say in I John 1:3-7 about the source of our fellowship, or relationship, with each other as Christians:

> We proclaim to you what we have seen and heard, so that you may also have fellowship with us. And our fellowship is with the Father and His Son, Jesus Christ. We write this to make our joy complete. This is the message we have heard from Him and declare to you: God is light; in Him there is no darkness at all. If we claim to have fellowship with Him yet walk in the darkness, we lie and do not live by the truth. But if we walk in the light, as He is in the light, we have fellowship with one another, and the blood of Jesus, His Son, purifies us from all sin.

John appears to be deeply concerned that we understand, first of all, that we really have no relationship (fellowship) with one another unless we are first brought into that primary relationship with God through Christ. Secondly, he wants us to know that fellowship is an active relationship, not

6. Arndt and Gingrich, pp. 439-440.

some static or passive concept. It is one of walking in Christ-likeness (in the light)—obviously a growing experience. Thirdly, if we have established that primary relationship, and we are continuing and growing in it, we also have fellowship with one another; and we find a purifying application of Jesus' redeeming blood in that shared relationship.

This concept of participating in the fellowship requires some further development as well. Examine I Corinthians 10:16 and its use of the word to point out our active participation with one another in the Lord's Supper, even as we participate in the body and the blood of Christ. Philippians 3:10 speaks of our fellowship in sharing suffering. II Corinthians 8:4 describes fellowship in the sense of taking part in the relief of the saints. Without carrying the matter any further, the point of all of this is to say that "fellowship," as defined in its New Testament usage, is an extremely active term. Yet, the church today has tended to re-translate it into a passive sense.

In this same vein, the New Testament concept of worship has also been seriously misunderstood. Two Greek words are translated "worship" in our English versions of the Bible. The first word means to prostrate oneself, to fall down before, or to do obeisance to God. The second word denotes the idea of serving God.[7] In Matthew 4:10b, quoting Deuteronomy 6:13, Jesus refutes the temptation of Satan by citing the command of God, "Worship the Lord your God, and serve Him only." The verse integrally links both of these words in describing our relationship to God. In Romans 12:1 we are admonished by Paul, "Therefore, I urge you, brothers, in view of God's mercy, to offer your bodies as

7. Arndt and Gingrich, pp. 468, 723-724.

living sacrifices, holy and pleasing to God—which is your spiritual worship." The concept here of worship is obviously a very active experience involving every aspect of our lives. Yet, the modern church has persisted in transforming the New Testament concept of worship into a passive experience on Sunday mornings, in which the church leadership is expected to perform before an audience of spectators and critics. What a counterfeit substitute for worship!

It might also be pointed out that this concept has then extended beyond the "worship service" to permeate the congregation's viewpoint of its total Christian experience (or worship). Leadership is hired or elected to perform ministry on behalf of the church, and the congregation settles back to be served. It is this notion which has largely incapacitated most churches. It is 180 degrees off-center from the New Testament concept reflected in Ephesians 4:11-16 and I Corinthians 12:12-27. In these passages the church is pictured as a living, growing body, with each member being gifted by God to perform a function vital to the body. The concept is re-stated in I Peter 2:5, 9 where the church is described first as "living stones . . . being built into a spiritual house to be a royal priesthood, offering spiritual sacrifices acceptable to God through Jesus Christ"; and then, "you are a chosen people, a royal priesthood, a holy nation, a people belonging to God, that you may declare the praises of Him who called you out of darkness into His wonderful light." Rather than the leaders being the performers and the congregation being the spectators and critics, the New Testament picture is one in which all the members of the congregation are the performers, and the leaders are the coaches. No one is permitted the role of spectator or sideline critic!

There is an urgent need for us to rediscover this vital concept of the essence of the church. The church has never been, nor can it ever be, a static organization. Nor can it be one in which ministry is delegated to a few. It is either a living, active and interactive organism, growing into Christ-likeness, or it is not the church at all—regardless of the name it wears.

The Church in Purpose

Almost every venture or organization has been initiated by the vision of some individual or small group. Yet many of these begin to go astray, to flounder or to go under as time passes and the vision of the initiator(s) is lost. The church is no exception. Conceived by God and initiated through the ministry of the apostles, acting under Jesus' authority, the church found its local expression all over the world. In the process of adapting to their local and contemporary cultures, however, many of these churches forgot, somewhere in the process, their reason for being.

It is a sad, but accurate, commentary on current editions of the church to note that most have a very vague or ill-defined sense of purpose. An examination of their leadership structure, their function and their performance all contribute to this evaluation. The majority just continue to exist, listlessly plodding along an aimless course which is bound for nowhere. The leadership is hard-pressed to devise any statement of mission or purpose, and those which are written bear little resemblance to the actual congregational priorities. This can be easily confirmed by comparing these statements of mission with the priorities reflected in the annual budget and the activities scheduled for the congregation in its weekly bulletin. These two printed pieces speak volumes about a church's real sense of mission. There is definitely no lack of busy-ness in most of these churches, but there is a serious deficiency in the area of purposeful activity and financial priorities!

The church has also too often turned into a battleground, being torn asunder by conflicting personalities and controversial issues. Any church which has an ill-defined sense of purpose is particularly susceptible to such conflict. Joe Ellis makes an excellent point:

> The millers who once ran gristmills had to be careful to keep grain between the millstones at all times. Otherwise, the great stones would grind each other to pieces. The mill would destroy itself if not engaged in its intended function. A parallel may be seen in the relationships among Christians. If the church is not properly engaged in accomplishing its purpose, it may grind destructively upon itself. This is one reason churches become embroiled in internal friction and sometimes manifest relationships that are as corrosive as those that exist among people of the world.[8]

If we are to comprehend the role of the leadership in the New Testament church we must be willing and able to develop an accurate and adequate mission statement for the church. Ted Engstrom and Edward Dayton give some sound reasons for the development of such a statement by the leaders of every church. They list seven benefits to be derived:

1. It gives us a reason for being, an explanation to ourselves and others as to why we exist as an organization.
2. It helps us to place boundaries around our ministry and thus define what we will do and what we will not do.

---

8. Joe S. Ellis, *The Church On Purpose* (Cincinnati: Standard Publishing Company, 1982), p. 72.

3. It describes the need that we are attempting to meet in the world.
4. It gives a general description of how we are going to respond to that need.
5. It acts as the hook on which the primary objectives of the organization can be hung.
6. It helps to form the basis for the ethos (or culture) of the organization.
7. It helps us to communicate to those outside the organization what we are all about.[9]

While Engstrom and Dayton are specifically writing about the development of statements of purpose for Christian organizations, there is obviously an equally important application to the church itself. A church without a clear sense of purpose will tend to tear itself apart, with each member and leader owning his own agenda and list of priorities.

How does a church go about developing such a statement of mission? Its leadership might begin by working together to compose four paragraphs which explain: (1) Why our church exists; (2) What we are to accomplish; (3) How we propose to accomplish these objectives; and (4) Within what boundaries we propose to implement this plan.

Rather than looking internally or to cultural examples, such as the corporate model, political government or the local Elks Lodge for a pattern for the church, a committed re-examination of the New Testament is certainly the preferable starting point. Far too many leaders have been more committed to the imposition of Robert's Rules of Order on the church's structure and operation than they have been

9. Ted W. Engstrom and Edward R. Dayton, "Defining the Mission," *Christian Leadership Letter*, June, 1984, pp. 1-2.

to the recapturing of the New Testament's guidelines. Contrary to evident popular belief, Robert had no apostolic commission or inspiration when he devised his rules, and they have little or no value to the church. Certainly Paul, who antedated Robert by numerous centuries, was making no reference to that particular set of rules when he admonished the church at Corinth to do things "in a fitting and orderly way" (I Cor 14:40).

James Murch summarizes some of the New Testament guidelines as follows:

> The functions of a local church, according to the New Testament, are (a) to glorify Christ (Eph 5:25-27); (b) to worship God in spirit and in truth (Heb 10:19-25); (c) to preach the Gospel (I Cor 15:1-11); (d) to observe the sacraments of baptism and the Lord's Supper (Rom. 6; I Cor 11); (e) to supply instruction in righteousness (Eph 4:11-16); (f) to exercise discipline (II Thess 3:6-15); (g) to provide fellowship and Christian growth (Rom 15:1-7; Eph 2:14-22); (h) to minister to the unfortunate (James 1:27; Acts 6:1-7); and (j) to promote Christian unity (I Cor 1:10; Rom 14:19).[10]

Certainly a primary focus in any serious quest to understand the New Testament purpose of the church should be a study of Jesus' Great Commission, found in Matthew 28:18-20. After citing His unique credentials to authorize such a statement of mission for the church, He proceeded to outline a three-point agenda: (1) Make disciples of all nations; (2) Baptize them in the name of the Father, Son and Holy Spirit; and (3) Teach them everything He had taught. The

10. James DeForest Murch, *The Free Church* (n.c.: Restoration Press, 1966), p. 20.

scope of the commission was world-wide. It would recognize no racial, sexual, political or geographical boundaries in its application (Gal 3:26-28). It was also cyclical in nature. It was to be repeatedly applied to all who were discipled, baptized and taught—that they might do the same to others. This commission given by Jesus immediately before His ascension into Heaven remains the marching orders for the church. In essence, our business in this world, as Christians and as the church, is that of evangelism and edification. No substitute agenda has ever been approved.

When the essential New Testament purpose and functions of the church are considered, it becomes evident why no structure beyond the local church is authorized. When that functions properly, nothing else is needed. The known world was permeated with the gospel in that first generation with nothing more than local churches functioning, either by themselves, or in cooperation with others. There was in that system a flexibility and workability which effectively adapted to some of the most difficult circumstances anyone could conceive.

Jesus' prayer for His immediate disciples and for all subsequent believers, found in John 17:1-26, reflects the same plan and purpose for the church as the Great Commission. Most importantly, both passages of Scripture bear the promise of divine assistance with the mission He has given the church to accomplish. Were it not for this element of the covenant, the leadership of the church would have to declare its divinely-assigned task to be "Mission Impossible." Unfortunately, most churches seem to forget this divine element in the equation and seek to operate solely within the limits of their visible resources. The relatively few churches who in fact have actually believed and claimed this promise have embarked on the most incredible spiritual adventure ever experienced by man.

When God is our partner in a venture, we dare not think small! Yet, the Apostle Paul's declaration in II Corinthians 5:7, "We live by faith, not by sight," actually characterizes the leadership of very few churches. There is far greater concern about fiscal responsibility, potential liability and consideration of the probabilities of success. When will we learn that God specializes in the impossible?! It would appear that there is an underlying principle found in all of Scripture which tells us that *God never does for man that which he can do for himself.* But when man has done all that he can do, God then steps in and does the rest. As long as man hovers within the safety of his sight and his visible resources, relatively little will ever be accomplished. God blesses faith, not sight! He does not expect us to be able to guarantee success. He only asks us to trust Him and to start moving. He will open the doors and supply the resources needed to accomplish His purposes.

Such has been the exciting discovery of those churches who have dared to align themselves with God's purpose and to walk by faith. One vibrant, growing church in point has adopted a hard-and-fast principle: leadership is never permitted to ask concerning a proposed ministry, "What will it cost?" or "Can we afford it?" until the primary question has been answered: "Is this what God wants this church to do at this time?" If the answer to that question is a definite "Yes," cost and affordability become superfluous considerations. If God wants it done, He will provide a way! How God must weep over the myriad doors of opportunity He opens before churches, but which are slammed shut and nailed closed by faithless church leadership! Their hypocritical petitions for God's blessings upon their leadership and churches will never be honored.

The Lordship of Jesus

Particularly at issue here is the Lordship of Jesus. One might well ask in the church, "Who is the boss?" Where, indeed, does the ultimate authority lie? Jesus is unequivocal on that subject: "All authority in heaven and on earth has been given to me" (Matt 28:18). On the Mount of Transfiguration it was the voice of God which declared to the apostles, "This is My Son, whom I love; with Him I am well pleased. Listen to Him!" (Matt 17:5). When the disciples asked about doing works required by God, Jesus answered, "The work of God is this: to believe in the One He has sent" (John 6:29). Again, in John 14:6, Jesus states, "I am the way and the truth and the life. No one comes to the Father except through Me." Ephesians 1:22, 23 says of Christ, "And God placed all things under His feet and appointed Him to be head over everything for the church, which is His body, the fulness of Him who fills everything in every way." In a similar vein, Colossians 1:18 states, "And He is the head of the body, the church; He is the beginning and the firstborn from among the dead, so that in everything He might have the supremacy." Then Philippians 2:9-11 reminds us:

> Therefore God exalted Him to the highest place and gave Him the name that is above every name, that in the name of Jesus every knee should bow, in heaven and on earth and under the earth, and every tongue confess that Jesus Christ is Lord, to the glory of the Father.

Somehow we have become confused in our thinking and have equated believing in Jesus and professing Him with simply believing He can save us from our sins and accepting His role as Savior. The passages cited above are not talking about Jesus as Savior, but accepting Jesus as Lord. How dare we set up any leadership structure in the church which is permitted to take upon itself the authority to write any different agenda for the church than the one commissioned by the Christ, in whom God has vested all authority? Either He is Lord and sets the agenda, or He is not really Lord at all! Many wax eloquently about His Lordship and point to His name over the church door, but the piercing indictment of Jesus echoes down through the ages to find application in those churches today: "Why do you call me, 'Lord, Lord,' and do not do what I say?" (Luke 6:46). Jesus demands far more of His church than a verbal tribute to His title and authority. He requires faith and obedience!

One of the most devastating intrusions from our culture into the thinking of the church has been the widely-held notion that the church is intended to operate as a democracy. We have hallowed majority votes by the congregation in all matters before the church, and have devised the election of leaders who are perceived to be the representatives of the people, responsible for reflecting their preferences and interests in all decisions. Nothing could be further from the New Testament pattern! The church is, and always has been, a monarchy under the authority and rule of King Jesus (I Tim 1:17; 6:15; Rev 17:14; 19:16). When the church evolves into a democratic institution, Jesus ceases to be Lord, and it ceases to be His church.

Functions of Leadership

The primary emphasis in the New Testament is upon the

functions of church leadership, rather than official titles. In view of the essential nature of the church as a functioning body of believers who are all to be personally growing and involved in ministry, leaders in the church were those who actually led all of the other members in the accomplishment of the church's mission. It is a picture of the more mature leading the less mature toward Christ-likeness and fruitful ministry.

It would appear, from a comprehensive study, that the New Testament presents at least four general functions of all church leadership: *EXAMPLE* - The first responsibility of a functioning leadership is to lead by example. Jesus first set the example and taught this "follow me" style of leadership to His disciples (Matt 8:22; 9:9; 16:24; 19:21; Mark 1:7; 2:14; 8:34; 10:21; Luke 5:27; 9:23, 59; 14:27; 18:22; John 1:43; 12:26). The Apostle Paul also repeatedly and unashamedly called attention to the example he set before the churches, urging them to follow that example. Many church leaders, including elders and deacons, are hesitant and self-conscious about having others look at them as examples. They recognize their own imperfections. Paul had imperfections, too, but he recognized the fact that he had grown spiritually since becoming a Christian, and that he was ahead of those he needed to lead in many ways. He frankly admitted his failings, along with his commitment to keep growing. Then he attempted to lead by example in the areas where he had grown and was succeeding in modelling the Christian lifestyle (I Cor 11:1; Phil 3:12-17). The Lord calls growing Christians to help others to grow with them, sharing that which they have already learned and experienced. That is leadership!

NURTURE - The second basic function of church leadership is that of nurture. Note the numerous references in the

New Testament to the innocent, weak and vulnerable condition of new Christians, described as "infants" or "babies" (Eph 4:14; I Cor 3:1; I Peter 2:2). Church leadership has the responsibility of rearing these spiritual infants to maturity, "like a mother caring for her little children . . . encouraging, comforting and urging you to live lives worthy of God, who calls you into His kingdom and glory" (I Thess 2:7, 12). This nurturing involves far more than simply feeding the infants. It entails all the responsibilities of spiritual parenting. It includes creating a caring, sharing, ministering kind of experience for each child of God in which he can grow. It involves patiently living through both successes and failures in the growing process. As in physical parenting, it requires the cleaning up of messes and accidental spills, the changing of the dirty diapers, warming bottles at all hours of the night, losing some sleep and even having to deal with the problems of spiritual adolescence. Instant maturity would be a relief to all parents, but it never happens that way—physically or spiritually. It takes years of love, patience, encouragement and wisdom, combined with loving discipline and forgiveness, to be able to succeed in this spiritual parenting task entrusted to the church's leaders.

EQUIPPING - The third function of leadership is that of equipping God's people for ministry (Eph 4:12). Leading the church does not mean doing their ministry for them. The genius of the church is the fact that it is designed to be a fellowship (a working together) of ministers. It is a priesthood of all believers (I Peter 2:9). Both I Corinthians 12 and Ephesians 4 present the concept of a body made up of many parts, all of which are functioning together in ministry. How is this to be accomplished, though? Leadership has the responsibility of not only telling Christians that they are gifted, and helping them to recognize those gifts or abilities from God, but also equipping them to actually use their gifts in functions of ministry. This does not necessarily mean that all equipping must be done "in house" by the leadership of a particular church. There are the shared resources of Bible college, Christian camps, conventions, conferences, area seminars and guest "equippers" who can be used to augment the local leaders' equipping skills. But those leaders have the responsibility to see that the job gets done for every member. Church leadership has tended to make a specialty of pounding square pegs into round holes. Operating from crisis to crisis, they fill vacancies in the essential programs with whoever happens to be close at hand and available, whether or not they have either the gifts or the training needed to successfully function in those positions. Then the most willing are so overloaded with an unbelievable diversity of jobs that they either do not do any of their jobs well, or they burn out and eventually quit. How much better the divinely-sanctioned plan of discovering and equipping all of the gifted in the church, and placing them in ministries where God intended them to be! Our personnel crises would be over.

SERVICE - The fourth function of leadership is that of service (Matt 20:25-28). Such leadership can be dangerous, dirty, degrading and self-denying—"even as the Son of man came not to be served but to serve, and to give His life as a ransom for many" (Matt 20:28). Unlike the worldly leaders who "lord it over" the people, the greatest in Christ's kingdom would be the one who had learned to be the servant of all. A professional football team has in its locker room the slogan written on the wall: "WHATEVER IT TAKES!" That needs to be the slogan of church leaders.

Whatever it takes to meet people at the point of their need, and to help them up from there, that is what is called for from the leader. Some of the New Testament translators have done the church a grave injustice by suggesting autocratic and authoritarian leadership styles in their translation of verses like Romans 12:8; I Timothy 3:4, 12; and Hebrews 13:7, 17, 24 with the use of the word "rule." The two Greek words so translated both more accurately convey the idea of simply leading. The words recognize the responsibility of the leader to manage, or be at the head of, those he is charged with leading; but they also carry the concept of being concerned about and caring for the needs of those they are leading.[11] The message of the New Testament is very clear. The church leader is called to step down from any egotistical pedestal where he or others may conceive him to stand, and to get down among the people. He is to get down where they are hurting, falling and failing, and to pick them up, brush them off and lift them back on their way toward growth as he helps them to discover God's answers, forgiveness, strength, hope and love.

Qualifications for Leadership

As previously stated, the New Testament picture of leadership is one in which the more mature are leading the less mature into spiritual maturity (Christ-likeness) and the accomplishment of the mission and ministry of the church. Since this is the case, the qualifications for church leadership naturally relate to spiritual maturity.

---

11. Arndt and Gingrich, p. 344, 713-714.

Galatians 5:22-26 gives a good measuring rod for spiritual growth and maturity by listing the fruit of the Spirit. Those who are to lead the church should evidence the growth of these fruit in their lives. Jesus so admonished His disciples, "Thus by their fruit you will recognize them" (Matt 7:16). The church has always been plagued by false prophets and self-serving individuals who wish to wrest control in order to lead the church in directions designed for their personal profit or aggrandizement. Hence, John admonished the church in his day, "Dear friends, do not believe every spirit, but test the spirits to see whether they are from God, because many false prophets have gone out into the world" (I John 4:1). The admonition of the apostles in Acts 6:3 to choose men from among themselves "who are known to be full of the Spirit and wisdom" is still an applicable admonition and yardstick for any modern church to use in taking the spiritual measure of those they would select for leadership. This is the point Ron Finlay makes when he says:

> The Holy Spirit makes elders (Acts 20:28). The "qualifications" listed in I Timothy 3 and Titus 1 should be understood as guidelines to the church so that it might understand how to recognize this activity of the Spirit. The congregation is instructed to be sensitive to these characteristics being demonstrated by a man and his family (I Tim 3:2, 3; Titus 1:6).[12]

The point is a good one. Church leadership must be conceived as being neither self-made nor congregation-made. In fact, leaders cannot be created by either election or appointment. They are the product of the activity of the Holy Spirit

---

12. Ron Finlay, "The Eldership," *Christian Standard*, September 9, 1979, p. 818.

working within their lives. Upon the basis of the visible evidence of this activity, they are to be selected for leadership in Christ's church.

Specific sets of qualifications for church leaders are given in I Timothy 3; II Timothy 2-4; Titus 1-2 and other such passages. These will be examined and discussed at length in the following chapters. Suffice it to say, though, that all of these qualifications involve the selection of people for leadership whose lives exhibit the marks of Christian maturity. Carl Malm correctly observes, "Restoring New Testament Christianity requires restoring a New Testament leadership of Spirit-filled men who actively serve their people and set a worthy example for them to follow. See I Peter 5:1-3."[13] To this affirmation Stan Paregien adds the following word of caution:

> To appoint unqualified men with the idea of letting them "grow into the qualifications" is like appointing a polygamist with ten wives and waiting for nine of them to die! Anytime a congregation ignores the lifestyle outlined for elders and deacons in the Scriptures and appoints unqualified men, that congregation is already in trouble and headed for much more. It is far better to have only two godly elders than to have two dozen half-hearted office holders![14]

Positions of Leadership

Last, and probably of least importance, we come to the consideration of the New Testament positions of leadership.

---

13. Carl Malm, "Restoring the Life of the New Testament Church," *Christian Standard*, July 31, 1977, p. 695.

14. Stan Paregien, 'The Appointment of Elders and Deacons," *The Restoration Herald*, June, 1976, p. 113.

Significantly, this is where most people want to begin. There is a prevalent preoccupation with titles and positions, and far too little concern about qualifications and the performance of the essential functions of leadership. One is reminded of Robert Richardson's observation in 1836:

> I conceive it important to notice this, because we American Christians, in spite of our republicanism and our Christianity too, are so excessively fond of titles of distinction, that notwithstanding we profess to have repudiated the lordly and aristocratic designations so much in vogue among the European nations from whom we derive our origin, we seem delighted with the best substitutes we can find. . . . Hence, we have professed Christians wearing the military titles of Captain, Major, Colonel, etc., and many who bear the name of Elder, Ruler, Bishop, or Deacon, who cannot fill—do not fill, and perhaps never have filled such offices. This anti-Christian practice appears to thrive most, as we might naturally expect, in our QUEENLY cities, and in my opinion ought to be reprobated by all who plead for a "sound speech that cannot be condemned."[15]

Times, it would seem, have not changed a great deal. We still have those who are evidently only concerned about wearing a title, rather than actually functioning as church leaders.

The New Testament lists at least fifteen different positions of leadership in the church. These include: apostles, prophets, teachers, evangelists, pastors, elders, bishops, deacons, miracle workers, healers, tongues-speakers, helpers and administrators. This number includes, however, some positions of a temporary or passing nature, along with others

15. Robert Richardson, "Offices," *Millennial Harbinger*, September, 1836, p. 425.

which are alternative designations for the same persons. The matter is further confused by the fact that most of these terms have both specific and general connotations. The word "apostle" is used, for example, in the specific sense to identify the twelve specially chosen disciples of Jesus, along with Paul; but it is also used generally to describe one who was sent somewhere—such as a missionary (Matt 10:2-4; Mark 3:13-19; Luke 6:12-16; Acts 1:12-13; I Cor 15:8; Acts 13:1; 14:14; 15:13, 22; Gal 1:19). It becomes apparent that, unless one approaches the New Testament with some preconceptions of a simple, exclusive order of leadership, it will not easily be found there.

Part of the difficulty lies in our tendency to think in terms of officers and titles, rather than of functions. Most simply stated, when something in God's will needed to be accomplished, a person was designated to do it. He or she might do it only once, for a brief period of time, or for a lifetime. Once the task was accomplished, no one else would be called upon to do it unless it needed to be done again to fulfill God's purposes. Along this line, O. L. Shelton has written:

> The work of all . . . was functional, not official. The needs of the congregations, or groups of Christians, created the work which was essential to the "building up of the body of Christ." People were appointed to perform the services that met the needs.[16]

Such a revolutionary concept is unheard of within our federal government's bureaucratic system, where offices come into existence to meet a need in time, but remain in

---

16. O. L. Shelton, *The Church Functioning Effectively* (St. Louis: The Bethany Press, 1946), p. 28.

existence in perpetuity, even though the need ceased to exist twenty years ago. Sadly, the same situation can exist within the church if this New Testament concept of the temporary functions is overlooked.

A startling discovery is made when one tries to find the term "office" anywhere in the New Testament. While many translators have arbitrarily taken the liberty of inserting the word into several passages (Acts 1:20; Rom 11:13; 12:4; I Tim 3:1, 10), it does *NOT* appear in the original Greek text. In fact, the term "office" is never used anywhere within the pages of the New Testament in application to any position of leadership in the church! Only in the case of Jesus (Heb 5-7), who is described as a high priest after the order of Melchizadek, and of the Jewish priesthood (Luke 1:8) is such a term used. Its absence is deliberate and significant, although few seem to be aware of it. J. W. McGarvey, back in 1870, acknowledged that it might be absent, but considered the continued use of the word with application to church leaders as only a matter of semantics.[17] Doubtless, the translators shared his opinion, which is a reflection upon how deeply our culture has affected our thinking concerning leadership concepts. There is definitely a Greek word for "office," but it is not used by the inspired writers to describe church leaders. A study of the Greek in each of these instances in the New Testament reveals that the actual word used is a term of specific function (overseeing, serving, etc.).

Herein, then, lies the source of much of our current confusion and impotence. We have insisted on taking functions and making them into offices, simply because that is the way it is done in our culture. We have gone so far as to

17. J. W. McGarvey, *A Treatise on the Eldership* (1870: reprint, Murfreesboro: DeHoff Publications, 1962), p. 10.

even insert it into the text of our New Testaments to give the concept of offices some semblance of legitimacy. We have gone too far, and we have suffered the consequences! While many regard as a type of blasphemy the title "Reverend" applied to a pastor's name, due to its only Scriptural application to God, there ought to be even greater horror over the appropriation of the term "Office" in its widespread application to positions of church leadership. The New Testament church has only one Officer—Jesus! It is time to cast off preconceptions and to take a fresh look at the New Testament, considering the possibility that one might function without an office to meet needs with ministry—however revolutionary that may be to us.

TEMPORARY FUNCTIONS - Don DeWelt lists apostles (in the specific sense of the twelve) and prophets as being temporary functionaries in the church. He defines the apostles' duties as:

1. To bear witness in behalf of Christ.
2. To reveal the laws or truths of Christ's Church.
3. To demonstrate the deity of Jesus and their own apostleship by various miraculous signs and wonders.
4. To confer on others the power to work miracles.[18]

The nature of their duties was temporary, and they died without appointing successors as apostles. More will be said about the ministry of apostles, both in the specific and general sense, in the next chapter. Prophets in the church are mentioned in Acts 11:27-28; 13:1; 15:32; 21:10-11; and I Corinthians 14:1-40. Understanding the I Corinthians 13:9-10 "that which is perfect" to apply to the New Testament,

---

18. Don DeWelt, *The Church in the Bible* (Joplin: College Press, 1958), pp. 79-80.

DeWelt believes the prophetic function of the church to have also passed out of existence with the necessity for it.[19] To this list Murch also adds miracle-workers and tongues-speakers who, he says, "likewise fulfilled a purpose until the revelation of God was completed and the Word of Faith was available to all in the New Testament."[20] This is not, however, to deny in any way that God has continued to work in miraculous ways throughout history or in the church today; but to note that the special functionaries who were uniquely gifted in these ways to accredit and propagate the initial message completed their mission without leaving successors.

PERMANENT POSITIONS - When churches selected leaders from their own numbers they were generally known as elders or bishops (used interchangeably) and deacons. The elder is the most commonly mentioned congregational leader in the New Testament (Acts 11:30; 14:23; 15:2, 4, 6, 22, 23; 20:17; I Tim 5:17, 19; Titus 1:5, 6; I Peter 5:1). The second leader most often cited is the deacon (Phil 1:1; I Tim 3:8-12; Rom 16:1).

To appreciate the terminology used concerning the church leadership one must appreciate the fact that many of the early churches were begun in synagogues. Murch says:

> Church historians have marked many similarities between the synagogues and the local churches of the early Christian community. There were many instances in which Jewish Christians continued to meet in their accustomed synagogues worshipping on the seventh day in their usual manner and then after sundown, when the first day (the day of Christ's resurrection and the establishment of the Church) had come,

---

19. DeWelt, p. 84.
20. Murch, *The Free Church*, p. 21.

> they observed the Lord's Supper, sang their Christian hymns, joined in common worship and listened to a Gospel sermon.[21]

Tenney adds: "Wherever the missionaries of the first century proclaimed their message, they were able, with few exceptions, to begin in the local synagogue, and they usually obtained a hearing from the proselytes if they did not from the Jews themselves."[22]

The significance of this is seen in the fact that the leaders of the synagogues had such similar designations as the church came to use for its leaders. The synagogues had elders, a ruling elder, overseer (bishop), almoners (in charge of benevolence), and the Shelih Hetsebur or minister, often called the Angel of the Assembly (cf. Rev 1:16ff.). The overseer was so called because it was his duty to stand beside the one reading the Scriptures to make certain they were read correctly.[23] While the roles within the church did not remain identical to those in the synagogue, it is interesting to note their origin.

Evangelists are also mentioned as a part of the church leadership in the New Testament (Acts 21:8; Rom 1:15; Eph 4:11; II Tim 4:5). These, it seems, were the missionaries of the churches, going out to preach the gospel and to organize new congregations in other places. They broke the new ground with their preaching and teaching.

Finally, in the Ephesians 4:11 list of leadership positions there is an interesting linking of the pastors and teachers,

---

21. Murch, pp. 15-16.
22. Merrill C. Tenney, *New Testament Times* (Grand Rapids: William B. Eerdmans Company, 1965), p. 90.
23. Alexander Campbell, *Family Culture* (London: Hall and Company, 1850), p. 312.

one of several in the New Testament. The indication is that although others might function in these ways at times, there were some who did these together in a special way in the local church. These were quite often paid, full-time positions (I Tim 5:17-18), and those who so served were also called ministers (Col 4:7). More will be said about each of these positions in the following chapters.

In the Ephesians 4:11 listing of positions, or functions, which God found essential for the infant church to be able to grow into maturity and to equip its members for accomplishing ministry, there is a noteworthy progression: apostles, prophets, evangelists, pastors and teachers. Neither elders nor deacons are mentioned in the list, but we should not necessarily see them excluded by it. The list is simply one of major preaching, teaching and equipping functions. There was in the early church, as there should be today, an overlapping of functions; hence our confusion over titles. An apostle might prophesy, evangelize, preach, teach or pastor. Peter the apostle could say in I Peter 5:1, "So I exhort the elders among you, as a fellow elder." An elder or a deacon might function in several capacities at one or different times, including some of these teaching-equipping roles. At what point did an evangelist cease to be an evangelist and become a pastor or teacher in a new church? Again, our difficulties come from wanting to freeze and categorize leadership into exclusive offices. The New Testament does not permit that. The church required many functions of leadership to begin it and to help it grow in each new location. The New Testament emphasis is upon the supplying of those essential functions, rather than the development of a stereotyped structure with exclusive titles which could be duplicated ten or twenty centuries later.

In Summary

Rather than clearly defining a detailed, reproduceable organizational chart and pattern for church leadership, the New Testament presents some basic guidelines and a number of key principles which should be observed in selecting leadership. This enables the church to preserve its unique identity and nature, and to accomplish its mission in any and every cultural, political, geographical and historical setting it may encounter. In essence, the church is an identifiable group of people in a particular place who are bound together in a common relationship and task because of their mutual relationship and commitment to Christ. It is divinely designed to function as a body, in which every person serves as an important and functioning part. The church's primary mission is a dual responsibility of evangelism and edification. It is under a continuing commission to make disciples, baptize and teach, to the end that those who are so discipled, baptized and taught will be able to extend that same ministry to others. The church is not a democracy, but a monarchy under the exclusive authority of Jesus. As Lord of His church, His agenda is the only one that counts. Leadership of the church exists to function under His authority and direction in the accomplishment of His mission for the church.

Since every member is intended to be a successfully functioning part of the body, leadership is charged with the responsibility of setting an example, parenting the spiritually immature, equipping each member for ministry according to his gifts, and serving in whatever way necessary to meet people at their point of need with the love and mercy of God. Since leadership must therefore consist of the more spiritually mature who will be able to lead those who are less mature into Christ-likeness and fruitful ministry, it is vitally important that the church examine those proposed for leadership for the marks of spiritual growth and maturity before they approve their selection. Leadership qualifications must be produced by the work of the Holy Spirit in lives. They cannot be accomplished by a vote. They can only be recognized and approved.

Finally, God established both temporary and permanent positions of leadership among those so qualified; but His emphasis has always been upon the function of that leadership, rather than the recognition of exclusive titles or offices. There is often an over-lapping of leadership functions, preventing any exclusive ownership of labels or official titles. He who would lead in the kingdom of God must first learn to serve, even as Jesus came to serve and to lay His life down for sinful men. Herein is the essence of Christian leadership.

3

THE EVANGELISTIC MISSIONARY

The Mission of the Apostles

The mission and purpose for the church was, as we have noted, delivered first to the apostles (Matt 28:18-20). Hence, it also became their purpose as apostles. They were commissioned to first persuade people to follow Christ. They were to baptize them as a demonstration of their commitment to the Lordship of Jesus and in acceptance of His forgiveness of sin (Acts 2:38). Then they were to instruct them in the ways of the Lord, that they might grow into Christ-likeness and continue to extend the same ministry to others.

The apostles' mission was one of both evangelism and edification. While one might be tempted to emphasize the evangelistic ministry of the apostles, pointing to the beginning of the church at Jerusalem on Pentecost and the tremendous number of decisions made on that day (Acts 2:41), the daily additions thereafter (Acts 2:47), the rapid growth of the church (Acts 4:4), the conversion of the large number of Jewish priests (Acts 6:7), or the many other conversions recorded in the Book of Acts, the apostles did not neglect the second facet of their mission. They were well aware of the fact that spiritual infants will die, just as will physical infants, without food and care, so they nurtured them on the milk of the Word of God (I Peter 2:1-3). Immediately following the statement in Acts concerning the 3,000 additions to the church on Pentecost comes the statement, "They devoted themselves to the apostles' teaching and to the fellowship, to the breaking of bread and to prayer" (Acts 2:42).

Beyond the testimony of Acts to the edification ministry of the apostles is the authorship of the bulk of the New Testament books by the apostles. Two of the four gospels, which document much of what Jesus did and said, were penned by apostles; and the other two were obviously written with apostolic input and direction. In addition to his gospel, the Apostle John contributed three instructive letters, plus the Book of Revelation. Peter added two letters of encouragement and instruction to scattered Christians who were feeling the effects of persecution and having to deal with the messages of false prophets. The Apostle Paul was the most prolific of the apostolic writers, though, as his teaching epistles were addressed to individuals and churches who were serving the Lord over much of the known world.

Joe Ellis comments, "Dynamic individuals and vital groups of people have at least one characteristic in common: they know where they are going, they have a plan for getting there, and they work wholeheartedly at the job. Successful people have a clear, strong sense of purpose, around which they center their lives."[1] Certainly this applies to the apostles! It would have been easy for them to have become sidetracked in their mission, had they not had a strong sense of purpose. Acts 6:1-6 records the account of a huge problem which arose early in the life of the Jerusalem church concerning the benevolent ministry to the widows. It is significant that the apostles refused to allow the development of this ministry—however important or essential it was—to sidetrack them from their primary mission. "It would not be right for us to neglect the ministry of the Word of God in order to wait on tables," they said. "Brothers, choose seven men from among you who are known to be full of the Holy Spirit and wisdom. We will turn this responsibility over to them and will give our attention to the ministry of the Word" (Acts 6:2-4).

The apostles wisely chose to delegate the other areas of ministry, that they might be effective in the one to which they had been called. There is a valuable lesson in this for any servant of the Lord who would attempt to do everything for everybody. Had the apostles yielded to that temptation, they would have both diluted their own effectiveness in their primary ministries and have cheated the other members of the body out of their opportunities for sharing in the ministry of the church.

Even the apostles, however, had those times when they momentarily forgot their purpose and priorities, when they

---

1. Joe S. Ellis, *The Church on Purpose* (Cincinnati: Standard Publishing Company, 1982), p. 18.

were influenced by peer pressure and prejudice. Galatians 2:11-21 records a case in point, describing a situation at Antioch when the Apostle Paul had to correct the Apostle Peter. Peter, it seems, had been unduly influenced by Jewish friends to separate himself from the Gentile Christians, thus creating the distinct impression that—regardless of what Jesus had done on the cross for their redemption—the Gentiles were still some kind of second-class citizens in the kingdom. Paul had to remind him, ". . . if righteousness could be gained through the law, Christ died for nothing" (Gal 2:21b). How much is taught—both positively and negatively—by the example we set! Peter had the words and the phrases right, but his actions were not always consistent with his profession. According to Paul, neither were his (Rom 7:21-25). The wonder of it all is that God could take a handful of fumbling, failing men, instill them with a mission and a sense of purpose, and change a world through their efforts! It could happen only through His power.

The Plan of the Apostles

The apostles were not left without a plan. Acts 1:8 records the last words of Jesus to His apostles before He ascended: "You will receive power when the Holy Spirit comes on you; and you will be my witness in Jerusalem, and in all Judea and Samaria, and to the ends of the earth."

A POWER - Two key elements immediately appear when one studies the plan Jesus gave them. First of all, they were to go and accomplish this "Mission Impossible" with the power of the Holy Spirit. They would have to rely on Him for inspiration: "But the Counselor, the Holy Spirit, whom the Father will send in my name, will teach you all things and will remind you of everything I said to you" (John 14:26). Again in John 16:12-15 Jesus said:

> I have much more to say to you, more than you can now bear. But when He, the Spirit of truth, comes, He will guide you into all truth. He will not speak on His own, He will speak only what He hears, and He will tell you what is yet to come. He will bring glory to Me by taking from what is mine and making it known to you. All that belongs to the Father is mine. That is why I said the Spirit will take from what is mine and make it known to you.

When one realizes how forgetful and confused we all become at times, simply because we are all human, we can only thank God for this miraculous provision made for those apostles. They would be able to get it right! Their written accounts, along with their preaching and teaching, could be trusted. It had the divine stamp of approval and accreditation on it, for it was all edited by the Holy Spirit.

Beyond providing accurate recall for the apostles, the Holy Spirit was going to also handle the responsibility for getting the results. In describing the Christian's armor in Ephesians 6:10-18, the Apostle Paul begins by saying, "Finally, be strong in the Lord and in His mighty power" (v. 10). And then in verse 17 he describes the Christian's offensive weapon as "the sword of the Spirit, which is the Word of God." Hebrews 4:12 uses the same figure of speech: "For the Word of God is living and active. Sharper than any double-edged sword, it penetrates even to dividing soul and spirit, joints and marrow; it judges the thoughts and attitudes of the heart." Even more explicitly, Jesus explained to His apostles in John 16:7-11:

> But I tell you the truth: It is for your good that I am going away. Unless I go away, the Counselor will not come to you;

> but if I go, I will send Him to you. When He comes, He will convict the world of guilt in regard to sin and righteousness and judgment: in regard to sin, because men do not believe in Me; in regard to righteousness, because I am going to the Father, where you can see Me no longer; and in regard to judgment, because the prince of this world now stands condemned.

From the time the gospel was first preached at Pentecost to the ministry of the present day church, the Holy Spirit has been active in and through the Word. He is the One assigned the responsibility for producing results! What a relief that should have been to the apostles! What a relief it should be to the church today! The apostles' job was that of preaching and teaching. God supplied the message and produced the results through His Holy Spirit's ministry. All the apostles had to do was to deliver the message!

So it is with the church today. Neither the apostles nor we were ever asked to try to manipulate people to produce spectacular or immediate results. That which God would not do in violating the free will of man, He certainly did not license among the apostles or among modern-day evangelists. We are reminded by the Parable of the Sower in Matthew 13:3-9, 18-23, that the Word of God is like seed which is sown. Its life and fruitfulness depends upon the soil where the seed lands. Within each seed is the same power to produce life and productivity, but the condition of each man's soil is left to him. The handlers of the Word have only been called to be sowers of the seed. But as the Apostle Paul noted, that is an exciting task; for we handle something which contains unprecedented power:

> I am not ashamed of the gospel, because it is the power of God for the salvation of everyone who believes: first for the

> Jew, then for the Gentile. For in the gospel a righteousness from God is revealed, a righteousness that is by faith from first to last, just as it is written: "The righteous will live by faith" (Rom 1:16-17).

The gospel message must be both heard and understood for its power to be unleashed. Here again the Holy Spirit's miraculous ministry was to come into play. There would be no way the apostles could become linguistically qualified to communicate effectively in all of the different languages they would need to reach the many different ethnic groups around the world. Even as the church began on Pentecost in Jerusalem there were gathered in that one city, "Parthians, Medes and Elamites; residents of Mesopotamia, Judea and Cappadocia, Pontus and Asia, Phrygia and Pamphylia, Egypt and the parts of Libya near Cyrene; visitors from Rome (both Jews and converts to Judaism); Cretans and Arabs . . ." (Acts 2:9-11). According to Acts 2:4-12, these people who were from all over the world were each miraculously enabled to hear in their own native language God's message of salvation. This, according to verse 4, was one of the consequences of the apostles' having been filled with and empowered by the Holy Spirit.

Much confusion has been generated by the translators' insistence upon rendering the gift "tongues," rather than "languages." It is quite clear in the Acts 2 context that this remarkable power given to the apostles was an enabling tool for the purpose of accomplishing communication with those who could not otherwise understand them. Those cults which have arisen out of this confusion, who have persisted in making a counterfeit "tongues" experience a test of spirituality and an entrance rite into their sect, have totally missed the point. Whenever this ability has been misunderstood or misused, it has created division among God's people. I Corinthians 12-14 was penned by Paul to deal with this specific problem. It obviously had become a big problem in Corinth. Some who either had, or claimed to have, this spiritual power were, in their worship in the church in Corinth, speaking in foreign languages to show off before the folk at home. It was creating havoc in the worship and division among the brethren. Paul writes in I Corinthians 14:7-12, 18-20 these words of reprimand:

> Even in the case of lifeless things that make sounds, such as the flute or harp, how will anyone know what tune is being played unless there is a distinction in the notes? Again, if the trumpet does not sound a clear call, who will get ready for battle? So it is with you. Unless you speak intelligible words with your tongue, how will anyone know what you are saying? You will just be speaking into the air. Undoubtedly there are all sorts of languages in the world, yet none of them is without meaning. If then I do not grasp the meaning of what someone is saying, I am a foreigner to the speaker, and he is a foreigner to me. So it is with you. Since you are eager to have spiritual gifts, try to excel in the gifts that build up the church. . . . I thank God that I speak in tongues more than all of you. But in the church I would rather speak five intelligible words to instruct others than ten thousand words in a tongue. Brothers, stop thinking like children. In regard to evil be infants, but in your thinking be adults.

In conclusion Paul says, "Tongues, then, are a sign, not for believers but for unbelievers . . ." (v. 22). The gift was an evangelistic, linguistic tool to enable the apostles to communicate their message to all peoples. Those who claim the gift today should either get out on a mission field with the unbelievers who speak that language, and need to be discipled for Christ, or they should shut up, according to

Paul. It has no place in the church at home. What a marvelous, miraculous tool it was, however, when it was used as it was intended!

A STRATEGY - The second element of the plan involved a strategy. The apostles were instructed to begin their witnessing for Christ in Jerusalem, and then to move on to Judea, Samaria, and to the ends of the earth. In other words, they were to begin where they were, and then to reach out in ever-widening concentric circles until they had witnessed to the world. Note again that Jesus did not make them responsible for winning all the world, but for witnessing to it.

It is always a glamorous temptation to try to succeed with a plan somewhere else. Somehow it always looks easier almost anywhere but where we are. Jesus knew that, so He refused to give the apostles or the church that option. Their mission was to begin at home in Jerusalem—the capital of Judaism and the seat of persecution. It was here that Jesus had been—only a few weeks before—tried and crucified. It was here that most of the harassment and persecution for the early church would find its source. If there was really power in the divinely-inspired message, it would have to work and be proven to them here in Jerusalem. If the apostles could succeed here, they could succeed anywhere; but if they refused to try here, they would be powerless anywhere else.

Neither did the plan allow the apostles to quit after witnessing at home. Theirs was a world-wide mission, beginning at home, but systematically stretching out, step-by-step, to reach the farthest beings on earth. It required bridging prejudices and fears. Judea included "home folk." They were Jews. Samaria was a different matter entirely. Despised half-breeds lived there. Self-respecting Jews would travel an extra day's journey to avoid having to even pass through Samaria on their way from Judea to Galilee. The Samaritans, along with all the Gentiles, however, would have to be included in their witnessing and their fellowship. That would be an especially tough lesson for apostles like Peter to learn (Acts 10:1-48; Gal 2:11-21). In that company entitled to receive the gospel would even be the hated occupation force, the Romans. In fact, the first Gentile Christian to be converted would be a commander of the occupation forces at Caesarea, Cornelius (Acts 10). From there the gospel would travel even to Caesar's own household (Phil 4:22). If they would but deliver the message, according to the strategy, the gospel contained the power to save all who would believe—anywhere!

The Methods of the Apostles

A study of the apostles' missionary methods yields some rather interesting characteristics. First of all, their ministries were marked with *boldness*. Though they had been given a mission most would consider to be absolutely impossible, they tackled it with a confidence which spoke of their belief in the promise of the abiding presence of Jesus and the enabling power of the Holy Spirit. They really believed that they were *not* alone in this task, and that if they did their part, God would supply the rest which was needed to enable them to succeed. Paul could write with ringing confidence, after years of experience as an apostle, "I can do everything through Him who gives me strength" (Phil 4:13). The account of Peter's Spirit-filled message found in Acts 4:8-12, as he and John boldly responded to charges against them before the Jewish Sanhedrin, is an excellent example.

Each trial they faced was viewed as God's opportunity, rather than as an insurmountable obstacle in their path; and they boldly used it to proclaim Jesus. They refused to be intimidated, even by this high court, when they were commanded to cease speaking and teaching in the name of Jesus. To this Supreme Court order they responded, "Judge for yourselves whether it is right in God's sight to obey you rather than God. For we cannot help speaking about what we have seen and heard" (Acts 4:19-20). Now that is boldness!

Time after time in the Book of Acts we witness the apostles' boldness. Church leadership today needs to take a lesson from the apostolic method of approaching difficult and seemingly impossible tasks. It would appear that the majority of today's churches are led by cautious, fearful men who have seldom if ever personally dared to walk by faith, much less ever consider leading the church in venturing out on faith. They would rather do anything else than to take any chances or to risk exposing themselves or the church to danger, possible failure or any undue liability risks. True, it is all right for the missionaries they support to hazzard their very lives; but playing it safe is the only way to go back in the home church. With such leadership the church would have surely died and become extinct in the first century! The apostles led boldly, and the church survived, in spite of the most determined attempts in history to exterminate Christianity.

Secondly, the apostles went to *the cities* with their mission and message. Beginning at Jerusalem, the capital city of the Jews, we see them next going to the city of Samaria in Acts 8. Then we begin to see the names of cities like Damascus, Joppa, Caesarea, Syrian Antioch, Paphos,

Pisidian Antioch, Iconium, Lystra, Derbe, Philippi, Thessalonica, Berea, Athens, Corinth, Ephesus, Troas and Rome. These were population centers of the day. True, smaller villages were also reached, but the apostles' primary thrust was to reach the cities. Here they would find the leaders and the majority of the people.

It is somewhat startling to realize that the thrust of modern missions has largely focused on rural areas, rather than urban. We have gone to the out-of-the-way places and have majored in bush evangelism. In so doing, we have largely neglected the great population centers of the world. Even in the United States, our churches are found more often in the country villages than in the major cities.

Of course the cities are difficult! Ask the Apostle Paul how difficult he found the cities to be where he sought to minister. Five times he was severely flogged, enduring 39 lashes. Three times he was beaten with rods. Once he was stoned. He was frequently imprisoned. He had to stay on the move constantly, due to all of the dangers he faced in the cities (II Cor 11:23-26). Yet, he persisted in going to the cities. And in every city he visited, he left an infant church. What a remarkable record!

No, evangelizing the cities has never been an easy or a popular task. The apostles would have been the first to admit it. Yet, had they neglected the cities in favor of an easier rural ministry, they would have never accomplished the task they were given of reaching the world for Christ. Neither will the church today reach the world in its generation if its thrust remains primarily a rural one.

Thirdly, the apostolic method was to begin by speaking in the synagogues wherever possible. Acts 14:1 is a typical statement: "At Iconium Paul and Barnabas went as usual into the Jewish synagogue. There they spoke so effectively that a great number of Jews and Gentiles believed." It made sense to try to begin first with those who might be *the most receptive to the gospel.* Those who attended the synagogue already had an existing relationship with God. Consequently, as we have already noted, the majority of the early churches began in the synagogues, with the Christians having their worship after the Jewish worship had concluded.

There is much to be said for the apostles' wisdom in looking for a most receptive audience as a beginning point. Even at the Areopagus in Athens Paul sought to find some *common ground* with his audience as a beginning point for their receptivity and understanding (Acts 17:16-34). They were religious people. He gave them credit for that. Among their many altars he had also found one with an inscription, "To An Unknown God." He then proceeded to tell them about the God they did not know. Paul's presentation before King Agrippa in Acts 26:1-29 is another case in point. He did everything possible to emphasize common ground as the point for a positive beginning and understanding of the message.

It would seem that there is today too little effort being put into understanding the person or the community's context, in order to find that common ground on which to build a foundation for faith and understanding. There is far too much reliance upon a simplified, standardized, multi-purpose text and message track to be used in all situations. It seems to assume that everyone is starting from an irreligious base with no knowledge of God or His Word. How many people have been insulted and offended by such an approach! This was definitely not the apostolic method of evangelism. Perhaps we have tried too hard to make it easy for mass-produced evangelists, who have been taught to run along a single track to a pre-programmed response. Little wonder that many of these manipulated "decisions" so produced have been shallow and short-lived!

It should also come as little surprise to us that there has often been minimal identification with the religion of American missionaries in many cultures. It has been labelled, "The White Man's Religion." The apostles recognized that each person and each culture must own the message and their relationship with God, or it is not really theirs. That must begin with an attempt to understand the people and their culture, and to discover that which is held in common and ways to adapt the Christian experience to the unique circumstances, customs and needs found in each situation. Again, this method of evangelism is more difficult than the mass-produced, uniform versions, but it is far more effective in the long run in producing enduring decisions and indigenous churches.

Fourthly, the apostles sought out *the leaders* and attempted to evangelized them. It is significant to notice how many times the Scriptures take note of the conversion of leaders (Acts 6:7; 10:1; 13:1, 43; 16:14; 17:4, 12, 34; 18:7, 8, 24). This priority in the apostolic method of evangelism was undoubtedly a key factor in the relatively quick time new churches were able to function autonomously. Again today there appears to be a basic difference in approach. Both at home and abroad, few churches or missionaries are actively seeking to convert community or national leaders to Christ. Consequently, many churches struggle for years trying to make leaders out of followers. The apostles, however, recognized a basic principle: Win the leaders, and you will win their followers. In addition to that, they will be the most effective leaders for the church, if they have been converted and taught the ways of the Lord. There is, of course, real danger for any church which immediately places a natural leader in church leadership who does not yet possess the essential spiritual qualifications, or who does not understand the purpose and agenda the Lord has established for His church.

Finally, the apostolic method involved *follow-up*. After establishing churches on his first missionary journey, Paul and his companions "returned to Lystra, Iconium and Antioch, strengthening the disciples and encouraging them to remain true to the faith. 'We must go through many hardships to enter the kingdom of God,' they said. Paul and Barnabas appointed elders for them in each church and, with prayer and fasting, committed them to the Lord in whom they had put their trust" (Acts 14:21-23). The account continues to record the retracing of their steps through the churches before returning to Antioch of Syria, from which they had begun.

Acts 15:36 says, "Some time later Paul said to Barnabas, 'Let us go back and visit the brothers in all of the towns where we preached the Word of the Lord and see how they are doing.'" Barnabas and Mark then revisited Cyprus (Acts 15:39), while Paul and Silas went through Syria and Cilicia strengthening the churches (Acts 15:40-41). As a result, Acts 16:5 testifies, "So the churches were strengthened in the faith and grew daily in numbers."

In addition to these accounts, we find evidence of this principle in the letters of the apostles. These were mainly written for follow-up with the people to whom they had ministered, encouraging them, exhorting them and correcting them as needed. There will always be a need for follow-up in ministry. It is too easy to misunderstand, to forget, to grow lax and to become discouraged. Many ministries today break down at this point. What a blessing and a help the apostles' follow-up ministry must have been to their converts —and continues to be to us today!

The Qualifications for Apostles

The Apostles, in the specific sense of the twelve, were personally selected, trained and commissioned by Jesus for their mission. What was it that Jesus saw in these men which prompted Him to select them instead of others? We will probably never know for certain, especially since we really know very little about the background of each man. Foremost in their qualifications, however, beside the fact that Jesus saw each of them as potential leaders, was their willingness to leave everything and to follow Jesus wherever that would take them, and whatever that would cost them (Mark 1:16-20; 2:13-14; John 1:43). It is interesting to observe that God has never required perfect men for leadership, only growing and willing ones. This willingness to leave everything and to go wherever Jesus would take or send them was also a factor in the later selection of the Apostle Paul (Acts 22:21). In addition to Jesus' designation of the twelve as apostles (Luke 6:13-15), Paul was declared by the Lord to be "my chosen instrument to carry my name before the Gentiles and their kings and before the people of Israel" (Acts 9:15b). His apostleship is declared and vindicated in Romans 1:1; 11:13; I Corinthians 9:1; 15:9; II Corinthians 1:1; 11:5; Galatians 1:1; Ephesians 1:1; Colossians 1:1; I Timothy 1:1 and II Timothy 1:1.

In the general sense of the word, Barnabas is also identified as an apostle (Acts 14:4, 14), since he had been commissioned for missionary work by the church at Antioch, along with Paul, at the direction of the Holy Spirit (Acts 13:1-3). In addition, Adronicus and Junias are described as "outstanding among the apostles" in Romans 16:7. Paul also describes them in that same verse as his relatives who had shared prison with him, and notes that they had been in Christ before he was. Tradition adds that they were among the seventy who were sent out by Jesus (Luke 10:1-16).

We have already called attention to the fact that the New Testament mentions evangelists. The term is applied to Philip (Acts 21:8) and Timothy (II Tim 4:5) and is mentioned again in Ephesians 4:11. Paul also expresses a desire to "evangelize," a verb form of this same word, in Rome (Rom 1:15). From the activities of Philip, Timothy and Paul, W. R. Walker concludes: "The work of an evangelist would precede that of the pastor or teacher. Often, he seems to have been an itinerant."[2] He further adds: "Evangelists received their credentials from churches, as in the instance wherein the Antioch church sent Barnabas and Saul out as their representatives."[3]

Since these evangelists were also perceived to be the missionaries and ground-breakers of the church in establishing new churches, what is the difference between the apostle, in the general sense of the word (one who is sent), and the evangelist (one who goes and evangelizes)? The answer is obviously "none." We must once again be reminded that the New Testament concept of leadership does not revolve

---

2. W. R. Walker, *A Ministering Ministry* (Cincinnati: Standard Publishing Company, 1938), p. 113.
3. Walker, p. 115.

around exclusive titles or offices, but is concerned with the functions which need to be accomplished for the church to exist and to successfully fulfill His mission. Whatever we call them—evangelists, apostles, preachers or missionaries (the latter English term being derived from a Latin word equivalent to "apostle")—they were essential to the church's mission.

Don DeWelt finds ten qualifications stated in the New Testament for evangelists:

1. A man of righteousness, godliness, faith, love, patience, meekness and peace (I Tim 6:11; II Tim 2:22)
2. A man of purity (I Tim 4:12; 5:22)
3. A diligent student of God's Word (II Tim 2:15)
4. Gentle and apt to teach (II Tim 2:24)
5. A man of contentment (I Tim 6:6-10)
6. A man who avoids foolish questions (II Tim 2:16, 23; Titus 3:9-10; I Tim 6:3-5)
7. One who will conscientiously fulfill all his duties (I Tim 4:15-16; 6:12, 14, 20; II Tim 4:3-5)
8. One who is not ashamed of the testimony of the Lord (II Tim 2:1-8)
9. Willing to suffer hardship (II Tim 2:3; 4:5)
10. An example in all things (I Tim 4:12; Titus 2:7-8).[4]

It is apparent that these qualities would be desirable and expected of both the itinerant and the located minister of the Word. It is also equally apparent that they represent a standard so high that no man has likely ever attained it completely. As in the other standards defined in the New Testament for church leadership, they depict Christ-likeness, which comes only through spiritual growth. One who is

4. Don DeWelt, *The Church in the Bible* (Joplin: College Press, 1958), p. 94.

going to serve on the front lines of ministry for the church, beginning new churches, needs to epitomize the most mature, flexible, talented and reliable leadership the church can produce. The task is too difficult, hardships too prevalent, discouragement too frequent and the consequences too great to field immature or insecure novices.

The Preparation of Apostles

In addition to their willingness to follow Jesus wherever He led or sent them, the apostles obviously needed a thorough understanding of the message of Christ and the lifestyle expected of them and of the ones they would be leading. The Apostle Paul makes a point about the importance of this knowledge to his apostleship in II Corinthians 11:16 when he says, "I may not be a trained speaker, but I do have knowledge." He says of that knowledge of the gospel, "I did not receive it from any, nor was I taught it; rather, I received it from Jesus Christ" (Gal 1:12). So did the other twelve apostles which Jesus specially selected. Paul also mentions in Galatians 1:17 a period of time he spent in Arabia, which may have been the segment of his life in which the Lord was preparing him for his apostolic ministry. Acts 18:3 makes reference to his vocational training as a tentmaker, and Acts 22:3 cites his excellent general and religious education background, having studied under one of the leading scholars of the day, Gamaliel.

The other apostles had the privilege of spending three eventful years of daily living with the Master. What a unique and incomparable education that must have been! In addition to being taught directly His message and witnessing His miracles, they also had Jesus to study and to emulate as the perfect role model. He could, and did, show them what He was teaching them, as well as to tell them. They, too, as apostles would be required to become the role models for others whom they would lead in the ministries of evangelism and edification for the church.

Their three years of living with the Lord were, in fact, both an education and an internship combined. They learned by hearing, by helping and by doing. They learned how to set priorities in ministry. They learned about love and compassion. They learned about overcoming prejudice. They learned to be flexible. They learned what it was to have a sense of mission, and they learned about obedience—even when that obedience took you to a cross. In all of these cases, they learned as much by living with and watching the example of Jesus in the various circumstances He faced as they did by listening to His lessons. That is significant.

Not all of the others who were sent out as evangelists or missionaries had the privilege of a personal education and internship with Jesus. Nevertheless, it is important to take note of the fact that they had their training under the guidance of one of the apostles or the other church leaders. Just imagine what an education Timothy, Titus, Silas and others must have received as they traveled and lived with Paul! There was nothing theoretical about that education. It was practical from start to finish.

As thorough a Biblical training as possible, along with a solid internship with an experienced leader, should still be required of modern-day missionaries. Far too many ill-prepared novices have traveled around the world to attempt ministries in cultures they have not understood, attempted to teach people whose language they could not speak, and wasted enormous sums of money on ill-advised, untried or unworkable schemes. Most international corporations would *never* think of sending an employee to represent their companies in a foreign culture with less than ten times the preparation which the majority of churches require of the missionaries they support. They would regard it as a foolhardy risk of losing their market in that country. Studying the training these corporations require could teach us much which would have application to our preparation of missionaries—if we really believed the task we were sending them to do was half as important as these corporations are assigning to their people. The consequent messes which ill-prepared missionaries have created in country after country have both squandered the churches' financial resources, with little or no results at best, and have at worst become colossal embarrassments and a reproach to the New Testament church in these countries.

This indictment, based upon both years of study of missionaries' activities, as well as personal observation and participation, is not to say that qualified and prepared missionaries are not producing exciting and productive results around the world today. They definitely are! It is imperative, however, that we remove the blinders and face the facts, recognizing that our modern missionary failures may out-number our successes. Many people have been sent to the mission field simply because they were available and willing to go. Others have perceived failures at home to be God's direction to them to become a missionary. Most of these have no language training before they embark on their mission. They have not studied in any depth the culture they will be entering. They have no personal experience or knowledge of other missionaries' experience upon which they might base a workable strategy for their mission. Even their Bible education has often been minimal and weak. Many are psychologically unprepared for the kinds of stress they will have to face or the flexibility which will be required of them in order to succeed in another culture.

Few missionary candidates have had any internship whatsoever with an experienced missionary, and the internships experienced by the few have often been too brief and too poorly designed to really prepare them for service. The truth of the matter is that most Bible Colleges do the churches and their students an injustice by pretending to equip graduates for missionary service. Their required curriculum bears little resemblance to the New Testament pattern of preparation we have studied. Furthermore, many who teach missions courses on these campuses have either never served as missionaries anywhere, or they have already failed somewhere and come home to teach. Their theories and ineffective methods are being passed along to unsuspecting pupils who will naively repeat their inadequate performances before giving up and coming home in frustration and failure also. Such an assessment may seem negative and unfair, but a study of the practices, performances and statistics will prove it to be far more accurate than most will be willing to admit. Missions has become one of the favorite sacred cows of the Christian Churches. We can no longer afford to give it such a protected status.

There is an urgent need for the church and its colleges to determinedly return to New Testament standards for qualifications and preparation of those who are to be sent out as modern apostles. Willingness to go is not sufficient in itself. A couple of missionary courses will not suffice. A smattering of Bible knowledge is inadequate. Spiritual maturity must be required. Internships on mission fields with experienced, successful missionaries should be mandatory; and they should be required for a sufficiently long term to make possible learning by observation, assisting and actually doing the work. Certainly it will cost money and take more time to equip missionaries the New Testament way! But consider again the time and money corporations spend to equip their people. Is our task any less important? Of course not! It is time the church stopped settling for substandard preparation, based upon the faulty notion of economizing. It is a false economy! The cumulative savings which will be reaped from a return to New Testament standards, and the consequent improved stewardship of total missions dollars, will more than justify the apparent high initial expense involved.

The Partnership in Missions

Two churches in the New Testament particularly stand out in their relationship to missions and can serve as an example to us today. The first of these is the church at Antioch of Syria. Directed by the Holy Spirit, they set aside Barnabas and Saul for missionary service (Acts 13:1-3). It was in this same city that the disciples were first called Christians, according to Acts 11:26. The church there had found its beginning as a direct result of the persecution of Christians in Jerusalem at the time of Stephen's martyrdom. Christians from Jerusalem were scattered as far as Phoenicia, Cyprus and Antioch. Wherever they went, these Christians shared the message of Jesus, telling it mainly to the Jews. Some of them, however, went to Antioch and began also to invite Greeks to become Christians. God blessed this ministry, and a great number of people became believers

(Acts 11:19-21). The Jerusalem church was a little concerned, however, when the news reached them about this Gentile congregation, so they sent Barnabas to Antioch to check it out for them. We find Barnabas previously mentioned in Acts 4:36-37:

> Joseph, a Levite from Cyprus, whom the apostles called Barnabas (which means son of Encouragement) sold a field he owned and brought the money and put it at the apostles' feet.

Barnabas had evidently become a respected leader in the Jerusalem church, and the unique name the apostles bestowed upon him is indicative of his spiritual maturity and his commitment to ministry. Oh, that every leader could be so recognized as an encourager—not to mention possessing the same degree of financial commitment to the Lord's work! He was an excellent choice by the Jerusalem church for such a mission. Acts 12:23-24 says:

> When he arrived and saw the evidence of the grace of God, he was glad and encouraged them all to remain true to the Lord with all their hearts. He was a good man, full of the Holy Spirit and faith, and a great number of people were brought to the Lord.

What a remarkable account! Barnabas obviously went to Antioch with an open mind and a willingness to be used by the Lord however he might be needed. He was already a mature, experienced leader in the church, and he possessed the kind of ability and flexibility needed to fit right in with this Gentile group of believers. He rejoiced with them and encouraged them. Then he buckled down to work with them in ministry. Certainly the Gentile church was different from the Jewish church at Jerusalem. Many people would have had trouble accepting those differences, overcoming prejudices and adjusting to the many changes. He could rejoice with them and fit into their ministry.

Barnabas, however, realized that the opportunity and need for leadership at Antioch were greater than he could personally provide without limiting the ministry of the church. He was a man of faith and vision. So it was that he made a trip to Tarsus to look for Saul (later known as Paul) to come and help him. After Saul's dramatic conversion on the road to Damascus (Acts 9:1-19), this former hated and feared persecutor of Christians had found difficulty in gaining acceptance from those Christians. That was probably only to be expected. Again it had been Barnabas to the rescue! Acts 9:26-30 recounts:

> When he came to Jerusalem, he tried to join the disciples, but they were all afraid of him, not believing that he really was a disciple. But Barnabas took him and brought him to the apostles. He told them how Saul on his journey had seen the Lord and that the Lord had spoken to him, and how in Damascus he had preached fearlessly in the name of Jesus. So Saul stayed with them and moved about freely in Jerusalem, speaking boldly in the name of the Lord. He talked and debated with the Grecian Jews, but they tried to kill him. When the brothers learned of this, they took him down to Caesarea and sent him off to Tarsus.

Barnabas, who had placed his reputation on the line to first back this new Christian and to get him accepted in the fellowship at Jerusalem, now faced an opportunity and a need at Antioch; so he went to Tarsus to find Saul and to challenge him to a partnership in this ministry. Saul accepted that challenge and returned to Antioch with Barnabas. Acts 11:26 goes on to relate that the two of them worked with that church for an entire year and taught great numbers of people.

Isn't it amazing what God can do when leaders have a vision, when they are full of faith and the Holy Spirit, and when they are not concerned about building personal empires? Barnabas could have selfishly held on to the leadership at Antioch. He was popular and obviously successful. But Barnabas realized that the church's ministry must be bigger than any single man. He was willing to share that ministry for the glory of God.

Perhaps even more significantly, Barnabas had a concern about this gifted Christian leader in Tarsus who needed to be involved and growing if he were to be equipped for a ministry which he would lead on his own. He did something about that concern, and God blessed his decision. Oh, that other Christian leaders would follow his splendid example!

Acts 11:27-30 also closes that chapter with a most interesting account of the Antioch church's next move:

> During this time some prophets came down from Jerusalem to Antioch. One of them, named Agabus, stood up and through the Spirit predicted that a severe famine would spread over the entire Roman world. (This happened during the reign of Claudius.) The disciples, each according to his ability, decided to provide help for the brothers living in Judea. This they did, sending their gift to the elders by Barnabas and Saul.

There is a certain irony about the fact that this Gentile church, which had been such a concern to the Jerusalem elders, is now the church sending sacrificial offerings via Barnabas and Saul to their Jewish brethren in Judea!

This was not the end of the Antioch church's sending ministry. Under the Holy Spirit's guidance, the church entered into a period of united fasting and prayer as they set apart Paul and Barnabas for missionary service. It must have been an emotional and an impressive time as they joined together in placing their hands on these two men who had been loved and who had served among them so faithfully before sending them away. One can only speculate about the communication which must have taken place between this church and their missionaries during their travels. While mail service was extremely limited, and we have no copies of any letters Paul or Barnabas wrote to the church at Antioch, it is not out of line to assume that there were a number of these. It takes no speculation, however, to learn what these missionaries did upon returning from their first tour of service. Acts 14:26-28 testifies:

> From Attalia they sailed back to Antioch, where they had been committed to the grace of God for the work they had now completed. On arriving there, they gathered the church together and reported all that God had done through them and how He had opened the door of faith to the Gentiles. And they stayed there a long time with the disciples.

Acts 18:22-23 reports a similar return to Antioch for reporting and participation in ministry after Paul's second missionary journey. This pattern is highly significant. These missionaries had a relationship with the Antioch church which amounted to a partnership in ministry. They had learned to love and respect each other as they had worked together, and they were obviously in prayer for each other as they served separately. The missionaries were still considered a part of the church's family and ministry, even though these men would be serving in completely different parts of the world. It was only logical and proper that they should return to the Antioch church to report the results of their ministry, to become acquainted with the new members of the church who had been added in their absence, and to spend more time ministering there at home with the brethren.

This New Testament pattern concerning the missionary-church relationship has been largely ignored by most churches and missionaries today, to the detriment of both the missionary and the church. The majority of "direct support" missionaries (who receive their income directly from churches, rather than through an administrative organization) are not supported by a single church. Their support is pieced together from dozens of churches.

Consequently, missionaries are forced to use their "furlough" time galloping around the country from church to church, spending a Sunday morning or evening with each, and attempting to raise more funds in order to be able to return to their fields. This appalling situation is the result of a "shotgun support" philosophy of missions which is prevalent in the churches. The missionary funds in each church are divided up and sent out like a shotgun spray, with small particles going in a number of directions.

The consequences of this non-New Testament method of missions support are devastating. No single church is responsible for sending the missionary or maintaining any close personal relationship with him. No single church has the privilege of having their missionary come home and spend "a long time with the disciples" (Acts 14:26). The little particles of support require immense amounts of time and expense for missionaries to maintain regular reports and communication with each supporting church. A tremendous amount of funds, time and missionaries' energy is wasted in the necessary travel to all of these churches during furloughs to report in some brief way. When the missionary finally returns to his field of labor, he is usually exhausted and generally still struggling to make ends meet financially. Yet, this costly and wasteful method is extolled around the world as being New Testament in form and as amounting to better stewardship than having a missionary organization take out its administration overhead. It is neither.

Blessed indeed are those few missionaries who, according to the New Testament pattern, enjoy a sending and supporting "living link" relationship with a single church! Like the relationship Paul and Barnabas had with the Antioch church, there is a mutual love and respect which is built between the missionary and the church members. The missionary will not have to worry about prayer support or financial support when he is off serving in another part of the world, for his church family back at home really cares. They will always arise to the need when it is known, for they keenly feel their responsibilities as partners in ministry. With our shrunken world of relatively fast and economical air travel, it is even possible for local church leaders to visit and to work with their missionary on his mission field for brief periods of time. While at home on furlough, the missionary can rest, renew relationships, visit with family, get needed medical attention, counsel with the elders, get more education and share in the local ministry of the church. Those who have participated in this kind of New Testament missionary ministry over the years can testify that no funds are wasted, all are blessed, and that the method still works!

We would be remiss if we did not briefly mention one other church of the New Testament in connection with missions. Paul writes the following note of appreciation to the church at Philippi in Philippians 4:14-19.

> Yet it was good of you to share in my troubles. Moreover, as you Philippians know, in the early days of your acquaintance with the gospel, when I set out from Macedonia, not one church shared with me in the matter of giving and receiving, except you only; for even when I was in Thessalonica, you sent me aid again and again when I was in need. Not that I am looking for a gift, but I am looking for what may be credited to your account. I have received full payment and even more; I am amply supplied, now that I have received from Epaphroditus the gifts you sent. They are a fragrant offering, an acceptable sacrifice, pleasing to God. And my God will meet all your needs according to his glorious riches in Christ Jesus.

This Philippian church which Paul had begun in Lydia's home (Acts 16:13-15, 40) also shared a very special relationship with Paul. He wrote in Philippians 1:3-8:

> I thank my God every time I remember you. In all my prayers for all of you, I always pray with joy because of your partnership in the gospel from the first day until now, being confident of this, that he who began a good work in you will carry it on to completion until the day of Christ Jesus. It is right for me to feel this way about all of you, since I have you in my heart; for whether I am in chains or defending and confirming the gospel, all of you share in God's grace with me. God can testify how I long for all of you with the affection of Christ Jesus.

Again and again these brethren had sent Paul financial aid for his ministry. A missionary always has needs! There never seems to be enough to be able to do everything which could be done. It must have been such a time of rejoicing for Paul every time he received a letter and a gift from these beloved Christians at Philippi, especially since it was generally delivered by one of the church's leaders. Although they had not sent Paul out on his missionary service, they could yet have a part in his ministry, as well as the church at Antioch. They, in the process, would receive a blessing from their giving and God's blessing upon them. This is the sense of Paul's comments to them in his letter. Paul could appreciate their need to participate in such an outreach ministry and he was fully able to understand the blessing they would receive from it. Consequently, he took the time to write to them about his ministry, along with sending words of encouragement and instruction.

There are indeed churches today which cannot afford to send and support a missionary by themselves. On the other hand, there are other churches which are capable of sending and supporting a number of them. Those which cannot, however, yet need the blessing of participating in some missionary's ministry, as did the church at Philippi. They should not, though, take the relatively small amount and adopt the "shotgun support" approach with it. Their small particles will often cost the missionary more in time, postage and travel expense necessary to acknowledge, report and maintain their support than it is worth. Such churches need to be a partner and a blessing to some one missionary, rather than being a burden to many. Then, as they grow, so ought their missionary support and involvement to grow.

In Summary

The apostles' mission, like that of the church, is one of evangelism and edification, and bringing churches into existence according to Jesus' Great Commission. The plan delivered to them by Jesus involved an empowerment by the Holy Spirit, who would be integrally involved in numerous ways in their ministry. The plan also included a strategy for mission which required them to begin evangelism and edification where they were (Jerusalem) and to expand outward in ever-widening circles, until the world was reached for Christ. The apostles' ministry was marked by boldness. It is also noteworthy that they made the evangelizing of cities and leaders highest priorities in their ministries. They first sought the most receptive audiences, generally beginning in the synagogues, and worked at discovering common ground and an identification for their message with the culture of their hearers. Follow-up on converts and new churches was also an important aspect of the apostolic method of ministry.

Those who were involved in such missionary work first needed a willingness to leave everything in order to follow Jesus and to go where He would send them. Whether known as evangelists, apostles or missionaries, the New Testament qualifications required of them include spiritual maturity, flexibility and reliability. A thorough knowledge of the Word of God and a solid internship with an experienced leader on a mission field should be considered as minimal preparation for missionaries.

Finally, churches need to adopt a "living link" relationship with one or more missionaries for whom they are willing to send and support as partners in ministry, rather than wastefuly scattering support in many directions and requiring unreasonable expectations of missionaries in return. Now, as much as ever, the church needs to rediscover and return to the New Testament's missionary methods if it is to succeed in accomplishing its mission in this generation.

4

MINISTER, PREACHER, PASTOR OR WHAT?

The Angels of the Churches

In the Book of Revelation the Apostle John is instructed to write the following explanation for the vision he saw, in which a figure appeared "like a son of man" holding in his right hand seven stars, and stood among seven golden lampstands (Rev 1:12-16).

> The mystery of the seven stars that you saw in my right hand and of the golden lampstands is this: The seven stars are the angels of the seven churches, and the seven lampstands are the seven churches (Rev 1:20).

The seven churches had already been identified in verse 11 as Ephesus, Smyrna, Pergamum, Thyatira, Sardis, Philadelphia and Laodicea. The apostle had been instructed to send the scroll he was preparing to these churches. As we continue on in Revelation we read in succession how he was to address each epistle for the churches to "the angel" of the church in each city (Rev 2:1, 8, 12, 18; 3:1, 7, 14). For example, Revelation 2:1 reads: "To the angel of the church at Ephesus write: These are the words of Him who holds the seven stars in His right hand and walks among the seven golden lampstands." Then He continues on with a personal message for each church.

Who are these angels of the churches? We are aware that angels are the messengers of God, and we generally think of them as being supernatural creatures who live in heaven, and who return to heaven after fulfilling whatever mission God has assigned them on earth (Matt 1:20; 2:13, 19; 22:30; 24:36; 28:2; Mark 8:38; Luke 1:11, 13, 18, 38; 2:9, 10, 13, 15, 21; 22:43; John 20:12; Acts 5:19; 7:53; 10:22; 12:7, 23; II Cor 11:14; Gal 4:14; I Tim 3:16; Heb 1:6; I Peter 1:12; Rev 5:2; 14:10; 18:21). They appear in dazzling light (Luke 2:9; Acts 6:15; 7:30) and in white garments (Matt 28:3; Luke 24:4; John 20:12). In Matthew 18:11 Jesus appears to indicate that children have guardian angels. Psalm 91:11-12 is quoted in Luke 4:10-11 by Satan as he tempts Jesus, noting again the role of guardian angels. The reference to Peter's angel in Acts 12:15 is also interesting. In all of these references, however, there is still no mention of angels of churches, at least in the sense of these supernatural beings.

Considering the fact that John is instructed in Revelation 1:11 to send the scroll to the churches, instead of telling him to give it to angels to deliver, there would seem to be a far more logical explanation concerning these angels to whom the letters are addressed than postulating some additional order of supernatural creatures.

There are three closely-related Greek words involved in clarifying this problem. The verb involved means to announce or to deliver a message to someone. Mary Magdalene was doing this kind of "angeling" when she delivered the Easter message to the disciples, according to John 20:18. In one of the two noun forms, it means the message, the good news, as it is used in I John 1:5. The other noun form is applied to the one who delivers the message. In Luke 7:24 John sends such "angels," or messengers, to inquire of Jesus and to bring back His message. In Luke 9:52 Jesus sends "angels," which are identified as His disciples, ahead to a Samaritan village to prepare for His coming. Going back to the Old Testament, the Greek version also uses this word to describe Joshua's scouts (Josh 2:25; 7:22).[1]

With this foundation of Biblical usage of the word as it is applied to human messengers, as well as to the heavenly ones, it would appear logical that the epistles were addressed to the one who ordinarily delivered God's message to the church—the pastor, minister, preacher or whatever he may be called. While some may be hestitant to refer to their minister as "Angel Smith," the word "angel" is certainly a good and appropriate descriptive title for this church leader when it is properly understood. As we have often noted, the New Testament church did not concern itself with developing exclusive titles, but concentrated upon describing leaders according to the functions they performed in the church. The pastor delivered God's message, so that made him an angel. What difference did it make whether a natural or supernatural being made the delivery? The

1. William F. Arndt and F. Wilbur Gingrich, *A Greek-English Lexicon of the New Testament and Other Early Christian Literature* (Chicago: The University of Chicago Press, 1952), p. 7.

important thing was the message, not the person. The word "angel" could apply to either kind of messenger, but it could never be applied to one who was not involved in delivering the message. The function is the key.

Expressive and Implementive Leadership

God said to Israel through the prophet Jeremiah, "Then I will give you shepherds after my own heart, who will lead you with knowledge and understanding" (Jer 3:15). God said through the prophet Hosea, "A people without understanding will come to ruin!" (Hosea 4:14c). The Hebrew Psalmist sang to God, "Your Word is a lamp to my feet and a light for my path" (Ps 119:105). It is evident that God recognized the importance of having His word expressed continually before His people, that they might gain that essential knowledge and understanding, that their paths would be lighted, and that they would not come to useless ruin.

It is important to take note of the apostles' statement when they chose to delegate some of the ministry responsibilities to others in the Jerusalem church:

> It would not be right for us to neglect the ministry of the Word of God in order to wait on tables. Brothers, choose seven men from among you who are known to be full of the Holy Spirit and wisdom. We will turn this responsibility over to them and will give our attention to prayer and the ministry of the Word (Acts 6:2-4).

The apostles were in no way degrading the Christian ministry of benevolence. It was essential that these needs in the church be met; and the church needed to choose very carefully the ones they would set apart to administer this work. The apostles, however, realized the primacy of the ministry of the Word to the life of that Jerusalem church.

The apostles could have spent their time doing a hundred important and even essential things, but unless they provided the church with a vision—an understanding of what God wanted them to be, to become and to accomplish, the church would perish. This, then, was their primary job, and it—more than anything else—was essential to the church. Theirs was an *EXPRESSIVE leadership*. The rôle assigned to the seven was an *IMPLEMENTIVE leadership*.

In their best-selling book, *In Search of Excellence,* Thomas Peters and Robert Waterman come up with some interesting and revolutionary conclusions about what makes America's best-run companies so successful. They conclude, among other things, "It appears that the real role of the chief executive is to manage the values of the organization."[2] "Their role of the leader, then, is one of orchestrator and labeler: taking what can be gotten in the way of action and shaping it—generally after the fact—into lasting commitment to a new strategic direction. In short, he makes meanings."[3] In another place they speak of the leader's most important task as being that of instilling purpose.[4]

As earth-shaking as these conclusions have been to the business community, these modern business analysts have simply rediscovered the wheel, as far as the church is concerned. In every united activity of life there is the necessity of having someone provide expressive leadership—that kind of leadership which communicates a sense of meaning and

---

2. Thomas J. Peters and Robert H. Waterman, Jr., *In Search of Excellence* (New York: Harper and Row, 1982), p. 26.
3. Peters and Waterman, p. 75.
4. Peters and Waterman, p. 83.

understanding behind the entire endeavor. Without a clear sense of purpose, any venture will eventually flounder or get blown off course. With a clear, unifying and motivating comprehension of purpose, there is far less need for volumes of rules and regulations to govern those who have some part in the venture. Whether it be a giant corporation or the church, someone must serve as that visible, visionary leader, defining and holding to a course.

In the church God calls such expressive leaders to be first of all committed to the ministry of His Word. He expects those leaders to deliver His divinely-authored message of meaning and purpose for His kingdom without alteration, for it contains sufficient motivation and power to literally change the world when it is implanted in the hearts and the lives of the church. The church which has lost its message, though, has lost its sense of direction and its power.

As in the case of the incident cited in the Jerusalem church, there is a need for both expressive and implementive leadership within the church. The apostles recognized a very real need among the widows, and they pointed it out to the church, along with a recommended plan for meeting that need. It required, however, the selection of qualified and committed implementers before the problem was resolved. It is vitally important that this distinction in types of leadership for the church be understood. When God has gifted, called and prepared those for providing the expressive leadership for the church, they must not allow themselves to be detoured into investing their time and efforts into implementive leadership functions. On the other hand, those gifted, called and committed implementers should not have to be responsible for providing the expressive leadership for the church. Unfortunately, this difference is not understood in most churches, and the resulting leadership snags are enough to dishearten any church and to stall most progress.

The Position of Pastor

Whether termed the "angels" of the church, or known by some other designation, it is evident in the New Testament that the churches had those who served in visible leadership roles as God's messengers and ministers, providing a major part of the expressive leadership needed by a congregation. I Timothy 5:17-18 comments:

> The elders who direct the affairs of the church well are worthy of double honor, especially those whose work is preaching and teaching. For the Scripture says, "Do not muzzle the ox while he is treading out the grain," and "The worker deserves his wages."

From angel to ox may seem like quite a come-down, but the point concerning the one who delivers God's message is clear. I Corinthians 9:14 adds: "In the same way, the Lord has commanded that those who preach the gospel should receive their living from the gospel." Galatians 6:6 identifies the source of the income: "Anyone who receives instruction in the Word must share all good things with his instructor."

The precedent for such a paid professional expressive leadership among God's people is as old as the financial provisions made for the Levitical tribe from the tithes and offerings of the Hebrew people (Lev 2:3; 10:13; 27:21; Num 3:48; 5:9; 18:8-21; Deut 18:1-8; II Kings 12:16). From that tribe came those who served as priests and other full-time servants in the tabernacle and temple. We further note, coming back to the New Testament, that the Apostle

Paul claimed his right to be so supported in his ministry by those he served, though he did not always exercise that right (Acts 18:3; 20:34; I Cor 9:6-18; I Thess 2:9; II Thess 3:8-10).

It would appear that men such as Peter, Timothy, Titus, Tychicus, Epaphras, Aristarchus, Epaphroditus, Apollos and others mentioned by Paul in his various letters functioned in the position of pastor or minister among the churches at one time or another. In fact, Tychicus is described by Paul in Colossians 4:7 as "a beloved brother and faithful minister and fellow servant of the Lord."

What should they be called? Again we are reminded of the New Testament's emphasis upon functions of leaders, rather than upon official titles. There is, in fact, NO exclusive title which can be given for any position of New Testament leadership, due to the interrelation of functions within the body. Such a leader of the church as we have described could be called a *preacher* if he is proclaiming the Word of God (Rom 10:14); but so can that name be applied to anyone who preaches. After the stoning of Stephen in Acts 7, for example, a great persecution arose against the church at Jerusalem. Acts 8:4 says of the church members, "Those who had been scattered preached the word wherever they went." They preached; therefore they were preachers, by virtue of the function they performed. Such a church leader could be called an *evangelist* if he is evangelizing—telling the good news to those who have never yet heard or accepted (Eph 4:11). He could be called a *teacher* if he is instructing (James 3:1). He could be called a *minister* if he is serving the Lord by meeting someone's needs (I Tim 4:6). All of these terms, however, can be used generically to describe anyone who performs such functions.

A fifth designation for this leader, which is equally as generic and functional a term, is that of *pastor*. In spite of the aversion to it by early Restoration Movement leaders, due to its contemporary connotations among the denominations, it is a good, Scriptural word which is rich and full of meaning.

In order to understand and appreciate the term "pastor," there are again several related Greek words which come into play. The one noun describes the flock, especially referring to sheep; but it is also specifically applied to the church in the New Testament (Luke 12:32; Acts 20:28; I Peter 5:3). A very similar Greek word which is spelled only slightly differently, is also used with the same meaning in Matthew 16:31; Luke 2:8; John 10:16 and I Corinthians 9:7. The related verb, of course, means to herd, tend, lead, pasture, feed or care for the flock (Luke 17:7; Acts 20:28; I Cor 9:7; I Peter 5:2). This is what Jesus asked Peter to do to prove his love for Him (John 21:16). It is obviously a very broad term in the sense of its application, but applies to all that is involved in taking care of the needs of the sheep.

The other related Greek noun is the one translated "pastor" in Ephesians 4:11. It is used in other places, but is translated as "shepherd" when it is found in Matthew 9:36; 25:32; 26:31; Mark 6:34; 14:27; Luke 2:8, 15, 18, 20; John 10:2, 16; Hebrews 13:20; I Peter 2:25.[5] Perhaps no term is so inclusive in its rich meaning, when applied to the many different kinds of functions of this church leader, as that of pastor or shepherd. Certainly it would be wrong for any leader to appropriate this designation as his exclusive title, but it is an applicable, functional name which can be used to describe the church leader who serves in this capacity.

5. Arndt and Gingrich, pp. 690-691.

Throughout this book the various titles for this kind of church leader will be used interchangeably. If any of the Scriptural titles—pastor, preacher, minister, evangelist—make you uncomfortable, please substitute the term you prefer. As you do so, however, ask yourself why that term is unacceptable to you. Are you being as flexible in naming this kind of leader as the New Testament itself?

The Qualifications

Since the New Testament picture of church leadership involves the more mature leading the less mature toward spiritual maturity (Christ-likeness) and fruitful ministry, it is apparent that those who serve as pastors should be expected to exhibit in their lives the marks of spiritual maturity and fruitfulness. The same qualifications for an evangelist cited in chapter three equally apply to a minister. His life must exhibit the fruit of the Spirit (Gal 5:22-23; I Tim 6:11; II Tim 2:22).

No age limitations or prerequisites are stated in Scripture for preachers, recognizing that a person's chronological age may have no bearing whatsoever on his spiritual maturity or performance in leadership. One who would pastor, must be able to lead out of his own spiritual experience, in addition to being able to proclaim a verbal message. His life and reputation must be clean and exemplary (I Tim 4:12; 5:22; Titus 2:7-8). He must be a diligent student of the Word of God if he is to be able to accurately share that Word with others, instead of putting forth his own unsubstantiated opinions (II Tim 2:15). He must be capable of gentle instruction, able to present God's Word in a caring way to people whose needs he is able to sense and help meet (II Tim 2:24).

One who would be a pastor must have the capacity to find contentment and fulfillment in ministering to the needs of others, rather than in the pursuit of accumulating wealth or financial security (Phil 4:11-13; I Tim 6:6-10). He must be willing and able to avoid useless and divisive arguments (I Tim 6:3-5; II Tim 2:16; Titus 3:9-10). He cannot be a quitter. He must be committed to conscientiously persevering in his ministry, his message and his personal growth (I Tim 4:15-16; 6:11-20; II Tim 4:3-5). Even in the face of opposition and hardship, he must be willing to hold his course (II Tim 2:3; 4:5). He must be convinced of the value and the power of the gospel message (Rom 1:16-17; II Tim 2:1-8). Finally, he must be willing to help prepare and equip those who are capable of carrying that message on to others (Eph 4:11-16; II Tim 2:2).

Is a pastor also an elder? Peter identified himself to the elders he addressed in his letter as "a fellow elder" (I Peter 5:1). I Timothy 5:7 speaks of elders whose work is preaching and teaching. The positions should not be considered mutually exclusive, and the qualifications listed for elders in I Timothy 3:1-7 and Titus 1:6-9 ought to equally apply to a minister. There is, in fact, nothing in either of these passages which is not in harmony with the other qualifications listed above. More will be said about these elders' qualifications in the next chapter.

In addition to the spiritual maturity involved, the nature of the pastoral ministry requires special gifts or abilities and adequate preparation for church leadership (I Tim 4:14). Not everyone can or should be a pastor. In Ephesians 4:11, apostles, prophets, evangelists, pastors and teachers are listed as those specially gifted leaders chosen to perform an equipping ministry for the church. It almost goes without saying that a minister must be a leader, rather than a follower. He must be able to preach, teach, shepherd and equip people. These attributes involve both basic abilities and acquired knowledge and skills. Some people would never be comfortable or successful in the role of pastor, no matter how much educational preparation they were given, while others are "naturals." One must ask himself, "Has God so made me that I possess the necessary gifts to be a pastor?" If so, God has a claim on your life which ought to be considered before all others.

Simply being gifted, however, does not make one a minister, any more than Peter's raw abilities equipped him for service as an apostle. The potential was there when Jesus called him, but he lacked both the spiritual maturity and the educational preparation to be able to launch out on his own as a leader in ministry. It took three intensive years of training with the Lord before he was ready to lead; and even then it was only through the power of the Holy Spirit that he was able to accomplish anything.

The education Peter and the others received from Jesus was definitely not a passive, spectator-type experience. Certainly there were the lectures (cf. Matt 5-7), the questions (Matt 15:16) and the quizzes (Matt 16:16); but there was far more. There were the guided learning experiences which could only happen in an intern-type relationship (Matt 10:1-42; 14:25-33). From the nature of all of the recorded teaching of Jesus in the presence of His disciples, it is evident that they were given a very thorough Biblical education, along with a very practical course in Christian ministry.

A study relating to the training of those whom Paul selected to serve in ministry with him reveals a similar course of instruction, although there are fewer specific details given

(II Tim 3:14-17). It is obvious that, in the cases of both Jesus and Paul, they were concerned about their students achieving far more than the ability to recite facts. They were concentrating on meanings. A think tank group recently decided that one of the greatest problems facing today's youth is an episodic grasp of reality. They can see the parts, but not the whole. This can be a problem for any generation and in any learning process. What does all of this mean? How does it apply to life, death and eternity? Jesus and Paul wanted their learners to be able to take the pieces and to put them together to produce a meaningful design which would lead to the right conclusions. If they could not see the over-all picture, how could they lead others?

What constitutes adequate preparation to qualify a person for a preaching ministry today? Of course a good, solid comprehension of the Bible is foundational and essential. It is the core to being able to provide that expressive leadership for the church. More than simply being able to recite the words and to list the facts, however, there must be the ability developed to build an accurate and reliable theology—putting it all together into a meaningful, workable pattern. This is essential both for anchoring personal faith and for being able to help others to establish their faith through the turmoil and crises of life (Eph 4:14-16; I Peter 3:15). A solid general education in conjunction with the Biblical one is also essential in helping to develop an adequate theology which can be applied to the world in which we live. The particular culture and level of education in which one will be ministering may also dictate additional graduate education in order to establish and maintain communication and credibility with those who need to be reached. It may not help to have the answers if you don't understand the questions.

In addition to the formal education, a practical and sustained internship with an experienced pastor is an essential part of the learning process. There is value, in fact, in participating in an internship concurrently with the formal education, such as the pupils of Jesus and Paul had the privilege of doing. The one can enhance the other. The immediate practical needs and applications help to create inquiry and a healthy climate for continued learning. An internship should ideally last for several years, if we are to judge from the New Testament precedents. The longer the period of time, the greater opportunity the intern has to see and experience a number of different kinds of situations, and the chance to work through some crises. It is far better to work through these, building confidence and skills with the help of a patient and experienced guide than to have to fearfully face them on your own for the first time. Both the veteran minister and the church involved need to clearly understand that the internship is primarily an educational experience for the immediate benefit of the intern and the ultimate benefit of the church, rather than the other way around.

Having said all of this regarding qualifications and preparation for the pastoral ministry, let us recall that it was still the empowering ministry of the Holy Spirit in the lives of those whom Jesus and Paul prepared which made them effective. There is a temptation in many cases, then, to forego adequate educational preparation and to depend entirely upon the Spirit to provide everything. In the first place, if that had been enough, Jesus and Paul wasted years of their lives, which were invested in the equipping of others for ministry. In the second place, we would reiterate that underlying principle which seems to be a common thread in all of Biblical history—that God never does for man that which he can do for himself. God asks us to get ready and get moving. Then He takes care of the impossibilities facing us.

The Functions

Many centuries ago God said to the prophet Ezekiel:

> But if the watchman sees the sword coming and does not blow the trumpet to warn the people and the sword comes and takes the life of one of them, that man will be taken away because of his sin, but I will hold the watchman accountable for his blood. Son of man, I have made you a watchman for the house of Israel; so hear the word I speak and give them warning from me (Ezek 33:6, 7).

Indeed the prophets' voices were often the only warning signals sounded among the people to rouse them from their spiritual slumber and sinfulness. Mont Smith has long contended that the Old Testament prophets served as God's attorneys to argue His case before the people concerning the covenants they had made with Him and broken.[6] Over and over again the prophets' refrain reminded all who would listen of their covenant responsibilities, along with the blessings to be found in obedience and the penalties for disobedience (Jer 11:1-5).

So it is that God has also appointed His watchmen and attorneys to call the world and the church's attention to His new covenant through Jesus. Paul writes in II Corinthians 3:4-6:

---

6. Mont W. Smith, *What the Bible Says About Covenant* (Joplin: College Press, 1981), pp. 136, 156-168.

> Such confidence as this is ours through Christ before God. Not that we are competent to claim anything for ourselves, but our competence comes from God. He has made us competent as ministers of a new covenant—not of the letter but of the Spirit; for the letter kills, but the Spirit gives life.

The preacher's role corresponds in many ways to that of the Old Testament prophets. Both serve as the voice of God among His people—warning, reminding, encouraging and providing a vision of God's great plan and expectations for His people. Just as the Old Testament prophet's role was not primarily one of condemnation, but of seeking to reconcile people with the God they had forsaken, so a pastor also shares a similar ministry. Paul could write:

> But thanks be to God, who leads us in triumphal procession in Christ and through us spreads everywhere the fragrance of the knowledge of Him. For we are to God the aroma of Christ among those who are being saved and those who are perishing. To one we are the smell of death; to the other, the fragrance of life. And who is equal to such a task? (II Cor 2:14-17).

Again in II Corinthians 5:18-20 he wrote:

> All this is from God, who reconciled us to Himself through Christ and gave Himself in Christ, not counting men's sins against them. And He has committed to us the message of reconciliation. We are therefore Christ's ambassadors, as though God were making His appeal through us. We implore you on Christ's behalf: Be reconciled to God.

It is evident that such a ministry requires a heavy emphasis upon public preaching and teaching, as Paul instructed Timothy to do (I Tim 4:13). To this admonition he adds a solemn charge:

> In the presence of God and of Christ Jesus, who will judge the living and the dead, and in view of His appearing and His kingdom, I give you this charge: Preach the Word; be prepared in season and out of season; correct, rebuke and encourage—with great patience and careful instruction. For the time will come when men will not put up with sound doctrine. Instead, to suit their own desires, they will gather around them a great number of teachers to say what their itching ears want to hear. They will turn their ears away from the truth and turn aside to myths. But you, keep your head in all situations, endure hardship, do the work of an evangelist, discharge all the duties of your ministry (II Tim 4:1-5).

It is largely in his preaching and teaching roles that a pastor is able to provide expressive leadership for the church to which he ministers. Herein he is able to communicate purpose, help to hold a course and bring into focus the issues and circumstances facing his people in the light of God's eternal Word. Preaching and teaching must involve accurate application of spiritual truths to the contemporary context, or they are empty exercises or rhetoric.

Nor should a preacher shirk his responsibility for adequate preparation of this message on the excuse that the Holy Spirit will provide the message. While it is true that the Holy Spirit will work through the Word to convict men of sin and righteousness and judgment (John 16:8), God yet refuses to do for man what he can do for himself. God honors adequate preparation in every area of ministry, and He blesses prepared preaching and teaching. Many are the fresh insights revealed even in the course of delivering a message. Most unprepared messages, on the other hand, wind up as vain repetitions and so much hot air. Even worse, they produce little spiritual growth in the hearers due to the lack of any meat from the Word. Productive preaching requires the very best effort of the preacher in both preparation and delivery, plus the power and working of the Holy Spirit.

With that teaching and preaching comes another heavy responsibility. James warns: "Not many of you should presume to be teachers, my brothers, because you know that we who teach will be judged more strictly" (James 3:1). Paul wrote in I Corinthians 9:26-27: "Therefore I do not run like a man running aimlessly; I do not fight like a man beating the air. No, I beat my body and make it my slave so that after I have preached to others, I myself will not be disqualified for the prize." Consequently, he adds another solemn charge for Timothy:

> But you, man of God, flee from all this, and pursue righteousness, godliness, faith, love, endurance and gentleness. Fight the good fight of the faith. Take hold of the eternal life to which you were called when you made your good confession in the presence of many witnesses. In the sight of God, who gives life to everything, and of Christ Jesus, who while testifying before Pilate made the good confession, I charge you to keep this commandment without spot or blame until the appearing of our Lord Jesus Christ, which God will bring about in His own time—God, the blessed and only Ruler, the King of kings and Lord of lords, who alone is immortal and who lives in unapproachable light, whom no one has seen or can see. To Him be honor and might forever. Amen. (I Tim 6:11-16)

Not only is the factor of personal obedience and escaping personal condemnation involved here, the pastor's lifestyle is a key to the credibility given his verbal message. Actions always speak louder than words; and if his actions are not consistent with his message, his lifestyle will cancel out his message. It must both reinforce and demonstrate that which he teaches. Here again we see the "follow me" style of leadership and the setting of an example being essential to any real communication of the message by all church leadership.

The pastor is called to be a shepherd—tending, caring for, feeding and protecting the flock entrusted to him. God said of Israel's watchmen and shepherds:

> Israel's watchmen are blind, they all lack knowledge; they are all mute dogs, they cannot bark; they lie around and dream, they love to sleep. They are dogs with mighty appetites; they never have enough. They are shepherds who lack understanding; they all turn to their own way, each seeks his own gain. "Come," each one cries, "Let me get wine! Let us drink our fill of beer! And tomorrow will be like today, or even far better" (Isa 56:10-12).

The first verse of the next chapter says, then: "The righteous perish, and no one ponders in his heart . . ." (Isa 57:1). As a shepherd, a pastor is called to care—to ponder in his heart—to speak out and to act. He is called to lead his sheep, not to concentrate on serving his own interests. Peter says to elders and pastors:

> Be shepherds of God's flock that is under your care, serving as overseers—not because you must, but because you are willing, as God wants you to be, not greedy for money, but eager to serve; not lording it over those entrusted to you, but being examples to the flock. And when the Chief Shepherd appears, you will receive the crown of glory that will never fade away" (I Peter 5:2-4).

What a responsibility! What a high standard for service! The concept of being an under-shepherd with responsibility to the Chief Shepherd is a key one—and an awesome kind of accountability. One cannot help but recall Jesus' teaching in Matthew 10:1-18, in which He contrasts His role and performance as the Shepherd with that of the hireling. It serves as a dramatic reminder to the minister that he is called to be more than a hired hand who abandons his sheep and runs for his life when danger and hardship come. The shepherd is expected to stay with his sheep and to lay down his life for them if necessary. He is expected to care, even as the Chief Shepherd cared enough to give His life for those sheep. Little is accomplished of any enduring value in brief, hit-and-run ministries. It takes time to build relationships and trust, to grow together and to construct a lasting kind of ministry.

Finally, we are reminded again that a pastor is expected by divine design to be an equipper of Christians for ministry (Eph 4:11-12). He is intended to use his gifts and preparation—not to play the role of star performer—but to excel as a coach. It was not the apostles, prophets, evangelists, pastors or teachers who were designated to do the works of ministry for the church, but they who would equip the church members to do their own ministry, and thus build up the total body in the process. This is the intent of Paul's admonition to Timothy: "And the things you have heard me say in the presence of many witnesses entrust to reliable men who will also be qualified to teach others" (II Tim 2:2). Paul had equipped Timothy. Now Timothy was to become an equipper of others, who would equip still others. Both the church and a pastor must understand the need for his function in the expressive and equipping roles, or he will become hopelessly bogged down in a multitude of implementive tasks and be incapable of functioning as God intended him and as the church requires.

It should be noted, however, that many large churches are being built today with star performers. Their personal charisma, dynamic leadership style and firm management enable them to attract a following and to hold a course. In fact, many people are looking for this kind of church. Whoever has the biggest show, the most beautiful buildings and requires the least of them gets their vote, their membership and even their money. Such "success" is alluring to preachers and people alike. Many are the imitators and those clamoring to know how to duplicate these spectacular results. Unfortunately, this is not New Testament leadership, nor is the product usually a New Testament church. They are the personal kingdoms of their charismatic leaders. The problem is not a new one, and the warnings against such false teachers are many (Matt 5:19; 15:9; I Tim 1:7; 4:2; 6:3; II Tim 4:3; Titus 1:11; II Peter 2:1). Paul's words in II Timothy 4:10 are sad testimony to the fact that there were those leaders, even among those he had sought to train who, had fallen into this trap: "for Demas, because he loved this world, has deserted me and has gone to Thessalonica. . . ." The world may call it success, but God calls that failure. Satan must rejoice.

The degree to which a pastor can produce leaders, to which responsibilities for ministry can be transferred, is the measure of his ultimate success. Consequently, preachers would do well to analyze the percentage of their time they spend equipping others for ministry, versus the percentage of time they spend doing the ministry for others. How many now serve as elders, pastors, missionaries or other church leaders as a direct result of their recruitment, training and encouragement? The results of such an analysis should spur many pastors into a re-alignment of their priorities and a revision of their schedules; for many are the pastors who have equipped no one. In effect, they have robbed the churches they have served and have often left them destitute.

Multiple Ministry in the Church

In the one sense, according to that which we have discovered about the very nature of the church in Ephesus 4 and I Corinthians 12, there should be a multiple ministry in every church. The body is assuredly intended to consist of many working parts—all involved in important works of ministry. The term "multiple ministry," however, is more commonly understood today to apply to a multiple paid staff for the church. In addition to a pastor or senior minister there will be various associate ministers with responsibilities in evangelism, music, youth, Christian education, children's ministries, seniors' ministries and a variety of other specialized areas. The number and type will vary with the congregation's size and circumstances.

There is certainly Scriptural precedent for multiple staff ministries. The Jerusalem church is an obvious example. Most of the apostles shared for a time in its leadership. We have already noted the ministerial team of Barnabas and Saul, who served together with the church at Antioch. Paul seems to have always had associates serving with him in his ministries with the various churches, judging from the greetings and personal remarks at the beginning and the end of each of his letters.

It is interesting to speculate about the leadership position James, the brother of Jesus, had in the Jerusalem church along with the apostles (Acts 12:17; 15:13-21; 21:18). Paul refers to him, along with Peter and John as "pillars" of the Jerusalem congregation in Galatians 2:9, and refers to him again in the 12th verse of that same chapter. Whatever his position, he was obviously recognized as a key leader at Jerusalem, and we are indebted to him for his authorship of the very practical and helpful New Testament book bearing his name. In the introduction of that book he simply identifies himself as "James, a servant of God and of the Lord Jesus Christ" (James 1:1). Had he been writing today, would his title on the Jerusalem church's letterhead have read "Senior Minister"? Some take offense at this designation commonly used to identify the pastor, or leader of the team of ministers. Since "minister" and "servant" are equivalent, however, it is doubtful that James would have been overly-concerned about its application, had it been used in his day.

One of the prerequisites for a ministerial team in the New Testament was the selection of those who could work well together. Barnabas went to Tarsus to recruit Saul for that ministry with him at Antioch (Acts 11:25-26). Later, when Paul did not feel that he could work with Mark on a second missionary journey, after his apparent desertion on the first, Barnabas took Mark as his associate and went one way, while Paul took Silas as his associate and went another way (Acts 15:36-41). Both combinations worked well. It is important to any church today considering a multiple leadership staff to assemble a team which can work well together. This involves personalities, of course. But it also involves basic philosophies of ministry and methodology. It can be disastrous for a church to put together a team which is heading in opposite, or even different, directions. The team has to pull together, or they will pull apart; and the church may be torn in the process.

It is essential that a ministerial team have a leader. Someone must be in charge of coordinating the directions of the combined ministry. Whether he be called a pastor, senior minister, administrator or whatever, a leader must lead the team and be responsible for its united efforts. At Antioch, Barnabas would appear to have been the leader. He had preceded Saul in that ministry, and had recruited Saul to come and help him. In Jerusalem we see Peter and James most often mentioned as the leaders and spokesmen. Paul was unquestionably the leader of his later ministerial teams after leaving Antioch. In none of these cases, however, was it a dictatorial type of leadership, lording it over the others. It was simply a responsible, workable kind of leadership arrangement which produced results. There were those disappointments, like Demas, whose commitment and loyalty to the team ministry failed. It goes without saying that a strong sense of purpose and loyalty to each other is essential to the successful function of any such multiple ministry.

Finally, it is absolutely vital that multiple staff be added for the right reasons, and that they be given the right kind of responsibilities. Far too many churches add staff to do the work of ministry for them. They will call a youth minister, for example, and expect him to be the youth leader for a particular youth group (the high school youth sponsor). They will call a minister of evangelism and expect him to do the evangelism for the church. In each of these cases, these churches are hiring performers, or implementers. *No church can afford to hire enough performers to do its ministry for its members!* Whether it be a preacher or a minister of music, he should be called to a ministry of equipping and administering others. He must be a multiplier of himself as he equips others with his knowledge, experience and gifts, so they will be able to be successful in their ministries. A youth minister should be recruiting and equipping youth leaders to do the work of youth ministry, and he should coach them and coordinate their efforts. The minister of evangelism should be recruiting and equipping church members to do the work of winning others to Christ, and he should coordinate their efforts. The principle applies to every area of a church's multiple ministry. No church can afford to hire performers; it must call equippers and administrators to its leadership team.

This is not to say that the ministers do not participate directly in their area of ministry, or that they are to sit off in an uninvolved state, issuing orders. They need to demonstrate and to model, as well as to tell their learners how to do it. It is simply to say that these leaders must not be called to serve as the ones who will now do it all in their areas of expertise for the church. That defeats the divine design for the church, robs Christians of their opportunities of sharing in the ministry, and amounts to extremely poor stewardship of the Lord's money.

The Pastor and His People

One cannot help but be impressed with the very evident love Paul had for the churches he had served as he writes to them. He always begins by thanking God for them and for his remembrances of them. His letter to the Philippian brethren contains a section to which we called attention in the last chapter. It is worth looking at again in this context, for it has some important lessons to teach us:

> I thank my God every time I remember you. In all of my prayers for all of you, I always pray with joy because of your partnership in the gospel from the first day until now, being

> confident of this, that He who began a good work in you will carry it on to completion until the day of Christ Jesus. It is right for me to feel this way about all of you, since I have you in my heart; for whether I am in chains or defending and confirming the gospel, all of you share in God's grace with me. God can testify how I long for all of you with the affection of Christ Jesus (Phil 1:3-8).

That is a pastor's heart! He had truly become their shepherd. He had learned to care about them and to regard them with a kind of respect which saw them as valuable and indispensable partners in ministry. Moreover, he had developed a confidence in them as he had worked alongside them, equipped them and delegated to them the various areas of ministry. A preacher must learn to love and accept his people in spite of their blemishes and warts. He must develop the ability to see beyond their faults, failures and imperfections, to be able to see their abilities and potential. Above all, he must be able to see that upon which God has placed infinite value—the human soul—and remember that it was to redeem each soul that Christ died. He needs to repeatedly remind himself of the attitude of Christ, which he is called to imitate:

> Who, being in very nature God, did not consider equality with God something to be grasped, but made Himself nothing, taking the very nature of a servant, being made in human likeness. And being found in appearance as a man, He humbled Himself and became obedient to death—even death on a cross!" (Phil 2:5-8).

So a pastor is called to humble himself and to be able to serve like the Master. He is called to regard with love and value those who become a part of his flock. How very different this picture is from the viewpoint of many church leaders today! There are those who think of their members only as numbers to be counted and compared. There are those who think of their people only as objects to be manipulated and incomes to be tapped for their own advantage. There are those who trust no one in their congregations, and those who regard them with fear as adversaries. These can never be effective ministers.

Certainly there will be problems, conflicts, misunderstandings and hurt feelings in the course of working together. We are all human, and we all make mistakes. We as often misunderstand others as they misunderstand us. We all fail to live up to our own high expectations at times, just as we fail to live up to the expectations of others, and they to ours. Crises will consequently come in any relationship; but a relationship only has an opportunity to grow and be strengthened when all the persons involved are willing to stick with it, work through it and resolve the crisis, rather than quitting and running from it. The grass will indeed always look greener on the other side of the hill, and the problems appear to be fewer. But moving from pasture to pasture, one soon learns that problems are inherent in people and relationships everywhere. A pastor must resolve this in his mind and heart, or he will never be able to accomplish much in the ministry anywhere.

Likewise, the members of a church need to resolve some things in their minds about their relationships with preachers. They are not hired hands or paid performers. They are not emotionless puppets to be hired and fired at will whenever the crowd tires of them and wants to watch a different kind of show. They are not humanly capable of accomplishing everything everyone expects of them. (Just take a poll of the members' expectations, and add up the hours it would take per week to perform as expected.) Many of the congregation's expectations have nothing to do with the pastor's God-given tasks.

The New Testament has much to say to the church about its relationship to its leaders. Jesus, in Matthew 10:10 reminds us that "The worker is worth his keep." I Corinthians 9:14; Galatians 6:6; Philippians 4:14-15; and I Timothy 5:18 all serve as reminders of a congregation's responsibility to provide financially for the needs of its spiritual leaders. With tongue in cheek, it has been observed that many churches have adopted as their official prayer concerning their pastor, "You keep him humble, Lord, and we'll keep him poor." There is more truth than fiction in that! Selfishness and lack of consideration are the roots of this problem. One of the chief causes for ministers' moves today is the widespread failure of churches to provide a living wage, and to even keep up with inflation through raises. Few ministers will beg, nor should they have to; so they simply leave. Ironically, the next preacher always costs more than the church was paying the last one, not to mention the moving expenses and the effects of a change in pastors on the membership. In many cases, the last pastor would have remained had he been given the salary of his successor. All of this is to say that the church has a very definite obligation to provide generously and thoughtfully for its pastor—to care about him, even as God calls him to care about them.

That caring needs to go beyond financial support. It should involve prayer support of a pastor's ministry (Rom 15:30; I Thess 5:25). It should involve a willingness to get behind his leadership and to submit to his guidance (I Cor 16:16). It should include respect for him as a servant and representative of the Lord (Gal 4:14). Paul admonished the

Thessalonian church: "Now we ask you, brothers, to respect those who work hard among you in the Lord and who admonish you. Hold them in the highest regard in love because of their work. Live in peace with each other" (I Thess 5:12, 13).

The Philippian church had evidently sent their minister to help Paul in prison and to carry for them their gift of love to Paul. Paul writes a very moving note:

> But I think it is necessary to send back to you Epaphroditis, my brother, fellow worker and fellow soldier, who is also your messenger, whom you sent to take care of my needs. For he longs for all of you and is distressed because you heard he was ill. Indeed he was ill, and almost died. But God had mercy on him, and not on him only but also on me, to spare me sorrow upon sorrow. Therefore I am all the more eager to send him, so that you may be glad and I may have less anxiety. Welcome him in the Lord and honor men like him, because he almost died for the work of Christ, risking his life to make up for the help you could not give me (Phil 2:25-30).

Last of all we would call attention to the passages of I Timothy 5:17 and Hebrews 13:7, for they are both important and related. The first passage notes that those who serve in the preaching and teaching ministry are worthy of double honor. In the context, he is calling the church both to support the leaders financially and to protect these leaders from irresponsible charges. According to Paul's instruction, no accusation is to be brought unless it is brought by two or three actual witnesses (I Tim 5:19). There is a real need for the church to stand behind a pastor in this way. Many a ministry has been destroyed and a minister needlessly disgraced because a congregation permitted unfounded accusations to be spread about him. Rather than gossiping and permitting criticism about a minister, Hebrews 13:7 charges the church to "Remember your leaders, who spoke the Word of God to you. Consider the outcome of their way of life and imitate their faith."

Fortunate indeed is a pastor whose flock is providing for him physically, praying for his ministry, backing his leadership, protecting him from those who would falsely or maliciously accuse him, and who are attempting to imitate the example of Christ-likeness he is trying to model before them. May the number of such churches increase dramatically in our times!

In Summary

The church has been given messengers of God who are charged with the primary responsibilities of preaching and teaching His Word. Whether they be called angels, preachers, teachers, pastors, ministers or prophets, they are essential to the church as they provide expressive leadership. Through their ministry of the Word they are able to help the church maintain its focus on its divine purpose. Considering the scope of the responsibilities given such leaders, perhaps the term "pastor" is the most descriptive. While no title can be used exclusively, due to the overlapping of ministries, the pastor (or shepherd) designation may best describe the caring role he is called to assume over his flock, recognizing that he serves under the Chief Shepherd.

Special abilities, spiritual maturity and an adequate Biblical and general education, including an internship, are prerequisites for effective service as a minister. Even with such qualifications, he is yet dependent upon the power and ministry of the Holy Spirit for his success. As a leader he is called to be an equipper of others for works of ministry, rather than being the sole performer of ministry for them. Even when additional ministers are added, they too are called to be equippers and administrators, rather than merely performers. A pastor must learn to develop a shepherd's heart for his sheep. In turn, the members of the flock are reminded of their responsibilities toward their shepherd. When there is a spirit of mutual love, respect and support, the church is blessed, and the kingdom will grow.

5

AN EFFECTIVE ELDERSHIP

Authority or Responsibility?

Elders occupy a prominent and vitally important place in the New Testament's blueprint for church leadership. As we have already noted, elders are the most commonly mentioned congregational leaders (Acts 11:30; 14:23; 15:2, 4, 6, 22, 23; 20:17; I Tim 5:17, 19; Titus 1:5, 6; I Peter 5:1). The position of leadership in the church obviously has its origins in Jewish culture, and particularly in the synagogues, whose leaders were likewise known as elders.

We have also pointed out that the designation of "elder" is used interchangeably with that of "bishop," which means "overseer." It is so translated in the New International Version of the Bible (I Tim 3:1, 2; Titus 1:7). The third term, "shepherds," is applied to describe the elders in I Peter 5:1-4, reminding them that they serve as overseers and shepherds of their flocks under the Chief Shepherd, Jesus.

In the Restoration Movement there has always existed a mandate that each congregation must have elders. As Alexander Campbell wrote, "Every well-organized church has its eldership."[1] Furthermore, there has also existed a recognized rule, as stated by J. W. McGarvey, "Indeed, there must be none until they can have more than one who is qualified."[2] The first of these rules for the churches is apparently Scriptural—if a church, organized or disorganized, has qualified men who are willing to serve. The second rule, which was designed to prevent any single individual from having authority over a church, would be much harder to substantiate from Scripture. In fact, this second rule grew out of a prevalent perversion of the Scriptures concerning the role of elders.

Moses Lard, an early spokesman for the Restoration Movement and editor of *Lard's Quarterly,* maintained, as we have seen, "The overseers did not become such in virtue of their age, but in virtue of their special appointment to the office."[3] Then he took the matter one step further:

> Before the ordination the man is an elder, and after it an elder; but before the ordination he is an elder without authority. It is the act of ordination that gives office, that gives authority.[4]

---

1. Alexander Campbell, *The Christian System* (1835: rpt. Nashville: Gospel Advocate Company, 1956), p. 70.
2. J. W. McGarvey, *A Treatise on the Eldership* (1870; rpt. Murfreesboro: DeHoff Publications, 1962), p. 89.
3. Moses E. Lard, "Ordination of Church Officers," *Lard's Quarterly,* July, 1865, p. 351.
4. Lard, p. 360.

Lard was dead wrong on all counts! We have already demonstrated in chapter 2 the fact that *there is no office of elder*. The fact of the matter is that there is no office of anything in the church. Jesus is the church's only officer, according to the Scriptures. A church which creates any offices for its leaders is defying the authority of Lord Jesus. Furthermore, it ceases to be a New Testament church, no matter what name they paint on the church sign. The concept of leaders as officers has invaded the church from our culture. We have been so enamored by this pagan notion that leaders must be officers that we have even licensed our Bible translators to violate the text and to substitute this word for the Scriptural words of function which appear in the Greek version (Acts 1:20; Rom 11:13; 12:4; I Tim 3:1, 10). Far more than a matter of semantics, which we have tended to lightly excuse as our prerogative, this counterfeit concept of church leadership amounts to treason. It is also the source of many of our problems in the church today.

The second error Lard makes is his assertion that the act of ordaining a man to the eldership conveys upon him authority over the church. This concept has been unanimously upheld throughout the churches—without a shred of Scriptural evidence. In fact, *the assumption of authority by any church leader constitutes outright mutiny against Christ,* according to the Scriptures. Jesus said, "All authority in heaven and on earth has been given to Me" (Matt 28:18). If this be so, where does the church get its authority to convey on the elders by virtue of their election, appointment or ordination? The authority is either wrested from Christ and handed over to the elders, or there is no authority to give them. It is not a commodity which the church can manufacture and distribute. Jesus owns all the rights to it.

Lest we be accused of creating a tempest in a teapot over a fine point of trivia, or of straining the point of a single text, a careful examination of the use of the word "authority" in the New Testament is in order. The Greek word is *exousia*. It has a relatively wide range of meanings, which requires us to categorize the cases of its use in Scripture in order to comprehend the point.

The word is first used in relationship to free will and *the freedom of choice,* including personal rights of choice. In John 10:18 Jesus discusses His right, or choice, to lay down his life and to take it up again. In Acts 5:4 Peter points out that Ananias and Sapphira had the right of choice to do whatever they wished with the money they received from the property they had sold. In Romans 9:21 the potter's freedom of choice over what to do with his lump of clay is used as an example. I Corinthians 7:37 involves the making up of one's mind about marriage. I Corinthians 8:9 is a warning about exercising freedoms of choice without regard to their consequences which affect others. In I Corinthians 9:4, 5, 12 Paul is defending his rights concerning marriage and the expectation of financial support from the churches he serves. In Hebrews 13:10 the Christian is told he has an altar from which the Jewish priests have no right to eat. Revelation 13:5 speaks of the beast's limited freedom of activity and influence. Then in Revelation 22:14 those who wash their robes have the right to the tree of life and to entry into the holy city.

The second use of the word represents *the ability to do something.* Matthew 9:6, 8 and Mark 3:15 describe Jesus' ability or power to forgive sins and to drive out demons. John 1:12 discusses the right or ability of all who believe in Jesus to become the children of God. In Acts 8:19 Simon the Sorcerer is attempting to procure the ability to convey the powers of the Holy Spirit which he observed were passed on to others by the laying on of the hands of the Apostles. Revelation 9:19 refers to the source of the horses' power, and Revelation 13:2, 12 has to do with the abilities delegated to the first beast by the dragon, and to the second beast by the first. Luke 12:5 and Acts 1:7 both speak of God's power, and Acts 26:18 mentions Satan's power. Finally, Jesus' hearers conclude from His teaching that He must have extraordinary power (Matt 7:29; Mark 1:22).

The third use of the word involves *authority or absolute power.* This is the authority claimed by Jesus in Matthew 28:18, which we have cited. In Matthew 21:23, 24; Mark 11:28, 29, 33; and Luke 20:2, 8 Jesus' authority is questioned by the religious leaders of the Jews. In Matthew 10:1; Mark 6:7 and John 17:2 Jesus gives the twelve authority to drive out evil spirits and to heal every disease and sickness. In Acts 26:12 Paul recounts how he was traveling to Damascus at the time of his conversion under the commissioned authority of the chief priests. Then in Revelation 12:10 it again speaks of the authority of Christ.

The fourth category in which the word is used describes *the power exercised by rulers and others in high places by virtue of their office.* Concerning the actual ruling or official power, Matthew 8:9 quotes the centurion as declaring himself to be a man under authority; Luke 20:20 refers to the authority of the governor; Luke 19:17 describes the authority granted in the parable to govern 10 cities; and John 19:10, 11 is Pilate's declaration of his authority. Concerning the domain in which the power is executed, Luke 4:6 records Satan's attempt to tempt Jesus by offering Him his authority over the kingdoms of this world; in Luke 22:53 Jesus speaks of the reign of darkness; Luke 23:7 describes Herod's jurisdiction; Ephesians 2:22 is translated "kingdom of the air"; and Colossians 1:13 refers to the dominion of darkness. Concerning the bearers of authority, such as human officials and government, Luke 12:11; Romans 13:1, 2 and Titus 3:1 all speak of the Christian's responsibilities toward these. Then in Ephesians 1:21; 3:10; 6:12; Colossians 1:16; 2:10 and I Peter 3:22 it speaks of rulers and functionaries of the spirit world or heavenly realms.[5]

The fifth and final category centers on *the sign of authority to be worn on a woman's head.* The sole use of the word in this rather curious application is found in I Corinthians 11:10. Julia Staton says of this passage:

> In verses 5-10, was Paul speaking about veils, hats, or a certain way of fixing a woman's hair? Scholars are not sure. The Greek word could mean any one of them. At this point, we need to consider the customs of the time: (1) When in public, married women wore veils or their hair done up in a knot or braids on top of their heads ("covering on her head" could mean either). This was a sign to all that she was not available but belonged to and was under the leadership of her husband. (2) Available, unmarried women and prostitutes did not wear veils and wore their hair loose around their shoulders. (3) A woman had to shave her hair (or cut it off short) if found guilty of adultery. . . .
>
> In essence, Paul was saying: if a wife appears to the community as a loose woman, she is reflecting dishonor upon her husband's character as well as her own. A loving, caring, Christian wife would not wish to do such a thing; she would

5. William F. Arndt and F. Wilbur Gingrich, *A Greek-English Lexicon of the New Testament and Other Early Christian Literature* (Chicago: The University of Chicago Press, 1952), pp. 277-278.

instead want to show the world her pure relationship with her husband (v. 10).[6]

Two other Greek words are also questionably translated as "authority" in the New Testament. I Timothy 2:12 is Paul's statement concerning his refusal to permit women to "have authority over a man." This is an entirely different Greek verb, which is again used only this one time in Scripture. Its noun form means "master." In the verb form it appears to have been used in other contemporary literature to mean "to domineer over someone."[7] The second Greek word is found in Titus 2:15, where Paul tells Titus, "Encourage and rebuke with all authority." The word means a command, order or injunction. It is used elsewhere in Scripture in Romans 16:26; I Corinthians 7:25; I Timothy 1:1; and Titus 1:3. In each case it is translated as God's command. For example, Paul introduces himself as "an apostle of Christ Jesus by the command of God our Savior and of Christ our hope" (I Tim 1:1). So the concept involved in Paul's instruction to Titus is that he was to teach God's Word, with its applied encouragement and rebukes, realizing that he spoke for the Lord. He was communicating God's commands. He was granted no personal authority.

What is the point of all of this? We have taken the time and effort to examine every case in the New Testament where the word "authority" appears. *It is NEVER used in connection with any elder or other church leader.* There is never any indication that the church is granted any authority as a corporate body, either. Churches can prepare and

---

6. Julia Staton, *What the Bible Says About Women* (Joplin: College Press Publishing Company, 1980), pp. 127-128.

7. Arndt and Gingrich, p. 120.

revise their by-laws until eternity, and they can cast votes in a million congregational meetings; but none of that will ever add up to an ounce of authority to do anything. All authority is vested in Christ.

If elders have no authority, then, what do they have? *The elders have responsibility.* Jesus Christ is Lord (Eph 1:22-23; Phil 2:9-11). He decides the purpose, lays down the rules and writes the agenda for His church. The elders have the responsibility to uphold that agenda. They have no authority to revise it or to develop a substitute of their own. As the most mature spiritual leaders of a congregation, theirs is the greatest responsibility for leading all of the rest of the congregation in their growth toward Christ-likeness, fruitful ministry and the accomplishment of the church's mission and purpose.

The Development of a Hierarchy

Largely out of the widely-held misconceptions about the existence of an office and a delegated authority for elders, a multitude of other problems historically began to develop among the eldership. It is very similar to buttoning up a sweater. If you miss the match on the bottom button and its hole, everything else above that will come out wrong. Begin with a false premise, and you will almost always produce some false conclusions as a result.

We witnessed in chapter one's brief historical recap how the giant, corrupt monstrosity of the Roman Catholic hierarchy grew out of the local church's eldership. The evolution did not take long, for by the end of the second century an office of bishop, or head elder, began to emerge among the churches, with the bishop being regarded as superior to the other elders. Then, with the continued growth and influence of the big city churches, their bishops began to assert a regional authority. As we have seen, as early as Irenaeus (130-190), we have the notion proposed that bishops, by virtue of their office, were the successors to the apostles, and were therefore not responsible to their own churches. They existed by some divine right and were subject to no control other than that of their peers. This naturally resulted in the development of a collective episcopate, speaking to all of the churches through synods and councils.[8]

Once the concept of the council was established, the councils then claimed the authority to rule in all matters of faith, to determine the content of the New Testament and to devise a binding creed for the church. Having secured that ground, the councils could then claim the authority to brand any dissenters as heretics and to exclude them from the churches or punish them. It was next only a short step toward the declaration of a chief bishop to enforce the council's decrees, and a predictable next move to establish infallibility for his papal office. Such official, untouchable power for anyone—even church leaders—was bound to corrupt those in office. The moral bankruptcy, intolerant repression and inhuman atrocities which resulted next—all in the name of Christianity, defending the faith, and of church leadership—defy comparison with any pagan or communistic regime which has ever come into power. It is no wonder that this thousand-year reign by church leaders is yet known as The Dark Ages! It all began with a wrong first button: the concept of an office and authority for the eldership.

---

8. Arthur Cushman McGiffert, *A History of Christian Thought*, Vol. 1 (New York: Charles Scribner's Sons, 1954), p. 161.

Throughout the history of the Free Church we have also wrestled with the same problem. We keep trying to start with the wrong button! Any time you begin with the premise of offices and authority for church leadership, you wind up in the same place. We have witnessed the cycles time after time, as the minorities become the majorities, and the persecuted become the persecutors.

It all begins with the eldership of the local church. If, by virtue of an envisioned office and their election to it, the elders believe themselves to now be vested with authority, they will inevitably begin to sit in judgment of others, to create laws for the church ("elders' decisions") and to seek to enforce their edicts upon the membership. Invariably the elders will decide that the Scriptures are not plain enough or explicit enough to serve as a working manual for their church, so they will add their own legislative rulings to clarify and govern their own situation.

Almost every church has its lists of "Thou shalts" and "Thou shalt nots." True, they cannot be substantiated by a "Thus says the Lord"; but someone had to do something, didn't they? Some rules had to be made about drinking, dancing, movies, card playing, make-up, bazaars, approved version of the Bible, etc. No sir. We can't allow all of those silences of the Bible to exist on all of these important subjects. We will have to write and attach our own codicil to the Last Will and Testament of Jesus to correct these problems. By what authority? By virtue of the elders' office and authority!

Have we forgotten the solemn words of warning from the inspired Apostle John in Revelation 22:18-20? Have elders recently received some special exemption from the curses pronounced by the inspired Apostle Paul in Galatians 1:8-9? Shall we now, with the cults, proclaim some latter-day revelation to excuse our additions to Scripture? No, we just cite the elders' office, their authority, their vote and the fact that their action was duly recorded in the official Minutes of the Board of Elders and announced to the congregation. Shades of the Edicts of the Councils of Nicaea (335 & 787), Constantinople (448), Ephesus (431 & 449), Chalcedon (451), Lateran (1179), Lyons (1215), Pisa (1409), Constance (1414), Basel (1431), etc.! These notable elders' meetings began as early as the middle of the second century. It was only a matter of time before they began legislating upon matters of doctrine and discipline.[9] Just take a look at what they produced!

It was probably inevitable that the elders' concept of their office and authority would relegate a pastor to a lower rung on the ladder. A hierarchy works that way. At the top you have the coveted chief elders' office, The Chairman of the Board of Elders. Next you have the members of the Official Board of Elders. And then comes the pastor, if the Deacons have not already staked out that rung in the hierarchy. In any case, if the elders are in authority, they obviously have the responsibility of being over everyone else, including the preacher. Since his is the most audible voice and most visible position, a major concern of the elders must be to keep him in line. In effect, he must play the role of their puppet. He will act and speak according to their edicts, or he will be fired and a new puppet will be substituted.

The hierarchical order in the churches has been so widely and unquestioningly accepted that it will come as an incredulous shock to many to realize that *the New Testament never*

---

9. Albert Henry Newman, *A Manual of Church History*, Vol. 1 (Philadelphia: The Judson Press, 1957), pp. 294-295.

gives elders an office, grants them any authority or places them over a pastor. (Nor does it place him over them.) In fact, the New Testament recognizes NO hierarchy of leadership. When you start with the right button, you only come up with a picture of shared responsibility under the authority of Jesus Christ.

The Marks of Maturity

Specific sets of qualifications for Elders are given in I Timothy 3:1-7 and Titus 1:5-9. Gene Getz notes, however:

> As you study the passages in the New Testament which refer to elders or bishops, it becomes clear that both qualifications and functions are described. Significantly far more is said about qualifications than functions.[10]

Getz is, of course, referring to the absence of a specific job description for the elders in each church. The reason for the heavy emphasis upon the qualifications of elders is, as we have seen, the church's need to be certain that these men are indeed the most spiritually mature and committed Christian leaders available in the congregation. Theirs is the primary responsibility for leading the rest of the flock on toward maturity and ministry. It is disastrous to select as elders those who lack the marks of spiritual maturity, whose lives reflect stagnancy, rather than continuing growth, or who are unwilling to accept the grave responsibilities of leading a church. Getz, in his study of the Scriptures, discovers twenty of these qualifications, or marks of maturity, which are deemed desirable in elders:

---

10. Gene A. Getz, *Sharpening the Focus of the Church* (Chicago: Moody Press, 1974), p. 105.

1. Above reproach (I Tim 3:2 Titus 2:7)
2. Husband of one wife, not a bigamist (I Tim 3:2; Titus 1:6)
3. Temperate (I Tim 3:2; Titus 1:8)
4. Prudent (I Tim 3:2; Titus 1:8)
5. Respectable (I Tim 3:2)
6. Hospitable (I Tim 3:2; Titus 1:8)
7. Able to teach (I Tim 3:2; Titus 1:9)
8. Not given to wine (I Tim 3:3; Titus 1:9)
9. Not pugnacious, but gentle (I Tim 3:3; Titus 1:7)
10. Uncontentious (I Tim 3:3)
11. Free from the love of money (I Tim 3:3; Titus 1:7; I Peter 5:2)
12. One who manages his household well, keeping his children under control with all dignity (I Tim 3:4; Titus 1:6)
13. Not a new convert (I Tim 3:6)
14. A good reputation with those outside the church (I Tim 3:7)
15. Not self-willed (Titus 1:7)
16. Not quick-tempered (Titus 1:7)
17. Must love what is good (Titus 1:8)
18. Must be just (Titus 1:8)
19. Must be devout (Titus 1:8)
20. Must hold fast the faithful Word (Titus 1:9)[11]

It is doubtful that any leader in any church, with the exception of Jesus, ever exhibited completely the accomplishment of all twenty of these qualifications. Yet, the list is given as the standard, and the combined eldership should be a composite of these strengths pooled in leadership. The qualifications are not to be lowered or diluted, simply because no one can be found to fulfill all of them. Again, we are not given the perogative of altering the Scriptures to fit

---

11. Getz, pp. 105-107.

our convenience or contemporary viewpoints. The qualifications remain high because they are the marks of spiritual maturity. They are the measuring rod. They are fixed to remind leaders that they have not yet "arrived," and that they must keep growing and maturing if they are to lead the church—even after they have been selected as elders! The best men available—those who exhibit the greatest number of these marks of maturity—are to be appointed to lead.

We are reminded again of the earlier assertion that elders are made by the Holy Spirit, who has been operating in their lives. Congregational votes do not qualify men for the eldership. They can only recognize the work of the Spirit in their lives and so appoint them to the task.

Several of these marks of spiritual maturity we have listed perhaps bear some closer examination and clarification. We note that there are at least four of the qualifications which relate to a prospective elder's home life. If he is married, even in a polygamous society he must be a "one-woman" man. He and his wife should be modeling what a Christian marriage ought to be, with commitment and faithfulness to each other. This does not mean they will not have disagreements or misunderstandings in their marriage. Everyone does. It does mean, however, that they are committed enough to each other to work them out. It is also straining the text to insist that one who is not married could not serve as an elder. Imagine disqualifying Jesus or Paul! The stipulation simply applies to those who are married.

This is likewise true of the qualification pertaining to the conduct of a man's household and his relationship to his children. Must a man have children to be an elder? Certainly not! While the experience of rearing children would definitely be of value, it is ridiculous to push the requirement to the point of eliminating a man from consideration as an elder if he is childless. If he does have children, do they respect him and his leadership of the home? That is the point. Again, to legalistically interpret the requirement to have his children under control as meaning that they never disobey or make mistakes is to misunderstand Paul. No one is able to completely control anyone. But who is in charge in the household? Do the kids run it, making all the decisions; or does the father responsibly assume his role of leadership? This is not to imply in any way some kind of arbitrary, dictatorship. That kind of "control" is devastating to both a home and a church. A man who leads by his personal Christian lifestyle, who models for his family Christ-likeness in his speech and in the way he conducts himself at home, who insists upon respect and observance of Christian principles in his home, and who leads his family in worship and ministry is the kind of man who makes a good elder.

A third mark of maturity relating to the home is that of committed family finances. Jesus said, "For where your treasure is, there your heart will be also" (Matt 6:21). Where are a man's priorities in this area? If he is constantly driven to "get ahead" financially, he will not have the time or the commitment to function as an elder. He already has another master. Either he or his wife may have an obsession for material things, or they may have made financial commitments beyond that which they can meet. We live in an age when compulsive credit buying is destroying individuals and marriages. Whatever the particular circumstances, if money has been permitted to become the driving, ruling factor in a man's life, he is unfit for the eldership. Again, he already serves another master. His heart is with his treasure, or his perceived lack thereof. If, however, he has learned the kind of contentment Paul describes in Philippians 4:12-13, by having committed his finances to the Lord, and has learned to accept His sufficiency, he will make a good elder. His heart, too, will be with his money—invested in the Lord's work.

The fourth matter involving a prospective elder's home relates to his use of his home. Has he learned how to open it and use it for the Lord's work, or are he and his wife selfish about its use? Christian hospitality is definitely a mark of spiritual maturity. Hosting a Bible study or inviting into his home neighbors, church visitors, youth and other members for meals or activities are all valid ways in which Christian homes can and should be used fruitfully in ministry. Christian hospitality could also include housing visiting missionaries or speakers and providing a meeting place for church leaders. There are so many productive ways in which the home can be used for the Lord! A man who keeps his home as his private castle, though, should never be an elder. An important part of his life has been excluded from the Lordship of Christ.

A number of the other marks of maturity deal with how a man conducts himself in his relationship with others. Has he learned how to speak the truth in love (Eph 4:15)? Has he learned how to be patient, understanding, fair and forgiving with the faults and failures of others, or is he quick-tempered, argumentative and judgmental in his approach? Is he a critic and a pessimist, or has he learned how to see the good in people and to expect God's good in each situation (Rom 8:28)? An insensitive or a negative man can destroy a church if he is selected as an elder. So also can one who sees the eldership as an opportunity to rule or to manipulate people!

Several other marks of maturity have to do with a man's reputation. How do the people outside the church see him? Do they recognize him as a Christian by the way he lives, or has he established a different kind of reputation away from the church building? How do they judge his business ethics, for example? Is he respected by his neighbors and those who work with him? Within the church, how do people regard him? Do they recognize the fruit of the Spirit growing in his life (Gal 5:22-23)? Has he learned how to walk by faith in his personal life, so he will be able to lead the church in also walking by faith? Are the members willing to work with him and to follow his leadership? It is amazing how many churches select for elders men whom no one intends to follow! Such an election is an exercise in futility and frustration for all concerned.

Finally, and perhaps most important, how does the man regard the Word of God? Has he taken the time and effort to really know God's Word? Is he stable in his faith? Is he committed to upholding the Lordship of Christ and the principles of His Word, even in the face of unpopularity? Does he really believe in the power of the Word (Rom 1:16)? Unless he is firmly grounded in this category, the church who selects him is in real trouble! The widespread ignorance of the Bible, lack of commitment to its message and just basic lack of faith among elders of churches today is certainly one of their greatest handicaps. How can elders lead Christ's church if they do not know or really believe what He has said? Yet, many do not. They are bluffing it. As a result, the blind lead the blind; and their destiny is certain (Luke 6:39).

It is impossible to over-emphasize the importance of congregational responsibility in the matter of selecting qualified church leadership. Those churches who have fallen into the trap of thinking it really doesn't matter much whom they select have sealed their own fate. In a similar condition are those churches who have ill-advisedly established in their by-laws set numbers of officers which must be selected each year, and have included elders in those offices and numbers. These are two of the most foolish moves any church can make! The Holy Spirit does not operate by the numbers in anyone's by-laws, particularly when they have blasphemed His work of accrediting Christ as Lord by their rejection of His sole authority in the setting up of other officers for the church. Let us be reminded again that the Holy Spirit makes elders, not the church! Either they are qualified by the Holy Spirit's work in their lives, or they are not. Filling up the ballot with the names of unqualified candidates for elders, in order to meet the requirements of by-laws, is a guaranteed, fool-proof way to sabotage the ministry of any church. The time has come to distinguish the church from the Moose Lodge!

Paul Benjamin comments concerning his studies of the ways churches select their leaders:

> In America . . . the "come-to-church" emphasis often results in stress laid upon three weekly services and giving a tithe of one's net income. I have often referred to this system as the "three and ten" pattern. The main difficulty with the "three and ten" pattern is the limits which it places upon participation in the kingdom of God. Furthermore, it often stresses one's relationship to the congregation rather than a personal relationship to Christ. A man may rise to a position of leadership in a congregation, even with very poor attitudes, if he attends the right number of services, and gives his money.[12]

---

12. Paul Benjamin, *The Growing Church* (Lincoln: Lincoln College Press, 1972), p. 17.

Benjamin has long observed the practices of our churches, and he has accurately identified the criteria really used by nominating committees in more churches than anyone would like to admit. Even if mature men are selected, they often have no concept of what they ought to be doing. J. Vernon Jacobs writes:

> Elders not only need to be men whose lives are above reproach, but they need to be taught how to serve. Unfortunately in too many churches the elders are simply a part of the business board. They feel that if they are faithful in conducting the affairs of the church, they have done their duty. . . . Most elders are good men who have specialized in nothing.[13]

The Functions of the Elders

Such emphasis is placed upon the selection of qualified elders because God expects more of elders than of anyone else in the church. Paul reminds Titus to select carefully those who would be elders, for they are "entrusted with God's work" (Titus 1:7). That is an immense stewardship! They must answer to God for the spiritual family they have been called to lead, in addition to their role as spiritual leader of their own physical family.

In chapter two we discovered in the Biblical blueprint for church leadership that there are at least four primary functions of all leaders in the church:

1. Leading by example—the "follow me" style of leadership
2. Providing nurture—functioning as a spiritual parent

---

13. J. Vernon Jacobs, "The Elders: Kind Spiritual Guides," *Christian Standard*, September 9, 1979, p. 819.

3. Equipping members for ministry, according to their gifts
4. Serving whenever, wherever and however as required within the body of Christ to meet people at the point of their needs.

Suffice it to say that the elders are called to perform these functions to the greatest degree. While everyone who leads in any capacity in the church is called to help function in these ways, elders must lead the way in each of these areas. The rest of the church will reflect the style of leadership which the elders model for them—for better or for worse. They are the pacesetters for church leadership.

It is also helpful for us to compare this list of basic functions of leadership with those of others. Getz enumerates six functions of the eldership which he finds defined in the New Testament:

1. Shepherd the flock of God (I Peter 5:2; Acts 20:28; I Tim 3:5)
2. Not to lord it over those allotted to his charge, but to be an example to the flock (I Peter 5:3)
3. Teach and exhort (I Tim 3:2; Titus 1:9)
4. Refute those who contradict the truth (Titus 1:9-11)
5. Manage the church of God (I Tim 3:5; 5:17)
6. Pray for the sick (James 5:14-15)[14]

To this list Don DeWelt adds the responsibility of administering discipline. Citing I Thessalonians 5:12-13 and I Timothy 3:5, he says:

> Those references seem to include both instruction as well as corrective discipline in the work of the bishop. The task of the bishop is also to administer and labor for and love the church as a father loves, labors for and admonishes his

14. Getz, p. 107.

children. This can only be true when they show themselves worthy of such work.[15]

In each of these lists we see spiritual leaders who are to lead more as caring parents of the church family, than to serve as legislators, judges or policemen. They are men who labor under a heavy responsibility. They must give an accounting for what happens to each sheep added to their flock! If those sheep are lacking food, exercise, care or protection, who is to blame? The elders are to provide. The elders are their shepherds, and they serve under the Chief Shepherd who will one day return and demand an accounting for His sheep (I Peter 5:1-4). More will be said later in this chapter concerning the shepherding function of elders.

Finally, elders need to be reminded again that they are called to lead. They are to be men of action, not simply men of talk. They have the glorious opportunity of leading the church forward on a tremendous adventure of faith, growth and ministry. Oh, the countless valuable hours which are wasted by elders in fruitless talk! Elders' meetings, however long they may be, do not amount to a hill of beans unless they produce something which is going to actually accomplish ministry in the church. Jesus repeatedly criticized the religious leaders of His day for their pious but fruitless talk, and for their elaborately-reasoned legislative decisions which subverted and quenched the spirit of God's guidelines for living. How the Lord must weep over elders' meetings which are spent arguing irrelevant fine points of opinion, devising new rules and regulations for the church, and hassling over implementive leadership details!

---

15. Don DeWelt, *The Church in the Bible* (Joplin: College Press Publishing Company, 1958), pp. 103-104.

Elders have a habit of majoring in minors, and minoring in the majors. Many elders are obsessed with a need to control. The elders need to mind their own business, and leave the business of other leaders in the church to them. There is value in dividing the church's total ministry up into departments, and to having an elder chair each of these departments which relates directly to the spiritual growth of the church. The elders do not, however, have to know and vote on everything that happens in the church. They do not have to review every decision before any action can be taken. Elders who view their function as being "the watchdogs" who need to control everything and everyone can easily become the main bottleneck (and pain in the neck) in any church's ministry. Moreover, they can discourage anyone else from participating in ministry! Rather than concerning themselves with the growth of the church, they waste their time with its maintenance. In fact, so much time is spent by the elders of most churches on controlling and maintaining, that there is seldom time left to decisively lead the church forward as elders. Max Hickerson speaks strongly concerning this issue:

> Elders, you lose your leadership when you cease to lead. Too many times, when men get a big position, they start to rest on their laurels. They feel so comfortable that they just settle back and say, "Here we go now." At this point, the three "I" sins usually show up: indifference, ignorance, and indecision. Sometimes people settle down so hard they flatten out. Comfort comes as a guest, lingers to become a host, and stays to enslave us. We must continue to improve, to perfect, to better qualify ourselves. We can never let up.[16]

16. Max Hickerson, "Follow the Leaders," *Christian Standard*, July 5, 1973, p. 627.

The Ministering Team

This brings us rather naturally to our next point concerning the relationship between the elders and the minister. We have already established the fact that the elders are nowhere in Scripture given authority over a pastor, nor is he given authority over them. What, then, is to be their relationship?

It would appear from the New Testament that they are intended to share a team relationship. They are all elders, overseers, shepherds and spiritual parents charged with the responsibility of leading and caring for the family of God entrusted to them. While their functions may differ somewhat, with a pastor serving as a more visible full-time leader in the areas of preaching and teaching (I Tim 5:17), they are intended to be partners in providing the expressive leadership for the church.

Roy Willbern provides some excellent and thought-provoking observations from his perspective as an elder. He speaks of the mutual leadership which should be shared by preachers and elders. He points out that the elder "is a product of the congregation, has his roots in the congregation, and should be able to understand its needs, capacities, and life." On the other hand:

> The preacher, with superior theological education, devoting his full time and energies to the spiritual life of the church, views a problem through the eyes and mind conditioned by this background. . . . The preacher's personal investment in the association needs to be carefully remembered. His education has been long, specifically channelled and costly. His years of experience have further prepared him for a life of continuing service. His emotional and psychological security are tied to performing effectively in this ministry

> to which he has been called. . . . Elders leading properly must understand and use constructively the unique capacities of preachers. And preachers, using the forum and opportunity afforded them, must be conscious of the responsibility for leading placed upon the elders.[17]

Who could say it better? Now there is an elder who understands the New Testament concept of leadership and who would be a blessing to any church or pastor! This concept of mutuality of leadership is one we must recapture at any cost, or we will continue to destroy churches and leaders with our counterfeit substitutes. *The leadership of a pastor and the leadership of elders are BOTH essential.* The function of one does not exclude or depreciate the leadership of the other. They are intended to be a pastoral team, with each recognizing the strengths of the other. We have for too long tolerated the continuance of an adversary relationship in the churches between ministers and elders. The Lord has never approved this, and the church cannot afford it. It is time to re-discover and to re-establish the team ministry concept!

Shepherding the Flock

We have pointed out that both pastors and elders serve as shepherds of the flock under the Chief Shepherd, Jesus (I Peter 2:25; 5:1-4). How can this immense job be accomplished, though, unless they divide up in some way the responsibilities among themselves? How can every shepherd, for example, be responsible for every sheep? Some shepherding plan is essential. Elders in many churches choose to divide up the flock according to the geographical

---

17. Roy Willbern, "Who's in Charge Here, Anyway?" *Mission*, September, 1977, pp. 64-65.

areas where they live, with each elder becoming the shepherd of one of the areas. Others prefer to divide the families alphabetically. The New Testament certainly does not prescribe a single organizational method we must use, but it does make the pastor and elders in each church responsible for getting the job done—however they see best. To fail to organize the task in some way is to guarantee that it will never be accomplished. Every person who becomes a part of a church needs to be someone's specific responsibility. Anything or anyone that is everyone's business winds up, in practice, being nobody's business. That can be disastrous in the shepherding business!

In organizing a shepherding program, while the elders have the chief responsibility for seeing that everyone is shepherded, they need to remember that they are not intended to do it all. Others in leadership are also designed to participate in these functions of modeling, nurturing, equipping and serving. How leadership is to be organized to assist elders in any given church is left up to that church. Some prefer to organize the shepherding around age-graded Bible school classes, which has worked extremely well for the Southern Baptists. Others use the concept of neighborhood flocks, cells or Bible studies. Many are the organizational systems which will work. Designing and adopting a system, however, is only the first step. Many churches get that far—and no further. Any plan must still be worked, or it is absolutely useless. How many excellent plans have been scrapped as being unworkable or unproductive, simply because they were never really worked! Plans do NOT work themselves. PEOPLE MUST WORK PLANS. *It is the elders' job to help devise the shepherding plan, to implement the plan, to see that the plan is worked, and to stick to the plan.* That is no small job, but neither is the eldership!

An additional word to pastors is essential at this point. One of the key reasons shepherding plans are not worked is that the elders and those charged with shepherding are often scared to death about their inability to function as shepherds. They can easily envision scenarios which they would not know how to handle. They have had no training in understanding the dynamics of human relationships. Recognizing that they are unprepared in this area, they would rather do anything than to have to do the work of shepherding. This has nothing to do with their approval or disapproval of the shepherding program. They simply want to succeed in whatever they personally attempt. (We all do!) In other words, they fear failure; and it is only human to avoid getting into uncomfortable situations where you expect to fail. Consequently, a thousand other important things in their lives have a way of crowding out shepherding responsibilities.

Pastors and elders need to face this fear and acknowledge it. More importantly, they need to do something about it. Every minister in his preparation for the ministry is given a foundation of basic Biblical counseling principles, and is also given the opportunity to develop at least some minimal skills in this area of ministry. There is no reason why shepherding leaders in the church should be deprived of this knowledge of these skills. There are some excellent programs available now which can be used in the church to teach these principles and abilities.[18] Should this not be an essential part of the church's equipping ministry? It may, in fact, be the single most important element in determining the success or failure of a church's shepherding ministry.

---

18. Rex Johnson, *Equipping Christians for Ministry in Counseling* (Seal Beach: Innovations in Learning, 1981), An Assisted-Video Series.

The institution of such an equipping program could also be the key to unburdening ministers who, if they are the only one in the church with any counseling training, can easily wind up scheduled 10 hours per day with this one function of ministry alone! We are not proposing making psychologists out of either pastors or other shepherding leaders in the congregation. There is a definite need for Christian professionals—specialists to whom some problems can be referred. But there is also a need for teaching some basic Biblical principles and helping skills throughout the shepherding leadership in the local church. We will also discover, in the process of that equipping, that God has specially gifted a few of our people in this area; and they can be given additional training to help assist a minister with certain kinds of follow-up counseling which he does not have the time to do. In fact, they will often be able to do some of these things better than he or the elders can. This can sometimes be threatening to pastors and elders; but rather than being threatened by these gifted leaders, they should rejoice in the success of shared ministry and in the multiple gifts God has given within the church.

Yes, shepherding the flock is an immense, on-going job. Relatively few churches do a good job of it. That fact, however, should serve as no excuse or consolation among elders. The Chief Shepherd will not hold the elders of a church responsible for what they have or have not done in comparison to the performance of the elders of other churches, but in comparison to the standard and goals He has set. He has never promised to grade on the curve! But what a promise He does make to those who are faithful to their charge: "And when the Chief Shepherd appears, you will receive the crown of glory that will never fade away" (I Peter 5:4).

In Summary

We have come to understand that the concepts of an office and authority for elders are both unscriptural and amount to a challenge of the Lordship of Christ over His church. In Him is vested all authority. That is unconditional. To the elders He has delegated responsibility for the flock entrusted to them. Failure to perceive this distinction between authority and responsibility has perverted the position of elders and severely damaged and destroyed churches. A predictable cycle of developments has historically occurred century after century in the churches, always beginning with the establishment of offices and authority for elders. The church must restore the New Testament concept of the role of elders if it is to achieve its mission, or it will forever be derailed by its own leadership.

Congregations have a vitally important responsibility of selecting only the most spiritually mature and qualified men to serve as elders, recognizing that they do not qualify elders by their votes. Elders are prepared to serve through the operation of the Holy Spirit in their lives. Churches simply examine them for the Scriptural marks of their spiritual maturity, determine their willingness to serve, and then set them apart to lead as their elders.

Elders are to function as the primary spiritual leaders of a church by setting an example, serving as a spiritual parent to the church family, equipping members for ministry according to their gifts, and ministering in any way necessary to help meet people at the point of their needs with God's solutions. Theirs should be a team ministry with a pastor in providing the essential expressive leadership for the church. According to the New Testament, neither is in authority, and neither is to rule over the other. Functions and responsibilities of ministers and elders may differ, but they are to build upon the strengths of each other and to complement each other's leadership.

Finally, a major responsibility of both pastor and elders is the shepherding of the flock entrusted to them. The method of doing this is left up to each church to determine. Some plan and division of responsibilities, however, must be selected and worked, or the task will never be accomplished. That plan needs to involve the other leaders within the church, since they are also intended to be equipped and to share in the work of shepherding.

6

THE SERVANT LEADERS (DEACONS)

Officers or Servants?

As we seek to understand the New Testament pattern of leadership for the church, our study leads us to the conclusion that deacons are the second most commonly mentioned church leaders. Paul addresses his letter to the Philippian church: "To all the saints in Christ Jesus at Philippi, together with the overseers and deacons" (Phil 1:1). Then in his first letter to Timothy he says:

> Deacons, likewise, are to be men worthy of respect, sincere, not indulging in much wine, and not pursuing dishonest gain. They must keep hold of the deep truths of the faith with a clear conscience. They must first be tested; and then if there is nothing against them, let them serve as deacons. . . .

A deacon must be the husband of but one wife and must manage his children and his household well (I Tim 3:8-10, 12).

In the New International Version of the Bible, along with most other versions, these four verses (Phil 1:1, I Tim 3:8, 10, 12) are the only incidences in which the word "deacon" appears. The identical word, however, appears in Matthew 20:26; 22:13; 23:11; Mark 9:35; 10:43; John 2:5, 9; 12:26; Romans 13:4; 15:8; 16:1; I Corinthians 3:5; II Corinthians 3:6; 6:4; 11:15; Galatians 2:17; Ephesians 3:7; 6:21; Colossians 1:7, 23, 25; 4:7; I Thessalonians 3:2; I Timothy 4:6; and Titus 1:9. From these references it is obvious that this is one of Paul's favorite words. It seemed to him to be the embodiment of the Christian's Christ-like activity in serving others. He constantly applies the term to himself and his own ministry, along with that of his assistants. In most of these cases the Greek word *diakonos* is translated "servant" or "minister." This is indeed an accurate English translation of the word. It can also mean simply "helper."[1]

It is particularly interesting to note what the translators do with Romans 16:1, where the word is used to describe the position of a woman by the name of Phoebe in the church at Cenchrea. Some translate the word as "deaconess," while others simply render it "servant." Both are inappropriate, since the Greek gender of the word in this specific case is masculine. The feminine form of the word would be required in order to be able to translate it as "a woman servant" or as the commonly transliterated "deaconess."

---

1. William F. Arndt and F. Wilbur Gingrich, *A Greek-English Lexicon of the New Testament and Other Early Christian Literature* (Chicago: The University of Chicago Press, 1952), pp. 183-184.

The concept that women can serve, along with men, as deacons of the church is further supported by another look at the way in which the translators have treated I Timothy 3:11. This verse appears in the middle of the single section of the New Testament devoted to discussing deacon's qualifications. It is translated:

> In the same way, their wives are to be women of respect, not malicious talkers but temperate and trustworthy in everything.

The Greek word for "wife" is *gynê* and it also means "woman." The word occurs in the plural form in this instance.[2] It applies to any adult female (Matt 9:20; 13:33; 27:55; Luke 1:42; 13:11; Acts 5:14; 8:3; I Cor 11:3, 5, 6-15; 14:34, 35; I Tim 2:11). The same word is used to designate wives (Matt 5:28, 31, 32; 14:3; 18:25; Luke 1:5, 13, 18, 24; I Cor 7:2ff.; 9:5; Eph 5:22ff.; Col 3:18, 19) and to describe a widow (Luke 4:26) and a stepmother (I Cor 5:1).[3] Its use in the passage in question (I Tim 3:11) is without any possessive pronoun, such as the translators insert. Hence, the passage could be more accurately translated, "The women are to be women worthy of respect. . . ." In this case, it would apply to the women who serve as deacons. More will be said in chapter 8 concerning women in church leadership, but it is important for us to establish here the fact that women are specifically cited, and did evidently serve, as deacons in the New Testament church.

---

2. Zondervan, *The Analytical Greek Lexicon* (Grand Rapids: Zondervan Publishing House, 1970), p. 83.
3. Arndt and Gingrich, p. 167.

As we have noted, the Greek word for deacon can also mean simply "servant," "helper" or "minister." The word is, like the other words used to describe church leadership, one of function, rather than title. The position of deacon in the New Testament Church is especially one of function, and it is most appropriate that the name chosen to describe these individuals should have been that used to describe the lowliest functionary in that society. A servant was one who acted to meet the needs of others. In no way was his position considered to be honorary or official in that culture. The servant lived to do whatever the master needed to have done for himself, for his household or for his guests. He had no responsibilities for determining policy or for deciding whether or not his employer was right in those things he had directed to be accomplished. A servant produced as directed, or he no longer remained a servant.

Within the family of God, the church, there would exist from time to time many different needs which would have to be met. Servants, or deacons, would be needed to attend to these things as required. Some would be considered very important tasks, while others would be common and mundane. All, however, would be essential. The operation of a household and its servants, and the function of the church and its deacons, exist as an excellent and accurate parallel to help us comprehend the nature, role and relationship of the deacons. As in any household, there would be some tasks which would be of an ongoing nature. A cook, a gardener or a housekeeper might be required on a regular, continuing basis. Harvest workers, carpenters and house painters might be selected and brought in only as needed. Each would have an important task to accomplish, but who would employ a house painter for two or three years, when he would only be needed for a few days of work every couple of years?

Considering the background of this concept and its application to the church, it is absolutely ludicrous that the church should evolve a generic office with a rank and a stated term of office for the position of deacons. Yet, this pattern has almost uniformly been adopted by the churches and defended as being "New Testament." It is not. There is not a shred of evidence that any church in the New Testament ever conceived deacons to be officers of the church or elected them to serve for any kind of fixed terms. Deacons were people who were carefully selected to serve in implementive kinds of leadership, according to the particular needs of the church at the time, and in consideration of their particular abilities and Christian character. They served as long as the function was needed, or as long as they continued to function as required.

It is time we faced the fact that the current concept of the office of deacon is an extra-scriptural and anti-scriptural adoption by the church of a form lifted from the pagan culture surrounding us. We have completely changed essential implementive church leadership functions, as prescribed by the New Testament, into a mixed marriage of corporate and representative government forms, resulting in the creation of "the office of the deacon." Then we have further attempted to define the scope of this office and to include it as a part of the expressive leadership of the church. In many cases, churches have so "stacked the deck" that the greater number of deacons required by their by-laws can, and are given the right to, out-vote the elders on any issue. In so doing, we have effectively undermined and rendered unworkable the entire New Testament concept of church leadership.

Functions of Deacons

"What do the deacons do?" In most churches that question brings a shrug of the shoulders in response, until someone remembers to note that they do distribute the communion and take up the offering. Another volunteers the information that deacons are members of the official church board and are expected to attend its monthly meetings and to vote on all matters coming before the board. Still another will add that deacons serve on committees.

It comes as quite a shock to most church members—and even to most deacons—that there is no New Testament precedent or authority for any of these functions mentioned. The scriptures, for example, never require that an elder preside at the communion table, or that those who serve the communion or take up the offering have to be elected deacons. These concepts, which are vehemently affirmed and defended in many of the churches, are all additions we have written into the New Testament and have set in concrete. Where in the world did we get such ideas? Well, if you are going to have deacon officers for the church, you have to give them some domain, don't you? So we have staked out their territory and hallowed it by including its boundaries in our official by-laws. More will be said about church by-laws in chapter 7.

Judging from the qualifications for deacons listed in I Timothy 3:8-13, it certainly does not require a deacon to handle passing the communion or taking up the offering on Sundays! It must be admitted that anyone could function in taking care of these tasks. If a church does not have any more important needs to be served than these, they have no need of deacons. In fact, it is doubtful that some of the New Testament churches had any at all.

A great many churches have sought to differentiate the elders' and deacons' roles by declaring the elders to be in charge of the spiritual affairs of the church, while the deacons are charged with the physical. The decision, then, about what is spiritual and what is physical brings reminders of the ancient dilemmas of Gnostic theology and Docetism.[4] Such an attempt at this kind of separation of areas of ministry inevitably leads to problems. For example, the deacons almost invariably wind up in charge of the finance committee. Money is physical—right? WRONG!! While money itself may be a physical thing, stewardship and preparing church budgets are among the most spiritual concerns of the church's entire ministry. It was Jesus Himself who pointed out, "For where your treasure is, there your heart will be also" (Matt 6:21). Elders need to be integrally involved in making certain that the stewardship of money is clearly taught to be essential to every Christian's spiritual growth. Likewise, leaving the planning of church budgets to those who are not participants in the expressive leadership of the church is a certain road to spiritual disaster for any church. The setting of budgets then becomes an arbitrary mathematical exercise, rather than reflecting the faith and direction of the church's priorities in mission. If Jesus wept over the condition of Jerusalem, how much more must He weep over the horror stories of the acts of such finance and budget committees! No, the deacons do not belong in roles where they are providing the expressive leadership in church finances!

What, then, should deacons be doing? That will probably vary from church to church and from time to time in the life

4. Albert Henry Newman, *A Manual of Church History* (Chicago: Moody Press, 1974), p. 108.

of each church. What are the specific needs to be met within that family of God? In the Jerusalem church, which had by the time cited in Acts 6 grown to an estimated membership of 20,000 to 25,000, there was a problem in administering a program to take care of the needs of some of their widows.[5] It was a big problem! In fact, it required the selection of seven qualified men to handle it (Acts 6:1-7). In every sense of the word, these men were deacons. No, the title is not used; but seven men were selected to serve the church by taking the responsibility for this part of its ministry. As they served, they were "deaconing." How long did they serve? The Book of Acts does not tell us. In fact, although the names of two of the men appear later in other contexts of ministry, no further mention is made of the role of these deacons. They did the job that needed to be done, and the church moved on to attend to the rest of its ministry. This is probably a very accurate and typical kind of situation in which deacons were called into existence in the church. There is no evidence that churches elected a pool of versatile, multiple-purpose men without any specific responsibilities, who would serve if and when needed. There is definitely no indication that they were given any responsibilities related to overseeing the church's total ministry.

Every church needs to analyze its ongoing needs for implementive leadership. Then they need to select those who are most qualified by ability and Christian character to meet those needs. Implementive ministries for deacons in a church might include organizing and administering:

---

5. R. C. H. Lenski, *The Interpretation of St. Paul's Epistles to the Colossians, to the Thessalonians, to Timothy, to Titus and to Philemon* (Columbus: The Wartburg Press, 1946), p. 593.

1. An Audio-Visual Ministry
2. A Benevolence Ministry
3. A Bible School Ministry
4. A Big Brother or Big Sister Ministry
5. A Bus Ministry
6. A Children's Ministry
7. A Christian Camping Ministry
8. A Counseling Ministry
9. A Drama Ministry
10. A Maintenance Ministry
11. A Men's Fellowship Ministry
12. A Music Ministry
13. A Preschool or Child Care Ministry
14. A Puppets Ministry
15. A Recreation Ministry
16. A Scouting Ministry
17. A Seniors Ministry
18. A Singles Ministry
19. A Women's Fellowship Ministry
20. A Youth Ministry

This is only a suggested list of possibilities. If any of these exist as legitimate needs within a church, qualified people should be selected and be given the responsibility for organizing whatever ministries are required to meet those needs. As we have noted, the particular needs and opportunities of each congregation will vary. Not everyone who serves in each of these ministries needs to be a deacon. This is where the ministry of all believers comes in. The person or persons who will be responsible for organizing and administering the program, however, should probably be appointed as deacons. They are the key implementers, and they work under the supervision of the pastor and elders to help accomplish the total ministry of the church.

After their appointment as deacons, they must then be allowed to get their assigned job done, without having to continually check each step with some governing authority, and without having to be hamstrung by the lack of the necessary resources to do their job. If it costs money, what will it cost? That amount needs to be approved and set aside for them to get the task accomplished. To do anything less is absurd, and speaks of lack of trust of those appointed to the task. *Church budgets need to be set on this basis.*

Then there will be those other special crises, opportunities and needs which will arise in the life of a congregation. They will exist only for a time, and they may never happen again. When they do arise, the best qualified people again need to be selected and appointed for the task, and be given the enabling resources to get the job done. When it is done, there is no need for them to continue to serve in that capacity. What about the remainder of their term of office and their position on the church board? No term should be specified for them, no office created, nor any position given on a board. The entire subject of the church board will also be discussed in chapter 7, so no further elaboration on the board relationship will be given here. Suffice it to say that church boards are another wondrous cultural addition we have made in the evolution of "The New Testament Church," again hallowed by our by-laws.

Qualifications for Deacons

Getz finds nine qualifications for Deacons in the I Timothy 3:8-12 passage:

1. A man of dignity (v. 8)
2. Not double-tongued (v. 8)

3. Not addicted to much wine (v. 8)
4. Not fond of sordid gain (v. 8)
5. Holding to the mystery of the faith with a clear conscience (v. 9)
6. Beyond reproach (v. 10)
7. Men whose wives are dignified, not malicious gossips, but temperate, faithful in all things (v. 11)
8. Husbands of only one wife (v. 12)
9. Good managers of their children and their own households (v. 12)[6]

The qualifications which have seemingly attracted the greatest attention in most churches have been those related to a man's marital state. Many have been those excluded from service as a deacon because they were not married, or they were widowed or re-married. We have already alluded to the fact that the translation of verse 11 is questionable, and that it is subject to another very reasonable interpretation—namely an application to women who may be considered for service as deacons. We noted the absence of any possessive pronoun such as that used by translators to render the passage as "their wives," and we pointed out the legitimate application of this word to any adult woman. We have also cited the instance of the reference to Phoebe in Romans 16:1, who served as a deacon of the church at Cenchrea.

The main thrust of the list of qualifications given for deacons is to assure that the implementive leaders, as well as the expressive leaders, will be the right kind of people. In addition to their abilities as implementers, they must necessarily demonstrate the Christian lifestyle one would

6. Gene A. Getz, *Sharpening the Focus of the Church* (Chicago: Moody Press, 1974), p. 108.

expect of a church leader. They must not be a reproach to the church by serving as a visible contradiction of its message.

The first word in verse 8 used to describe the qualities to be found in those who would be appointed to serve as deacons has been variously translated as "grave," "dignified," "serious" and "worthy of respect." The latter translation is probably the most accurate representation of the Greek word used here. *Semnos* carries the idea that a person has proven himself and his Christian character. Therefore such a person has earned the respect of others.[7] How many times have church leaders complained that they are not properly respected by members of their congregations—as if their respect should automatically come as a requirement upon the people by virtue of their office and title?! Such leaders have placed the cart before the horse. Before a deacon candidate is selected to serve, he is expected to have earned the respect of the people. It is a prerequisite for deacons, not a consequence of election.

It is the height of folly to place someone in a leadership position who has not, in the people's minds, earned credibililty and the right to lead. No one will follow him! Imagine the plight of those Jerusalem deacons, had they not been men whose judgment and administrative leadership had been trusted, as they developed that church's extensive benevolence program. That trust was the key to their effectiveness as leaders. The apostles would have only compounded the problem which existed if they had appointed those who lacked the respect of the people. Consequently, they asked the congregation to choose from among them men whose judgment they would honor and whom they would be willing

7. Arndt and Gingrich, p. 754.

to follow. It worked! Numerous churches today, however, come to mind in which this qualification has obviously been ignored. These congregations have repeatedly repudiated the plans and proposals of their leadership.

The second word Paul uses in verse 8 is an interesting one. The Amplified Version renders it, "not shifty and double-talkers, but sincere in what they say." That is not a bad explanation of Paul's meaning. *Dilogos* means "double-tongued" or "insincere."[8] *Logos* means "speaking" or "word." For example, John refers to Jesus repeatedly in John 1:1-14 as the *Logos*—God's ultimate word and revelation to man. *Dilogos* means literally "two-worded."

Deacons, in other words, need to be able to be counted on to be the kind of people who will always speak with sincerity and integrity. Their word is their bond; it can be trusted. Note in verse 11, with reference to the women, the same use of *semnos* (worthy of respect), but this time followed by *diabolos,* meaning "ones who slander."[9] The thoughts are parallel. The deacon, whether man or woman, must be the kind of person who can be trusted to speak truthfully and with integrity, whether standing before you or speaking behind your back.

Both of these Greek words which are used in warning could also sustain the idea of tale-bearing, or gossiping—a tendency which could also be devastating to a deacon's function and leadership.[10] The deacon must be able to maintain confidences and use good judgment and discretion in what he says.

---

8. Arndt and Gingrich, p. 197.
9. Arndt and Gingrich, p. 181.
10. Donald Guthrie, *The Pastoral Epistles* (Grand Rapids: Wm. B. Eerdmans Publishing Company, 1957), p. 83.

The other two warnings about the character of prospective deacons in verse 8 deal with those who are addicted to, or who "cling to" much wine (the common alcoholic beverage of Jesus' day), and those who are eager for dishonorable gain. Both of these attributes are dangerous and would certainly disqualify a person from Christian leadership. They testify to his having transferred his dependence and confidence from the Lord to alcohol as an escape, or to money as the means to gain power and independence, rather than by faith trusting the Lord to provide as needed by His grace.

The word regarding the relationship to money is the same one used with reference to elders in I Peter 5:2 and is very similar to the one employed in relationship to the qualification of the elders in I Timothy 3:3, meaning "not loving money." One who has become dependent upon, and who cannot be parted from, his wine or his money has indeed made them his lords. As Jesus said, "No servant can serve two masters. Either he will hate the one and love the other, or he will be devoted to the one and despise the other. You cannot serve God and Money" (Luke 16:13). That statement did not set well with the religious leaders Jesus was addressing, according to the following verses, for they "loved money" (v. 14).

It is evident that many who have been elected to church leadership also "love money." A few have succumbed to the temptation to siphon off church funds into their own pockets. Far more common, however, are those who have such a preoccupation with their own money-making ventures that they grossly neglect the ministries of the church for which they have been made responsible. Others are so fearful that God will be unable to provide to see His purposes accomplished, that they refuse to allow the church to move ahead an inch by faith, insisting upon having cash in hand for everything before any action can be taken. These leaders will paralyze a church in its tracks!

Still other leaders jealously guard their church's funds as they guard their own, insisting upon hoarding them and compounding them by earning the highest rate of savings interest available, rather than putting them to work in ministry. The great tragedy is that these kinds of leaders and churches are not the rare exceptions. They tend to be the rule. Some may exclaim, "God preserve the church from such leaders!" Let us remember, however, that the church is given the responsibility for preserving itself from them by carefully selecting those who have their financial priorities straight BEFORE they are appointed to lead!

Although deacons are not charged with the expressive leadership of the church, they must be tuned into its mission and be committed to the same principles and goals as the expressive leaders. "They must keep hold of the deep truths of the faith with a clear conscience" (v. 9) speaks to this issue. Does the person being considered as a prospective deacon really believe the gospel? Is he or she wholly committed to the implementation of Scriptural principles and the accomplishment of divine purposes, or do some personal reservations and doubts still exist? The truth of the matter is that many church leaders are elected who actually believe very little of the Christian message. They are not really certain that the principles and goals espoused by Jesus and His apostles are valid or still work—if they ever did. Consequently, they each come into leadership owning a different agenda for the church which reflects their personal creed.

Many are the problems witnessed in churches where the implementive and expressive leaders are tracking in different directions! Unless both are deeply committed to the Lordship of Christ in all things, to the accomplishment of His purposes for the church, and to a chosen, workable plan of action, continual conflict and stalemates can be expected. It can be demonstrated over and over again in actual case studies of churches that very little is ever achieved in such situations. Everyone is operating by a different agenda and a separate set of rules. This is particularly a problem, as we will see, for churches who have adopted the church board concept.

Those who would serve as deacons must also be tested. Lenski notes that Paul uses here his favorite word for testing —that which was employed regarding the testing of coins, metals, etc., "but he does not use the aorist imperative to express a formal and set test, but the present imperative which indicates a testing that covers some time." He adds, "This does not indicate a period of probation, that men were tried out in the office before permanent appointment was made, but a constant testing so that, when deacons were later needed, such men may be nominated as candidates."[11]

Lenski's point is an important one. How many churches have elected men to serve as deacons in order to "get them more involved in the church?" If their commitment has already been tested and found lacking, the last place in the world where they should be is in church leadership! Yet, this refrain is heard in the nominating committees in the majority of the churches; and the consequent watering down of the

11. Lenski, pp. 597-598.

quality of church leadership is the evident, direct result. Let them FIRST be tested; and then if they are NOT found lacking, let them serve—not the other way around!

How are they to be tested? It is absolutely inconceivable to many church leaders and members that anyone should be expected to do anything in the ministry of the church without an office and an official title. From this perspective, it would be impossible to pre-test anyone. Fortunately, though, that notion does not reflect, as we have seen, the New Testament concept of the ministry of the church. The Scriptures teach us that everyone in the church is intended to be involved in works of ministry according to their God-given abilities. Consequently, there are multitudes of opportunities to observe candidates for service as deacons as they actually function in ministry. Assign them jobs in established areas of ministry. How do they fulfill their responsibilities? Check out their lifestyles at home and on the job. Are they polygamists, child abusers, irresponsible parents or lacking the ability to manage their homes? Are they actually living their faith in their homes and on their jobs, or simply verbalizing it at church? Are they really interested in serving the Lord, or are they just looking for the prestige of a title and a position in a ruling church hierarchy? These are questions which need to be answered before anyone is appointed to church leadership. If no problems are observed in their performance or their motives, if they are found to be stable and trustworthy, and their abilities are needed in the leadership of the church, let them be appointed deacons and be put to work helping to expand the church's ministry!

Finally in verse 13 it speaks of the rewards of faithful and fruitful service. Those who so serve "gain an excellent standing and great assurance in their faith in Christ Jesus." What is this excellent standing? Lenski comments:

> To have served excellently for some time places one beyond any timidity or hesitation and makes him act with boldness and assurance. The acquisition of such boldness in faith, the blessed faith that rests in Christ Jesus, is the most satisfying reward and the incentive to proceed on this tried course.[12]

From a leadership standpoint, successful service also inspires others to continue to follow such proven leadership. No one wants to follow a loser. They all want to be winners. They want some assurance that their leader is capable and can produce before they commit their time and talents to help. The proven leader has a far better chance of getting his followers to take steps of faith and to move ahead into new areas of endeavor than does the new leader whose potential and judgment may still be questioned.

Moving Through the Chairs

Some interpreters believe that Paul was suggesting that the excellent standing achieved by successful deacons places them in line for a promotion to the eldership. While this may or may not be true in specific instances, there is no implication of such a progression in I Timothy 3:13. There is simply no connection which can be made from this text.

It is interesting to observe, however, that a great number of churches have adopted the assumption that the deaconate is the training ground for the eldership, and that the goal of all deacons should be to become elders. This expectation has grown more out of an association with the local Moose or Elks Lodges than from any responsible exegesis of the Scriptures. While the Masons, Elks and Eagles may expect

12. Lenski, p. 604.

to "move through the chairs" of lodge leadership, there is no such progression of musical chairs to be played in church leadership.

Some churches have even gone so far as to write into their by-laws requirements for serving a certain number of years as a deacon before being "advanced" to the eldership. This has fostered, in many cases, an expected automatic kind of upward movement in a hierarchy which they have created, once an individual has served the required number of years as an "apprentice" of the elders.

It is important to reiterate the principle of differing function between elders and deacons. One serves primarily in expressive leadership, and the other serves in implementive leadership. The fact is that most deacons probably should never be elders. A successful implementer does not necessarily make a good expressive leader. To attempt to place him in a position of expressive leadership may be trying to fit a square peg into a round hole. It may not be intended to fit. Conversely, a person may make an excellent expressive leader, but be a lousy implementer. He may be totally frustrated at the job of implementing a program to meet a need. So why must we insist upon mixing the two and requiring a person in church leadership to succeed at both? Few are that talented. Furthermore, automatic moving through the chairs may destroy the eldership and the church by placing people in roles of elders who are unqualified and who are incapable of providing the essential expressive leadership the church requires.

There are many areas, however, in which the elders and the deacons desperately need each other and must work together. None is more important than in the shepherding program of the church. In the first place, the shepherding endeavor needs to be interrelated with every aspect of the ministry of the church in order to be effective. It cannot stand in isolation as a separate and autonomous program and ever hope to succeed. Church members must be viewed from the standpoint of their total involvement in the ministries of the church, and must be directed into the particular ministries which will meet their needs and will give them the essential opportunities they require to grow and to serve. The deacons will be leading most of these areas. Consequently, a close working relationship between the elders and the deacons helps to assure that church members will not be "lost through the cracks." Human resources and areas of need in ministry will be more closely matched as a result of that cooperation among the leaders.

In addition, in most churches no elder is capable of keeping track of and ministering to everyone in his entire flock without some assistance. It is certainly appropriate that deacons should be assigned to each elder to serve as his shepherding assistants for his flock. These deacons can each take a segment of an elder's flock—several families, at least—and make a point of regularly checking on them to learn of their special needs. Many of those needs the deacon will be able to deal with directly, while others may require referral to the supervising elder for his attention and follow-up.

Most people who have been involved with construction to any degree are aware of the fact that architects at times design some features of buildings which may look very good on paper, but which prove totally unworkable—or at least impractical—when they are built. Working closely with a good contractor (the one who has to build the architect's design and make it work) during the design stage, however, can save immense amounts of money and produce a far more functional building. The contractor, while he may lack the vision and ability to develop the building's design, is capable of pointing out to the architect a number of different ways in which something can be constructed, many times at less cost and that would work better. Some of these suggestions may not fit the design or function of the building, and need to be discarded. Others may enhance the design more than any solution envisioned by the architect. They simply view the same project from two different perspectives. Unfortunately, few architects are willing to work in this way with contractors during the design stage, and the owners suffer for their lack of cooperative endeavor and often must live with an inferior building as a result.

This is an apt illustration of the relationship between elders and deacons. Both need to recognize the strengths each is capable of bringing into the design stage. The expertise of the deacons needs to be sought at this point, rather than independently adopting a totally elder-designed program and insisting that it be implemented in that form by the deacons, whether it is workable or not. Instead of having to encounter and deal with the deacons' resistance to its final implementation because of its flaws, how much better it is to approach them early in the planning process with an explanation of the need, a description of the basic design of the program being proposed to meet that need, and the question, "Now what can you tell us that will help us to design a plan that will work?" Any church whose elders are willing to work in this way with the deacons will find far less conflict and far more accomplished in the long run.

Enlarging the Vision

One of the key benefits of a cooperative relationship in planning between the expressive and the implementive leadership is an enlarged vision for the church. The elders help the deacons to understand better the needs and the goals of the church. With a greater vision of the "whys" behind the plans and programs, the implementers are willing to work harder to achieve the goals and to feel that they, too, own those goals. Besides helping to refine the elders' plans and to make them more workable, the deacons also contribute to enlarging the elders' vision. They will many times point out problems and needs which the elders have not recognized. In addition, they often see how a program could be designed a little differently and be able, as a result, to offer expanded ministries which had never occurred to the elders. The net result is planning which will be more solid and more visionary than either group could produce on its own.

In the matter of vision, one of the reasons churches suffer from limited vision is that they have traditionally failed to enlarge their image concerning the roles of deacons. Rather than seeing them as both men and women, there has been a resolute insistence upon limiting deacons' positions to only the men of the church. Rather than understanding them to be the vitally important implementers envisioned in the New Testament, the church has insisted upon casting them in insignificant, impotent and ill-defined offices, or have attempted to push them into board memberships in which they are expected to perform expressive functions.

Deacons who are given specific responsibilities to implement programs have generally found they are not provided or trusted with the necessary financial means to get the job done. Though many times these same deacons may be entrusted with the administration of millions of dollars by pagans in their secular jobs, the church board is unwilling to trust them with more than $50 (if that much) without advance itemization and board approval of anticipated expenditures for every step. This is ridiculous! More than that, it makes the church the laughing stock of the world.

It is time the church expanded its vision concerning the deacons. They are not some kind of useless fifth wheel running along behind the wagon, nor are they intended to be pressed into the cultural mold of being made representative officers on governing boards in order to give them some identity and purpose. They are not the bottom rung on a hierarchical ladder of church rulers. They are not simply serving some probationary period as deacon until they can finally become elders. Deacons need to be recognized as the capable, qualified implementers who can be put in charge of a project to make it happen! This is as Scriptural as the example given in Acts 6:1-7.

In Summary

The New Testament portrays the role of deacons to be one of implementation. They are servants, as their name implies, rather than being officers, as churches have made them. Their servanthood, however, makes them no less leaders. The position is clearly described in the New Testament as having been occupied by both men and women in the first century churches.

Deacons will function in different ways as required by the specific needs of each congregation. There is no Scriptural foundation for the notion that they are to be in charge of the physical and the elders in charge of the spiritual in the church, however those areas may be conceived. They are instead to be given the responsibility for organizing and implementing specific programs which are in accordance with the church's purpose and are designed to meet real needs which exist. These obviously involve both the physical and spiritual aspects of the church's ministry. They are the people, though, who can be put in charge to get the job done.

Deacons must be selected on the basis of their tested Christian lifestyle and commitment to the Lordship of Christ, along with their proven ability to function successfully in implementive leadership. They should not be elected as deacons to "get them more involved in the church"; nor should they be appointed as leaders of programs before they have earned the respect of those who will be expected to follow their leadership. The church has a definite responsibility to test every prospective deacon before he is appointed to lead, rather than expecting to use his service as a deacon as a probationary period leading to some higher and more important office. A progression from deacon to elder is not prescribed in the New Testament, and many deacons should never be expected to serve as elders.

Finally, there ought to exist a close cooperation and working relationship between the elders and the deacons. This is especially true in the shepherding ministry of the church. It is also important, however, in many other areas of their functions, including the designing of workable programs to meet the needs of the church and to accomplish its mission.

The New Testament appears to have a far more important image of the role of deacons than do the majority of churches today. They have bought a counterfeit substitute which has been imported from our culture. The Scriptural vision of deacons needs to be recaptured if the church is to realize its potential and to accomplish its mission.

7

THE CHURCH BOARD: BANE OR BLESSING?

Democracy or Monarchy?

Of all of the modern developments in church leadership, probably none is as curious or as devastating an invention as that of the official church board. Before considering the development or function of the board, however, it is vitally important that we review a very basic and key question: "Is the church a democracy or a monarchy?"

As idealistic and egocentric youth we typically go through a stage where we labor under the unrealistic notion that we have some inalienable right to exist in a kind of free state in which we can do whatever we wish without having to be responsible to anyone. It does not take too many years of living to recognize that such a state exists only as a figment of the imagination. While there are those who spend a good segment of their lifetime rebelliously battling all authorities and insisting upon "doing their own thing," most of us learn that we must eventually face responsibility and deal with accountability to someone in every facet of our lives.

Even in a "free" country such as the United States we have learned that freedom is not free. Our ability to function as a society with any kind of assurances concerning our personal safety and the exercise of our legitimate rights is dependent upon our adherence to laws which have been established, and upon our willingness to do whatever is necessary to preserve our way of life. The preservation of that freedom has cost thousands of men and women their lives. Though free men, their sense of duty caused them to serve to the ultimate degree of even laying down their lives. This is indeed a paradox, but it is one of many we learn to accept in life as we grow up.

In the church we have often become so enamored with the concept of the autonomy of the local congregation that we forget the lessons we have learned about freedom and responsibility. We begin to think of the church as "our church" and to assert rights to decide its course which we have never been given. Our problem is compounded by the fact that the church exists in a political context in which many decisions are made by popular vote, and representatives are elected by the people to act in their behalf in the making and enforcing of laws. It is a government "of the people, by the people, and for the people." Although it is full of flaws and has often failed to achieve our aims for it, we believe it to be perhaps the best political system ever designed by men. We are proud of our country.

It is only natural, therefore, that we should be tempted to transplant our political system into the church. The difficulty exists in the fact that the church already has a system designed for it. While democracy may be a great political invention of men, therein lies the problem. The church is a divine institution, rather than a human one. The One who conceived it and established it had His own plan for its function. Rather than establishing it as a democracy, He designed it as a monarchy; and He made His only Son King. In Him was vested all authority.

Since its beginning, no one has ever been authorized to change the political structure of the church. It still exists today as a monarchy, even in the midst of a democratic society. Some may produce counterfeit models with democratic systems inserted, but they can never be certified or accepted by God as genuine. The church of Christ must always remain His kingdom, or it is not His church.

As pointed out in chapter 2 in our examination of the Biblical Blueprint for church leadership, the church is indeed divinely designed as a monarchy with King Jesus as absolute Lord over His kingdom. To Him has been given all authority in heaven and on earth (Matt 28:18). He is described as "the Head of the body, the church" in Colossians 1:18. In like manner, Ephesians 1:22-23 proclaims concerning Christ, "And God placed all things under His feet and appointed Him to be head over everything for the church, which is His body, the fullness of Him who fills everything in every way."

Much is made in the New Testament about the Lordship of Christ, and rightly so. While many may live an entire lifetime ignoring or rejecting Jesus' credentials, Philippians 2:9-11 affirms that one day every person will be forced to acknowledge that Jesus is Lord. At both His baptism and on the Mount of Transfiguration God made a point of calling attention to Jesus as His Son, the One who must be heard (Matt 3:17; 17:5).

The Apostle John begins his Gospel with a wonderful section concerning Jesus as the Word:

> In the beginning was the Word, and the Word was with God, and the Word was God. He was with God in the beginning. Through Him all things were made; without Him nothing was made that has been made. In Him was life, and that life was the light of men. The light shines in the darkness, but the darkness has not understood it. . . . The true light that gives light to every man was coming into the world. He was in the world, and though the world was made through Him, the world did not recognize Him. He came to that which was His own, but His own did not receive Him. Yet to all who received Him, to those who believed in His name, He gave the right to become children of God—children born not of natural descent, nor of human decision or a husband's will, but born of God.
>
> The Word became flesh and lived for a while among us. We have seen His glory, the glory of the one and only Son, who came from the Father, full of grace and truth (John 1:1-5, 9-14).

John's point is clear, even though he never names Jesus in this section. He wants all who read his Gospel to understand that this One who came to walk with men for a time was like no other. He was eternal. He had a part in creating everything that is. He came as God's ultimate Word about redemption and a restored relationship which sin had broken. He came with the unmistakable glory and the authority which identified Him as the Son of God. Great men such as John the Baptizer would come and witness to Him, but none would be like Him. He was the one ultimately to be heard and accepted. And to those who accepted Him by faith He gave the power to become a part of the family of God in a whole new sense. They would, by God's choice, become His children, members of His family, which is the church.

The Development of the Board

Perhaps the most unlikely creature to be evolved by the Restoration Movement in its developing concept of church leadership has been the Official Board of the church. In an endeavor committed to the restoration of the New Testament faith and practice, its development is a particular enigma. In fact, it has always proven to be something of a theological embarrassment to the movement; and since no Scriptural apology can be made for its existence, little has ever been written about it. In the first one hundred years of the weekly *Christian Standard,* so scarce was any reference to it that there is not even an entry or category for it in that journal's index. Perhaps even more amazing is the fact that, in almost two hundred years of writing by Restoration Movement leaders, no one has ever addressed its origins. David I. McWhirter, the Director of the Library and Archives of the Disciples of Christ Historical Society in Nashville—probably the most complete collection of documents of the Restoration Movement to be found anywhere in the world—writes:

> In checking our holdings I find that we have approximately ten books which talk about the Church Board. I am quite sure that none of these discuss the origin of the Church Board but simply tell how it should work. In talking over your topic here at the Society several of us are in agreement that the Church Board probably developed rather gradually. There was probably no "first" Church Board as such.[1]

---

1. Letter from David I. McWhirter, Director of the Library and Archives, Disciples of Christ Historical Society, Nashville, Tennessee, November 21, 1979.

Now isn't that remarkable? In a movement committed to restoring the church of the New Testament, something as big and important as the church board was allowed to develop and to exist within the church with its origins going unquestioned and uninvestigated for all these years!

In a national poll of church leaders around the country who were asked, "Where did the church board in the Christian Churches originate?" similar responses to that from Nashville were received. No one really knew. Amazingly, the question did not even appear to be of any great consequence to most. The board has been around for so long that it has seemingly been accepted as an inevitable part of church polity, for better or for worse.

Where did we get the church board? Historians Charles and Mary Beard provide probably the best clue to its origin in this country. They write concerning the American colonies: "It may be said that the corporation of capitalists—the instrument employed in commercial undertakings—was the agency which planted the first successful colonies and molded their early polity in church and state and economy."[2] The Beard's summary statement about the corporate structure molding the early American church polity is an important one. In fact, that concept became so deeply ingrained that it eventually helped to mold the Restoration Movement's concept of leadership. More than one Restoration leader argued points of polity based on the corporate example. W. R. Walker is a case in point:

> Bishops, or overseers . . . are necessary to the organized life of a congregation. The position of the overseers in a

---

2. Charles A. and Mary R. Beard, *The Rise of American Civilization*, rev. ed., (New York: The Macmillan Company, 1934), p. 36.

> local church is quite similar to that of the superintendents of different departments in a modern business or industrial enterprise. To them there is delegated the responsibility for the execution of the plans endorsed by the stockholders—the individual members of the local congregation. Their duties are outlined and assigned by those whose interests they represent.[3]

Along with the impression of the corporate form came also the influence of John Locke, whose concepts of representative government heavily impacted our American history and culture. It was this philosophy of government which led to the cultural necessity of translating all positions and functions into offices. The writings of both Thomas and Alexander Campbell, for example, contain frequent references to "offices" and "officers," even though they were endorsing a restoration of New Testament Christianity, including calling Biblical things by Biblical names. In an 1835 controversy over apostolic succession with Tennessee Bishop James H. Otey, Alexander Campbell very typically said:

> The Apostles never were one of three orders, nor one of two orders of offices in the kingdom of the Messiah, but all orders in one as respected the administration of the Reign of Heaven. Indeed, theirs was the authority to create and fill offices in the church. Under Christ they instituted the offices and gave directions for filling them with suitable persons. They originated the offices and gave instructions for the election and appointment of bishops and deacons in the Christian communities. . . . All these duties they assigned

---

3. W. R. Walker, *A Functioning Eldership* (Cincinnati: The Standard Publishing Company, 1940), p. 12.

> to the two offices of bishops and deacons as soon as they found persons competent to discharge them.[4]

We have earlier made reference to Robert Richardson's 1836 comment about the American Christians' fondness for titles of distinction, including those of the church offices of Elder and Deacon.[5] J. W. McGarvey, reflecting how deeply he had been influenced by Locke and his culture, argued in 1870:

> It is here objected by some, that we should not call the overseership an office, because Paul in this passage calls it a work: "If any man desire the overseership, he desires a good work." Undoubtedly it is a work; and so is every office in either church or State, unless it be a mere sinecure. The fact that it is a work makes it none the less an office. . . . The conclusion thus naturally and necessarily springing from these passages of Scripture will be confirmed as we proceed to develop the functions of the office. We will find that the elders or overseers of the church are charged with such duties, and entrusted with such authority as makes them officers of the church in the fullest sense of the term.[6]

Such flawed logic and exegesis by a man of McGarvey's ability and stature is surprising, but it represents the degree to which cultural influence can warp a person's perspective. Interestingly, it was in that same work that McGarvey referred to the Elders as a "board of Elders" and "the official Board." If he was not the first Restoration leader to use such terms,

---

4. Alexander Campbell, "To Dr. James Otey, Bishop of Tennessee—Letter II, *Millennial Harbinger*, July, 1835, p. 293.

5. Robert Richardson, "Offices," *Millennial Harbinger*, September, 1836, p. 426.

6. J. W. McGarvey, *A Treatise on the Eldership* (1870; rpt. Murfreesboro: DeHoff Publications, 1966), p. 17.

he was certainly one of the first to do so. Arguing for the necessity of their regular meeting as a board, he reasoned:

> The regularity with which the directors of banks, insurance companies, and corporations of like character, hold their meetings, is very well known. How then, can it be expected that the Elders of a church, who have the interests of many precious souls under their care, will be able to dispense with such meetings?[7]

J. W. McGarvey's premier position in use of the term, "the official board," in 1870 is rather ironical. Twenty-nine years later he seems aghast that this term is being used in the church and in a different way. His article on "The Official Board" in 1899 is the very first discussion of the subject in the *Christian Standard:*

> The newly coined expression which stands at the head of this article has had a great run since some genius invented it. Like many other unscriptural expressions, it seems to have no fixed meaning; and as a consequence, it breeds confusion. It seems to mean, in the lips of some, the elders and deacons acting as one body; in the lips of others, these officials and the preacher; in the lips of others, all these with the addition of the trustees and Sunday school superintendent, if not also the clerk, male or female, and the treasurer. What perogatives belong to this "Official Board" seems to be as uncertain as the membership.[8]

He continues in the article by referring the young pastor who had written him about the issue to the New Testament to learn more about elders and deacons:

---

7. McGarvey, p. 76.

8. J. W. McGarvey, "The Official Board," *Christian Standard*, May 6, 1899, p. 559.

> In so doing he will learn that these two classes of officials do not constitute what may properly be called a Board, with common functions; but that each has its special and separate duties. He will learn that the pastor so-called, or the young preacher serving the congregation, is not a member of either of these bodies, and that his relationship to both is that of cooperation and mutual helpfulness. As to the trustees, he will find no information at all in the Scriptures; for this office has been called into existence by a civil statute which requires that trustees shall be elected by every church which holds real estate, to hold and to transfer the same to the name of the church.[9]

The confusion in the minds of the churches over the evolution of the church board and its proper functions is evidenced in an article by J. H. Garrison in an 1892 edition of *The Christian-Evangelist.* He raised three questions:

> If the "Official Board" is called together to discuss disorderly members, the deacons are present and have an equal voice. What scriptural authority is there for this? If the "Official Board" meets to discuss the fitness of a candidate for the position of pastor and preacher, the deacons are present to help consider his qualifications. Where is this made a perogative of the deacon's office? What more voice have they on these questions than any other member of the congregation? On the other hand, if a bill for gas or coal oil is to be paid, the elders are a part of the body that orders the settlement. If a coal-house needs to be built, they have the same voice in the matter as the deacons. Where in the Word of God is it directed that they "should serve table"? The fact is that in many churches these offices are so hopelessly confused that the flock would never know which were deacons and

---

9. McGarvey, "The Official Board," p. 578.

which elders, if they did not notice a distinction at the Lord's Supper.[10]

The composition of the church board, as we have already seen, was a subject of much discussion and difference of opinion. With the local autonomy of the Christian Churches, each congregation was free to define the term and include as many officers and leaders in its application as they wished. Isaac Errett, who served as editor of the *Christian Standard*, registered his objection to the board for the following reason:

> A subscriber asks what officers of the church constitute the "Official Board." When church people talk of "the Official Board" they usually mean the elders and deacons of the congregation. With some churches, perhaps, the scope would extend to include the superintendent of the Sunday-school, president of the C.E., etc. The term "Official Board" is used for convenience, no doubt, but we confess to a dislike for it. It smacks entirely too much of current ecclesiasticism to be in harmony with the simplicity of New Testament order and phraseology.[11]

In order to help reduce the confusion and to argue the merits of the example set by his church, a church clerk reported in the *Christian Standard* in that same year of 1900 the practice of the First Christian Church of Wellsville, Ohio. Their board, he wrote, met monthly and was elected annually:

> The "Official Board" in many Christian Churches includes the trustees, elders and deacons only. In order to infuse

---

10. J. H. Garrison, "A Rambling Talk About Church Officers," *The Christian Evangelist*, January 21, 1892, p. 34.

11. Isaac Errett, "The Official Board," *Christian Standard*, January 13, 1900, p. 45.

> more life in all departments of church work at this place, it was decided, three years ago, to increase the membership of the Board, and it was thereafter to be known as the Church Board of the First Christian Church of Wellsville. It now includes the Board of Trustees, five; Board of Elders, six; Board of Deacons, twelve; one clerk, treasurer, financial secretary, superintendent of Sunday-school, president of C.W.B.M., president of Endeavor Society, pastor of church, and three deaconesses—total, thirty-three.[12]

The composition of the church board, since it has no scriptural basis or guidelines, has remained a debated issue. At the minimum, it has consisted in some churches as a unified board of elders and deacons. On the other end of the spectrum, one church served by the author included as voting members of the board any and all members of the congregation who cared to attend the monthly board meeting. The operation of the board has also varied greatly from church to church, with the meetings of the joint board taking the place of individual meetings of the elders and deacons in some churches. Consequently, lengthy and tumultuous sessions of the boards have become more the rule than the exception. Allan B. Philputt, pastor of the Central Christian Church of Indianapolis, Indiana, which was one of the largest churches in his state in 1900, wrote with pride concerning the functioning of his board:

> Its membership is large, but harmonious and loyal . . . representing all shades of thought and feeling, is careful to defer in all things to the sentiment of the church. A more courteous and businesslike body I have never seen. No protracted discussion is tolerated. No brother that acted in a captious

12. A. C. Van Dyke, "The Church Board," *Christian Standard,* April 7, 1900, p. 2.

> spirit, seeking to carry his point whether or not, would be re-elected when his time expired. Thirty minutes is as long as I have ever known a board meeting to continue. Usually 20 minutes is enough. There are certain committees which take care of details. The business of the church is well done. There are no heated arguments, no factional differences—simply an exchange of views.[13]

While many pastors and board members might look with envy at such a rare picture of board harmony and brevity of meetings, the first sentence written by Mr. Philputt is highly significant. It should not be overlooked in our examination of the evolution of the church board. As a "courteous and businesslike body" *it intentionally sought "to defer in all things to the sentiment of the church."* Where does this leave the Lordship of Christ over His church? A governing body has now been created by men for the church whose stated purpose is to represent the views and feelings of the church members, rather than those of its King. Does this not constitute treason? Furthermore, the board of this church was held up by its pastor as "A Model Board," the title of the article published in a major national journal for the churches of the Restoration Movement.

It is evident from these citations and historical references that the church board originated as an adaptation of our American culture. It reflected to some degree the corporate structure and the concept of representative government. In addition, its adoption as a leadership form in the Restoration Movement also obviously was influenced by the forms which were already in use among the denominations from whence the Movement had come.

---

13. Allan B. Philputt, "A Model Board," *The Christian Messenger*, December 28, 1900, p. 2.

Exactly when the first Christian Church board was constituted is difficult to pinpoint from available evidence. The best guess is that it evolved into an accepted form within the Christian Churches during the 1870's. Its acceptance was probably fueled by J. W. McGarvey's own reference in 1870 to the elders as "the official Board," and his culturally based exhortation for its meetings. From references in the church paper of the Webster City, Iowa, Christian Church, it is evident that the church began in 1892 with the concept inherent in its organizational structure. In an interesting news item in 1893, their new church board officers included a man as president, with women as vice president, treasurer and recording secretary. The committees of the board also consisted mainly of women.[14]

Still earlier, out in the Arizona Territory, the 1887 Articles of Incorporation of the First Church of Christ of Phoenix read:

> At a special meeting of the congregation of Christians or Disciples of Christ worshipping at Phoenix, Arizona, held on the 23rd day of April AD 1887, at Phoenix, Arizona, were present Thomas H. McMullin and T. F. Derrick, elders in said congregation, W. A. Hall, deacon thereof and members as follows. . . . The meeting organized for the transaction of business by choosing Elder Thomas H. McMullin as Chairman and H. A. Wilson as Secretary of the meeting. On motion, the congregation proceeded to elect three trustees to take charge of and title to the estate and property belonging to said church and that may hereafter be acquired by the same, and to manage in connection with the official board of Elders and Deacons the temporalities thereof as provided for by an Act of the Legislative Assembly of Arizona.[15]

---

14. Bruce Brown, "New Officers," *Webster City Christian*, July, 1893, p. 1.

15. Articles of Incorporation, First Church of Christ of Phoenix, Arizona, Arizona Territory, April 23, 1887, p. 1.

Also of interest is the fact that the articles of the Phoenix church provided that trustees would be elected for life, unless they resigned, moved from the Territory or were "removed for cause by the regular action of this congregation in accordance with its rules of discipline."

With the concept of "the official board" widely enough accepted by the Christian Churches in the 1880's to have been incorporated when the Phoenix church was organized in 1885, it is safe to assume that it must have begun at least a decade earlier back in the Mid-West. In any event, whatever its date of origin, it rapidly became accepted into the orthodoxy of the Restoration Movement, in spite of some early protests, as the mark of the well-organized Christian Church.

Bruce Brown, who served as pastor of the Central Christian Church in Denver, Colorado, commented in 1901 about the practices of his church in comparison with others:

> The deacons' meetings, the elders' meeting and the general board meeting for May were all well attended and a large amount of business was transacted. In some churches the board meetings are protracted to a late hour, and, by becoming veritable debating societies, are wearisome and tedious. By having matters of detail well digested by competent committees, or by the separate boards of elders and deacons, the general board meeting is harmonious, dignified and both religious and businesslike.[16]

In his classic book giving guidelines to churches for their most effective organization and function of church boards, O. L. Shelton suggested:

---

16. Bruce Brown, "Model Board Meetings," *The Christian Messenger*, May 24, 1901, p. 2.

> The meeting should be held in a room in the church that breathes the presence of God. It should have an atmosphere of worship and should create a spirit of reverence. Every meeting should open with a devotional period. The presence of God ought to be felt, and all that is done should be done as unto Him. There should be an orderly procedure. . . . All committees should make reports, and they should be in writing. . . . The meetings should be democratic. Each member has a responsibility and should feel that his presence and participation is important. . . . No one should be allowed to hold lightly the matter of attendance at the meeting of the church board. . . . The meeting should be concluded with a brief period of meditation and prayer.[17]

The official board has indeed evolved, has become thoroughly established and has gained unquestioning acceptance now in most churches. Perhaps McGarvey was right when he described it as "something that has crept into the churches like a thief in the dark."[18] But once it arrived, it became obvious that this thief had come to stay and to rule the house. After the initial shock of its entry, hardly a ripple has been felt in protest of it since the turn of the century. Its influential role as the primary seat of authority, control, direction and leadership in the churches has grown to the extent that there are now numerous churches whose elders and deacons seldom, if ever, meet as separate bodies. Since everything must eventually "go through the board," it is simply reasoned by many that other leadership meetings by groups are superfluous. The committee of the whole can take care of everything.

---

17. O. L. Shelton, *The Church Functioning Effectively* (St. Louis: The Bethany Press, 1946), p. 195.

18. J. W. McGarvey, "The Official Board," *Christian Standard*, April 23, 1910, p. 703.

Representative Government in the Church

English philosopher John Locke (1632-1704) had a powerful influence on the life and thought of the west. His theories impacted philosophy, psychology, education and religion. In no area, however, has his influence been felt more strongly on the American scene than in that of political theory. His classic *Two Treatises of Government,* published in 1690, were probably the most significant factors in shaping the political structure of the United States of America.

Without entering into an extensive analysis of Locke's political writings, it is sufficient to say that he is the father of representative government as we have come to know it. The U.S. Constitution and Bill of Rights embody most of his premises. As a people, we believe in these principles to the extent that we will defend them and even die to protect them. They are ingrained in us from the time we are born, and we depend upon their preservation until we die. A Supreme Court exists to guarantee their proper application in every area of our society.

It is little wonder, therefore, that these concepts should profoundly color our perspective as we view issues of church leadership. With the church existing in such a democratic culture, and operating in accordance with its laws, it was probably inevitable that the political system should become transplanted in the church. Many writers have noted the fact that the Roman political structure became superimposed on the evolution of the Roman Catholic Church as well. History has simply repeated itself.

A keystone in the political theories of John Locke and the American political system is the concept of representative government. It is the duty of the elected representatives of the people to reflect the wishes and interests of those who elect them in the making of laws and in key decisions affecting the direction of the country. To a great extent, representative government exists as a giant weather vane which has its direction determined by the prevailing winds which blow.

When this political philosophy is transposed into the church and finds its application in the form of the church board, watch out! As we noted in the "Model Board" of the Indianapolis church, which was held up for national emulation, great care was taken "to defer in all things to the sentiment of the church." In other words, they were careful to set the course of the church, as its elected representatives, by the prevailing winds which blew in the congregation.

How much different from this is the New Testament concept of church leadership! It stands in direct contrast. Read again the inspired prescription of the Apostle Paul in Ephesians 4:11-16:

> It was He who gave some to be apostles, some to be prophets, some to be evangelists, and some to be pastors and teachers, to prepare God's people for works of service, so that the body of Christ may be built up until all reach unity in the faith and in the knowledge of the Son of God and become mature, attaining to the whole measure of the fullness of Christ.
>
> Then we will no longer be infants, tossed back and forth by the waves, and blown here and there by every wind of teaching and by the cunning and craftiness of men in their deceitful scheming. Instead, speaking the truth in love, we will in all things grow up into Him who is the Head, that is, Christ. From Him the whole body, joined together by every supporting ligament, grows and builds itself up in love, as each part does its work.

That which is lauded as exemplary leadership for the churches on the part of their "official boards" is specifically termed spiritual immaturity, or infancy, by Paul in verse 14. He does not call such weather vane action church leadership at all! To his way of thinking, it represents simply being blown about, and being unable to hold any course of its own. Such spiritual immaturity in leadership is always subject to "every wind of teaching and the cunning and craftiness of men in their deceitful scheming." To have made this the model for church leadership would have been utterly unthinkable for the apostle.

Paul clearly saw the marks of maturity, the unity of the church and the accomplishment of its mission as inseparably hinged to "the truth" taught and lived by Christ, "the Word." It made no difference what anyone else thought or taught. Jesus is Lord! The course for the church had to be set by its Head, Christ alone. "From Him the whole body, joined and held together by every supporting ligament, grows and builds itself up in love, as each part does its work" (v. 16).

Where does that leave representative government? It clearly has no place in determining the course of the church. Those who are the closest to the Lord in their spiritual maturity and understanding of His Word are to be set aside and charged with the task of providing the expressive leadership for the church—specifically that which will best represent the will of Christ. If that will is in conflict with the will of the majority of the church members, what has that to do with the course to be set? He was appointed by the Father to be the Lord of the church, not they. He was sent to die for the church, not they. He sits at the right hand of God and will judge the church, not they. If anything, Paul insists that the elders ignore the winds that blow within the church.

They are charged, and will be judged, by their ability to hold the Lord's course for the church entrusted to their care and leadership.

Effects of the Board System

The first rather obvious effect which is produced by the substitution of the man-made board system for the Scriptural pattern of church leadership is the shift of authority. No longer is Jesus in the driver's seat steering the course for the church. The most vocal and powerful church members or leaders now determine the course, as the board seeks to reflect the will of the people. Anyone who has a vendetta against the minister, another leader or a program can change the course of the church by rallying enough support. A board member who has just had a fight with his spouse or his boss can turn a board meeting into shambles and wind up, out of spite, killing any program or ministry being proposed. Rather than the Head being the Head, the tail now wags the dog.

Secondly, the course steered is generally an erratic one which bears little resemblance to that charted by the Scriptures for the church. Programs are often instituted which have little or no relationship to the mission of the church, and which may even be in conflict with that mission. Due to their popularity with the people, however, they take top priority in the schedule and in the expenditure of church finances. Carpets for the church building or cushions for the pews, for example, take precedence over the employing of a missionary, a youth minister or other personnel needed to expand outreach. Parties for the members definitely outrank calling programs and benevolence projects. Little thought is given to the development of a clear, Biblical statement of purpose for the church, or of formulating long-range goals or workable plans for the accomplishment of that mission.

The third effect is that of subverting the leadership of the elders. The majority vote decides every issue for the board. The elders are never in the majority. If the direction they are seeking to lead is not popular, even though it may be Scriptural, they can be voted down and their plans cancelled. When everything has to go through the board for approval, the board has supplanted the leadership of the elders.

Fourthly, the board system creates a classical example of a bottleneck, which is capable of discouraging the most committed and enthusiastic worker in the church. Like the "Mother, May I?" game, no movement can be made until it is authorized in the absolutely correct way. How many wrists have been slapped and spirits quenched of the zealous members who either never knew or forgot "the proper channels"? Even with all good intentions considered, NOTHING can happen until the board votes. In many churches, bills cannot even be paid until the board votes approval! How the Lord must weep!!

The fifth devastating effect of the board system is that wondrous device of assigning a proposal to a committee "for further study." If there is any indication a proposed program might be unpopular, controversial or too costly, there is no surer way to guarantee its demise than to bury it in a committee. The board has learned its lesson well from government and congressional example!

In the sixth place, the church board system reduces the concept of church leadership to one of attending meetings, arguing issues and casting votes. Board members are deluded into believing that they have actually performed leadership for the church by going through this prescribed ritual. As we have seen, this substitute exercise bears absolutely no resemblance to New Testament leadership.

Finally, the board system is often spiritually destroying the church leaders who comprise its membership. Dr. Robert Munger, of Fuller Theological Seminary, has produced some terrifying statistics from his studies of church boards. He has repeatedly asked board members to respond to the question, "Since serving on a Church Board, do you feel your spiritual life has improved or declined?" He reports that over 80% of the responses to that question consistently indicate that service on a church board has contributed to a spiritual decline in their lives![19] That statistic alone ought to shake us to our core.

Canon Laws and By-Laws

In the first chapter we traced some of the evolution of the Roman Catholic hierarchy. With the development of that hierarchy came obvious conflicts with the Scriptures. As we have seen, there has always existed something of a Free Church Movement which has sought to call the hierarchy to Scriptural accountability for its excesses and deviations from the prescribed course outlined in the Bible. The result was inevitable. The hierarchy, in order to protect its power and to excuse its practices, first claimed the right to make rules for the church on the basis of apostolic succession, and then proceeded to develop its own set of rules. These, as they grew in volume, became the substitute authority

19. Olan Hendrix, *Study Guide for Olan Hendrix Management Skills Seminar* (Glendale: Gospel Light Publications, 1975), p. 102.

for the church. Soon it was argued that the Bible must be viewed through the lens of the canon law, the "Corpus Juris Canonici," in order to correctly interpret its meaning and application. Priests were instructed far more in the canon law than they were in actual Scripture; and the only copies of the Bible were kept in Latin and chained in the cathedrals and monasteries, away from any inquisitive minds among the people who might challenge the practices or the conclusions of the hierarchy. Any who dared to challenge them were declared to be heretics and could be persecuted and killed, all in the name of preserving the faith.

It was Augustine, for example, who wrote in his controversy with the Donatists, these infamous words:

> Why therefore should not the Church use force in compelling her lost sons to return? . . . The Lord Himself said, "Go out into the highways and hedges and compel them to come in." . . . Wherefore if the power which the Church has received by divine appointment in its due season, through the religious character and faith of kings, be the instrument by which those who are found in the highways and hedges—that is, in heresies and schisms—are compelled to come in, then let them not find fault with being compelled.[20]

Such a construction of Luke 14:13 by so eminent a theologian as Augustine provided all of the apology the hierarchy needed. Armed with both ecclesiastical and civil authority, they instituted immediate persecution of the Donatists, including the imposition of the death penalty for anyone participating in a Donatist meeting. Members were deprived of all civil rights, and many were fined exorbitant

---

20. E. H. Broadbent, *The Pilgrim Church* (London: Pickering and Englis, Ltd., 1931), p. 27.

amounts. This was only the beginning of its brutal application as an instrument of the church leadership during the following centuries. The church, which had once been a persecuted minority, had now become the persecuting power against all who dared to challenge its interpretations of the Bible and the laws it had established for the conduct of the church. What a radical turn of events occurred in so short a period of history! This development, in fact, found its ultimate expression in the organizations of the Inquisition by papal decree in 1232, which gave the church a weapon by which it could systematically eradicate all who were deemed heretics.[21]

In essence, canon law was written to permit the hierarchy to do whatever they wished and in whatever manner they chose. Martin Luther (1483-1546) was a German Catholic monk and professor at the University of Wittenburg. Having become increasingly upset over the corruption of the clergy and the competitive sale of indulgences (the proceeds from which were divided between the seller-priest, the territorial prince and the Vatican), he on October 31, 1517, nailed 95 theses to the church door at Wittenburg. These were points of difference with the Scriptures which he wished to debate. Although he was determined to remain within the Roman Church and to reform it, he found himself eventually excommunicated and condemned to death, if he were ever to be apprehended. Probably his greatest contribution to the Free Church Movement was his translation of the Bible into the spoken German language of his day. Friedenthal says:

---

21. Virgil A. Olson, trans., *The Free Church Through the Ages*, by Gunnar Westin (Nashville: Broadman Press, 1958), p. 26.

> He undertook the work, knowing quite well that it was "beyond" him, because no one else had the courage to tackle it. It had to be done, people everywhere yearned for it to be done, but the Church did nothing to satisfy this desire.[22]

It did indeed prove to be a tremendous asset to all who yearned to understand for themselves the Word of God and to gain an understanding of the church of the New Testament. It was from this intense study in translating and applying the Scriptures, though, that Luther found so many discrepancies between the canon law and those Scriptures and produced his 95 theses which led to his branding as a heretic and his excommunication.

What has all of this to do with the adoption of by-laws for the churches today? The by-laws are written and exist as the canon laws for the modern church. While some argue their legal necessity, such an argument does not excuse in any way the hefty volumes produced by modern hierarchies. Any legal requirements of our society could be satisfied with far less, and certainly with something which more accurately reflects the actual teachings of the New Testament.

The fact of the matter is that modern church leaders have seized the excuse provided by the minimal requirements of civil authorities concerning corporations as an opportunity to speak authoritatively within the silences of the Bible. Even worse, they have often spoken in direct contradiction of the Bible, in order to justify a practice or to protect their power. Just as Martin Luther found that the canon law could

---

22. John Newell, trans., *Luther—His Life and Times,* by Richard Friedenthal (New York: Harcourt Brace Jovanovich, 1970), p. 313.

not stand up against a comparison with the Scriptures, so any serious Bible student today will find that 99% of the church by-laws which have been written cannot withstand the scrutiny of Scripture either.

Through the vehicle of the by-laws we have sought to set up and justify an entire hierarchical structure of offices, officers, terms, duties and jurisdictions. Though the New Testament knows no office of deacon, for example, we have created and defined one in the by-laws. We have established privileges, procedures, quorums, voting rights and restrictions, and a host of other regulations. We have set up systems of checks and balances similar to those we are accustomed to in democratic government.

It is through the by-laws that we have granted the license for the establishment of the church board. Here we have defined its composition, described its power, determined its committees and prescribed its officers and their terms. Here we have hallowed the concepts of representative government which we have transported from our culture into the church.

By what authority does the church do these things? At least 95 theses could be nailed to the front door of most churches. The only answers to be given, however, would have to be citations from the by-laws.

By-laws, like canon laws, have been written mainly to preserve control and to give justification to practices found to be inexcusable by the New Testament. They are defensive documents, for the most part. They have also been used, however, offensively as a license for persecution and excommunication from the body. They are the creedal statements which draw the lines around the fellowship.

It must be frankly admitted that the Restoration Movement has often been guilty of the most gross hypocrisy in its condemnation of the canon laws of the Roman Catholics and the creeds of the protestant denominations. Proclaiming to have no authority but Christ and no creed but the Bible, we have played ostrich with our head in the sand, refusing to recognize or admit our own flagrant additions to the Scriptures. Jesus said to the Pharisees:

> Why do you look at the speck of sawdust in your brother's eye and pay no attention to the plank in your own eye? How can you say to your brother, "Let me take the speck out of your eye," when all the time there is a plank in your own eye? You hypocrite, first take the plank out of your own eye, and then you will see clearly to remove the speck from your brother's eye (Matt 7:3-5).

Would Jesus be any more charitable toward us? Time and again the by-laws are elevated above the Scriptures in the Christian Churches to justify an action. How many pastors have protested a practice as being inconsistent with the New Testament, only to have the Chairman of the Board over-rule the objection with a citation of the by-laws?

The Future of the Board

Is there any redeeming value to be found within the church board? With all of the problems we have cited with the board and its negative effects, we would be forced to admit that there is no Biblical apology for its continued existence in its typical form. Neither is there any logical excuse for perpetuating any entity which is contradictory to the Lordship of Christ and the system of government He established for His church.

Certainly church boards will not be disposed of easily or quickly. If there were ever two sacred cows of the Christian

Churches, they would have to be the church board and the by-laws. Though both are totally extra-Scriptural, they are protected species in every sense of the expression.

A key reason churches will fight to the death to retain their church boards and by-laws is the issue of control. These are the primary means we have devised to control the church as we have attempted to control our society through our government. Our answer to every problem and potential excess has been the establishment of more regulations and more regulatory agencies. The volume of new laws and new policing forces devised each year in the United States staggers the imagination. Amazingly, we are discovering today that government regulation is not the answer to everything.

If the church is ever to realize its potential for growth and accomplishment of its mission in this world, it must be willing to de-regulate—to strip off some of the protective by-laws, committees and boards we have created. We have almost regulated the church to death. In some cases, in fact, we have succeeded in doing exactly that. In others, we have simply bound the church so tightly that it is unable to move to accomplish anything. It is certainly secure, though!

There is a danger, however, of throwing the baby out with the bath water. In the chapter on the deacons we mentioned the need for all leaders to work together, along with the need for the elders to secure the valuable input which implementive leadership could offer. There is a need for some coordinating and planning council. The right hand needs to know what the left hand is doing. It will not work for each member of the body to work independently of the others, nor will much be accomplished by a total segregation of leadership groups. The church will never need a church board, as it is presently defined. It does need some vehicle for accomplishing this essential communication and cooperation among leaders. If we can formulate such a forum without re-creating the present monster, with its officers and compulsion to control everything and everyone, we will have accomplished something constructive for the church.

One of the first objections always encountered in any effort to do away with the church board system, and to return to the New Testament pattern, is that the authority and control once vested in the greater number on the board is now being transferred to a few elders. This, however, reflects both a strong cultural bias and a misunderstanding of the Biblical blueprint for leadership. No one in the church is to be given the control or any authority. God left that all in Jesus' hands. All He gave the elders was responsibility —lots of it—and He intends to hold them accountable to Him for how they have handled those responsibilities.

What about checks and balances? What if . . .? We are simply not comfortable with de-regulation of the church. Perhaps the problem is that it requires too much faith on our part to turn people loose and to trust them to do the jobs we have asked them to do, without binding them with our controls. God is willing, however, to take that risk! Remember, He refuses to make us His puppets. He took a chance and gave us a free will. Rather than insisting upon the security we hope to assure with our elaborate regulations, checks and balances, He calls upon us to stretch and to exercise our faith instead. Rather than insisting upon having it our way with church leadership, He calls us to try it His way first. Amazingly—it works!!

In Summary

We have been reminded again that the church Christ established can never be a democracy. It is by divine design a monarchy with Jesus as King and Lord over all. The typical church board developed as a direct product of our American culture. It has no Biblical basis whatsoever. It exists as a challenge to the authority of Christ by substituting a representative government model into the church. In this model, the majority rules. Leadership is deemed to be successful when it reflects the wishes of those who elected them. Such leadership usually follows an erratic and inconsistent course, and will not effectively accomplish the purposes of Christ for His church.

The church board system produces numerous negative effects upon both the church and its leaders who comprise its membership. It finds its sole authority for existence within man-made church by-laws. There is a strong and valid parallel to be drawn between the canon laws of the Roman Catholics, the creeds of the protestant denominations and the by-laws of the Christian Churches. Each exists for much the same purpose. Each has produced some devastating results, and each falls before the scrutiny of the Scriptures.

There is no valid Scriptural apology for the continued existence of this kind of church board in any congregation. There is, however, an urgent need to de-regulate the church and to return to the New Testament structure and pattern for leadership. Though this change is a traumatic experience for most churches in our culture, it is essential if any church is serious about its quest to restore New Testament faith and practice, or if it ever hopes to accomplish the mission Christ gave it.

8

WOMEN IN LEADERSHIP?

Biblical Examples of Leadership

There has been much discussion concerning the low estate of women in Bible times. It has been pointed out over and over again that women were considered as property, rather than persons with rights, and that they were given no educational, vocational or economic opportunities to be able to assume any positions of leadership. To a degree there is some truth in that picture which has been painted. On the other hand, the case has also been grossly overstated in many instances, mainly by those who cannot conceive of a woman ever being accepted or approved by God in a position of church leadership. To make such a blanket affirmation of the lowly position given women in

Bible times is to ignore the many outstanding women who are clearly cited in the Bible as having served as leaders. A cursory review of some of them would help to refresh our memories as we address the subject of women in church leadership, and would serve to put our discussion into a proper Biblical perspective.

One cannot think of Abraham, for example, without also remembering *Sarah*. It was to both Abraham and Sarah that God made His promise in Genesis 17:15-16, changing her name as well as that of Abraham. God proclaimed that she would be a mother of nations and kings. She was significant in God's eyes! Even the prophet Isaiah mentions them both, rather than simply referring to Abraham as the father of Israel (Isa 51:2). Sarah was a beautiful woman. She was a wife and a mother, with the latter role coming miraculously late in life. She was even more, though. She was a partner in Abraham's great adventure of faith. Julia Staton says of her:

> God also thought of Sarah as an individual. He wanted her to have faith and trust in Him, just as much as He wanted Abraham to do so. It was evident that Sarah knew of the promise and her part in it, for she became frustrated when she felt she was not able to fulfill her responsibility. God's gentle rebuke of Sarah when she doubted for a moment that she could have a child (because of the couple's advanced age) showed that God expected her to trust Him as an individual in her own right: "And the Lord said . . . 'Why did Sarah laugh, saying "Shall I indeed bear a child, when I am so old?" 'Is anything too difficult for the Lord?' " (Gen 18:13, 14). Sarah was personally responsible to God. It was not that she found her identity from being Abraham's wife and only in that way was she known to God. When

> Sarah's faith had matured as it should have, God recognized it and praised her: "By faith even Sarah herself received ability to conceive, even beyond the proper time of life, since she considered Him faithful who had promised" (Heb 11:11).[1]

Miriam, the sister of Moses and Aaron, also stands out as a significant woman in the Old Testament. She was recognized by God and by her people as one of the key leaders of Israel. The prophet Micah speaks for God to Israel saying, "I brought you up out of Egypt and redeemed you from the land of slavery. I sent Moses to lead you, also Aaron and Miriam" (Mic 6:4). God actually sent a woman to help lead His people? As inconceivable as that may be to many church leaders today, that is exactly what the prophet said; and that is precisely what happened. In Exodus 15:20 Miriam is described as "the prophetess, Aaron's sister." As a female prophet, she served as God's mouthpiece to speak to His people. That verse also describes how she led all of the women in Israel in jubilant celebration of their successful escape from the Egyptians and their miraculous crossing through the Red Sea. Verse 21 even preserves for us Miriam's song of praise to God. Not all of Miriam's leadership was to be lauded, however. Numbers 12:1-2 tells us:

> Miriam and Aaron began to talk against Moses because of his Cushite wife, for he had married a Cushite. "Has the Lord spoken only through Moses?" they asked. "Hasn't He also spoken through us?" And the Lord heard them.

The following verses record God's confrontation with the two of them. Verses 9-10 recount:

> The anger of the Lord burned against them, and He left them. When the cloud lifted from above the Tent, there

1. Julia Staton, *What the Bible Says About Women* (Joplin: College Press Publishing Company, 1980), p. 51.

> stood Miriam—leprous, like snow. Aaron turned toward her and saw that she had leprosy.

Evidently Miriam had been the chief instigator of the jealous attack on Moses' primary position of leadership. She had sought to discredit him in the eyes of the people with gossip, falling into the old trap of trying to elevate herself by pulling down someone else. It never works. Quite often both persons are destroyed in the process. In this case, however, "the Lord heard this," and those four words spelled her downfall.

With the call to leadership comes the responsibility for supporting other leadership. Our omniscient God ALWAYS hears, and He refuses to tolerate the undercutting of other leadership by any leader—male or female. We may be successful in destroying someone else, but we will eventually have to pay for that destruction. A valuable leadership lesson is to be learned from the example God made of Miriam.

Rahab, whose story is told in Joshua 2:1-21, is another woman who, though beginning from the most disrespectable background, is cited in both the Old and New Testaments for her faith, courage and leadership. James points to Abraham and Rahab as examples of leaders who were justified in God's sight by their works, which demonstrated their faith. Of Rahab he says:

> In the same way, was not even Rahab the prostitute considered righteous for what she did when she gave lodging to the spies and sent them off in a different direction? As the body without the spirit is dead, so faith without deeds is dead" (James 2:25-26).

Certainly no one can speak of Bible leaders without recalling *Deborah*, the woman whose leadership of Israel caused her to be chronicled among the Judges. Deborah is described in Judges 4:4 as "a prophetess, the wife of Lappidoth," and the verse notes that she was "leading Israel at that time." People from all over the nation journeyed to the hill country of Ephraim, between Ramah and Bethel, to the place where she held court. There she settled their disputes. Not only did all of the people—both men and women—respect her as their leader, God also recognized her as Israel's primary leader and spoke directly to her concerning the messages which she was to deliver to the people. Judges is a most interesting account to be studied by those who claim that a woman should never be in leadership where men are concerned:

> She sent for Barak son of Abinoam from Kedesh in Naphtali and said to him, "The Lord, the God of Israel, commands you: 'Go, take with you ten thousand men of Naphtali and Zebulun and lead the way to Mount Tabor. I will lure Sisera, the commander of Jabin's army, with his chariots and his troops to the Kishon River and give him into your hands.'" Barak said to her, "If you go with me, I will go; but if you don't go with me, I won't go." "Very well," Deborah said, "I will go with you. But because of the way you are going about this, the honor will not be yours, for the Lord will hand Sisera over to a woman." So Deborah went with Barak to Kedesh, where he summoned Zebulun and Naphtali. Ten thousand men followed him, and Deborah also went with him (Judg 4:6-10).

How many times in history have men lacked the courage and commitment to act when needed, leaving the task of leadership to women? One does not have to read very many pages of history to find a host of examples. Deborah is an excellent case in point in Biblical history. There was no lack of men in Israel. There was simply a lack of faith, courage and vision among them. Deborah, on the other hand, was so respected and trusted for her wise, decisive leadership that the men of the nation would follow her wherever she would lead them. In this case, she provided the expressive leadership for the nation, and Barak and his troops provided the implementive leadership.

Deborah was obviously God's kind of leader! She had no qualms about leading the people—men or women—in getting the job done that God wanted done according to His directions. The remainder of chapter 4 leaves no doubt about who was providing the expressive leadership. Then in chapter 5 Deborah's song of victory and praise to God is recorded. The 31st verse ends the song with the comment, "Then the land had peace for forty years." It would not have happened, had it not been for the leadership of this remarkable woman.

Queen Esther must also be included in any list of courageous national leaders. Hers was the task of saving the entire nation of Israel from extinction. A treacherous scheme had been engineered by Persian enemies, and the annihilation of God's chosen people had already been decreed. She alone could accomplish the mission of saving them from certain destruction (Esther 4:14). She responded to the challenge by first leading Israel in a spiritual revival. For three days they joined her in a period of fasting on behalf of her leadership mission. Then she proceeded to act by faith. In consequence, Israel was spared; and her name was written indelibly on the pages of history as one of God's great leaders.

While many other women are mentioned in the Old Testament, these five women we have cited stand out as excellent examples of women whom God chose to use in leadership. Some served as leaders of women. Some functioned in ways that only women could be effective. Others stood above the men of their time in their faith and ability, and were used by God instead of men to lead the men, as well as the women. It is important to note that each bore the stamp of God's appointment and approval on their leadership, and some of them served as spokesmen for God.

Before leaving the Old Testament in our study of the roles of women, some mention of Proverbs 31 and the ideal woman described there is also appropriate. In this chapter is pictured a married woman of "noble character" (v. 10). She is a good and faithful wife, as well as being a responsible mother and a capable household manager (vs. 11-15, 21-23, 27-29). In this particular example, she also has careers in real estate and in farming, along with another career in the manufacture and merchandising of clothing (vs. 16-19, 24). She is a woman of self-confidence, strength and dignity (v. 25), and she is respected for her wisdom and teaching (v. 26). Above all, she is a woman of faith (v. 30). This is one remarkable lady! It is no wonder that her husband and children arise to praise her. It is significant to also note that they do not have any problem with her being recognized for her ability and accomplishments throughout the city. They are not jealous or intimidated by her success. They feel she deserves any acclaim she earns (v. 31).

It has been maintained by many pious church leaders that the place of women is solely in the home, rearing the children. Such an affirmation betrays a remarkable ignorance of both Scripture and history. It will undoubtedly come as a real shock to many of these people to realize that this notion of an exclusive home-bound mission for women is a product of our culture and our particular historical setting. It can be easily demonstrated that ours has been an exceptional period in history. There have been very few other times in which a family could afford to have a woman remain in the home, functioning only with domestic duties, while her husband went off to earn the living for the family. It has been necessary for women to work outside the home during most of human history, and businesses and careers for women have been the accepted norm. Susan Pollak, reviewing the work of anthropologist Maxine Margolis in determining why views concerning American women changed, comments:

> Starting around 1830, as mass-produced goods replaced homemade goods, women's domestic production lost its commercial value. Men left farms to work in factories and offices, and women were advised to focus on reproduction and the joys of motherhood. Women were told that they were "naturally domestic," yet needed training for their calling in life. In 1841, Catherine Beecher wrote, "Every woman should imbibe, from early youth, the impression, that she is training for the discharge of the most important, the most difficult, and the most sacred and interesting duties that can possibly employ the highest intellect." Thus, housework was transformed into "science" and the domestic sphere into a "sacred calling."
>
> By mid 19th century, all mention of fathers had disappeared from tracts in child rearing. Women had sole responsibility for child care, and "had it in their power to produce joy or misery," depending on how well they mothered.[2]

These changes have certainly not all been for the good. Besides developing some unique and unfair attitudes toward

---

2. Susan Pollak, "Reflections on Motherhood," *Psychology Today*, December, 1984, p. 14.

the roles women should play in business and in leadership, they have robbed generations of American youth of the important benefits to be found from co-parenting. The participation of both parents in child-rearing has characterized most other periods in history far more than our own. The roles played by fathers in other times have also been much closer to the expectations concerning their involvement found in the Bible in such passages as Deuteronomy 4:9; 6:20-25 and Ephesians 6:4.

In the New Testament era we first find three women associated with the birth of Christ who stand out in Luke's gospel. *Mary,* the remarkable woman chosen to give birth to the Son of God, must have been special in every way. She was "highly favored" in God's sight, and God was with her, according to the angel who was sent to announce the impending birth (Luke 1:28). She was deciared by inspiration of the Holy Spirit to be "blessed . . . among women" (Luke 1:42).

Mary was asked to lead the kind of life, and to play a role in history, which would be both the highest privilege accorded any human, and yet be one of the most difficult imaginable. She would have to undergo the public disgrace associated with a pregnancy before marriage in a society which was far less than sympathetic or tolerant. Even the experience of giving birth would be a difficult and degrading one, far from home. After having to endure an arduous journey aboard a donkey when at full term in her pregnancy, she then had to settle for a stable as the only possible delivery room for her baby. Then what must it have been like to have had to flee to Egypt to protect the life of her Son from a cruel king, only to eventually be forced to stand helplessly at the foot of a rugged cross, watching her own people unjustly crucify Him as a common criminal? Luke 1:35 contains the prophecy that a sword would pierce her soul, and it aptly describes the agony she must have suffered. Yes, Mary is definitely unique in all of history.

Elizabeth, the aged wife of Zechariah the priest, and a relative of Mary, also is a woman worthy of note. In the first place, she was chosen to miraculously give birth to John the Baptist, who would serve as the herald for the earthly ministry of the Lord. Besides the favor God showed to her in selecting her for such a significant role in history, the account recorded in Luke 1:41-45 indicates that the Holy Spirit filled her, and she spoke by inspiration to confirm God's special role for Mary.

The third key woman associated with the birth of Jesus is *Anna*, the daughter of Phanuel. Life had not been easy for her. She had shared a marriage for only seven years before her husband died. She lived in the loneliness of widowhood until she was eighty-four, when we discover her in Luke's account. Luke 1:36 also notes that she was a prophetess. As a spokesman for God, she was totally dedicated to her task. She literally lived in the temple, worshiping, fasting, praying and proclaiming God's message. As Jesus was brought to the temple on the eighth day after His birth, Luke takes notice of Anna's praise to God and her speaking to all who were present, concerning the redemption which would come through the Christ-child. It is interesting that God used both a man (Simeon) and a woman (Anna) to announce the significance of His birth in the great temple at Jerusalem (Luke 1:25-38).

A number of women are mentioned in the gospel accounts of the life and ministry of Jesus. Of particular note for her effective leadership was an un-named Samaritan woman at

Sychar. Jesus effectively used her to reach an entire village with his message. She was certainly an unlikely messenger to be chosen, but God has always specialized in using the insignificant and unlikely to accomplish His purposes. She was a much-married woman (5 times), and was not even married to the man with whom she was living. Yet, she was used by the Lord to announce to her village, "Come, see a man who told me everything I ever did. Could this be the Christ?" (John 4:39). She was definitely successful in her proclamation and invitation, for the next verse says, "They came out of the town and made their way toward Him" (v. 40). Any preacher would be envious of such results from his sermons!

Several women were included in the circle of the closest friends of Jesus. Mary and Martha, the sisters of Lazarus, who lived at Bethany, were evidently among the closest friends and students. Luke 10:38-42 records the story of one visit to their home, and John 11:1-44 tells of another visit at the time of the death of Lazarus. His miraculous resurrection was one of the most dramatic signs Jesus provided of His supernatural powers. We know very little about the ministry of Mary and Martha, but it is evident that they were women of great faith in Jesus. It is also obvious that Jesus had the highest regard for both of them from these accounts, as He invested His time in teaching them.

In the early church a number of names of women are mentioned as sharing in the ministry of the church. *Priscilla* and Aquila were a married team who made their living as tentmakers, while they assisted in the teaching ministry of the Apostle Paul. Their work is mentioned in Acts 18:18-28; Romans 16:3; I Corinthians 16:19; and II Timothy 4:19. Paul describes them as "my fellow workers in Christ Jesus," and says of them, "They risked their lives for me. Not only I but all the churches of the Gentiles are grateful to them" (Rom 16:3). It is particularly interesting to note that Priscilla's name appears first when the two of them are mentioned in all but one instance. She was definitely a vital part of the team, and perhaps even the more gifted of the pair.

Examining the Acts 18 passage, we also notice the key role this couple played in instructing Apollos. Having heard him speak in the synagogue, and recognizing his potential as a gospel preacher, "they invited him into their home and explained to him the way of God more adequately" (v. 26). Rather than challenging his errors or debating him in public, they wisely chose to use the hospitality of their home as an opportunity to instruct him further in a home Bible study. What a tremendous example they provide for us! God has not called leaders to publicly humiliate and to win arguments and debates over others. He has commissioned church leaders to LEAD, "speaking the truth in love," so that the whole body of believers might "in all things grow up into Him who is the Head, that is, Christ" (Eph 4:15). How easy it would have been for Priscilla and Aquila to have confronted Apollos in public, demonstrated their superior knowledge for the admiration of all, and to have destroyed this gifted young man! They chose the better course!!

The four single *daughters of Philip* are also mentioned in Acts 21:9. It will be recalled that he was one of the seven chosen by the Jerusalem church to organize and administer the welfare program for the widows. We also see him in Acts 8:4-8 preaching and performing miraculous signs in Samaria. Then in verses 26-40 we find God using him to convert and baptize the Ethiopian treasurer, and then travelling as an itinerant preacher in all of the towns from Azotus to Caesarea. The Acts 21 passage records the visit of Paul and his team to the home of Philip in Caesarea, and introduces him as "Philip the evangelist, one of the Seven." Evidently his unmarried daughters had chosen to follow in his footsteps, with his and God's approval, for they are introduced as "daughters who prophesied." Where and how they did this is not specified. It should not be overlooked that they and Priscilla were involved in expressive leadership, rather than implementive.

Phoebe served as a deacon in the church at Cenchrea, according to Romans 16:1. In the chapter on deacons we explained why it is incorrect to translate the word used here in this passage in any other way. We also referred to the passage in I Timothy 3:11 in which "the women" are included in the list of qualifications for deacons. It would appear that women did indeed serve as deacons in the church, functioning in numerous kinds of implementive ministry. We would caution once again, however, concerning the evolution of the role of deacon into an "office," whether it be for a male or female. The Scriptures do not permit this!

We do not know how Phoebe served, but she was highly commended by Paul. It is probable that she carried his letter to the Christians at Rome. He writes to them concerning her in Romans 16:1-2:

> I commend to you our sister Phoebe, a deacon of the church in Cenchrea. I ask you to receive her in the Lord in a way worthy of the saints and to give her any help she may need from you, for she has been a great help to many people, including me.

In that same chapter (Rom 16) a number of other women are mentioned, including *Priscilla* (v. 3); *Mary*, "who worked very hard for you" (v. 6), *Tryphena* and *Tryphosa*, "those women who work hard in the Lord" (v. 12); *Persis*, "my good friend . . . another woman who has worked very hard in the Lord" (v. 12); and *the mother of Rufus*, "who has been a mother to me" (v. 13). From this list it is apparent that Paul had many women who worked with him in his ministry, and that he valued their services highly. He encourages the Roman church to treat them with the highest respect and to help them in every way.

Numerous other women are mentioned in the New Testament. The influence of the faith and teaching of the mother and grandmother of Timothy, *Eunice* and *Lois*, are cited by Paul in II Timothy 1:5. Certainly *Lydia* is a key figure in the beginning of the great Philippian church. She provided not only a place for Paul and his team to stay, but also welcomed the young church into her home. The account in Acts 16:11-15 describes her as a successful businesswoman. She was "a dealer in purple cloth from the city of Thyatira, who was a worshiper of God" (v. 14). Luke records in verse 15:

> When she and the members of her household were baptized, she invited us to her home. "If you consider me a believer in the Lord," she said, "come and stay at my house." And she persuaded us.

What a great blessing this woman proved to be to the future of that church. Following their experience in prison, and the conversion of the jailer, verse 40 says: "After Paul and Silas came out of prison, they went to Lydia's house, where they met with the brothers and encouraged them. Then they left." The ministry of Lydia however, continued, to the glory of God and to the strengthening of that church.

Lydia was a woman who could have easily excused herself from opening her home. She had a business to run. It is likely that she was single. She could have cited many reasons why she did not need the extra work and trouble of playing hostess to a visiting group of missionaries in her home for an extended period of time. For one thing, it was politically dangerous. In the second place, what would it do to her reputation? Then who would want their home disrupted week after week to hold church services there? Lydia, however, counted it an honor and a privilege to have her home so used for the Lord. Oh, that more women today would exercise this kind of leadership!

Paul also has some interesting things to say about the role of older women in the church. In Titus 2:3-5 he instructs Timothy:

> Likewise, teach the older women to be reverent in the way they live, not to be slanderers or addicted to much wine, but to teach what is good. Then they can train the younger women to love their husbands and children, to be self-controlled and pure, to be busy at home, to be kind, and to be subject to their husbands, so that no one will malign the Word of God.

Paul is in no way implying that women are to be confined solely to the home. He is simply suggesting that the older Christian women live in such a way as to be able to teach by their word and example how Christian women ought to live. They ought to be devoted and submissive to their husbands, for they have made marriage commitments to them. They ought to treat their children with love. They ought not to be idle or contentious in the home. Their lives ought to reflect Christ. The bottom line is that the younger women should be taught by the older women to live in such a way that their lives and examples will not be a reproach to Christ and His Word.

Finally, we would note that women were intended to be integrally involved in the ministry and leadership of the church from its very beginning. On the day of Pentecost the Apostle Peter quotes the prophet Joel, pointing out that his prophecy is now being fulfilled in the establishment and function of the church:

> In the last days, God says, "I will pour out my Spirit on all people. Your sons and daughters will prophesy, your young men will see visions, your old men will dream dreams. Even on my servants, both men and women, I will pour out my Spirit in those days, and they will prophesy" (Acts 2:17-18).

Is it not interesting that in this passage God makes no difference between men and women, sons or daughters? Both would be used to speak His message in the church. Does this sound like God has changed the plan, as some would have us believe, between the Old and New Testaments? Peter is serving notice at the very beginning, as God speaks through him, that women will have an important place in the kingdom of God, His church. To this we must also add the Apostle Paul's affirmation in Galatians 3:28-29:

> There is neither Jew nor Greek, slave nor free, male nor female, for you are all one in Christ. If you belong to Christ, you are Abraham's seed, and heirs according to the promise.

It seems that it would be impossible to make the point with any greater clarity. It is stated by two apostles, both speaking under the inspiration of the Holy Spirit; and examples of the leadership of women abound in the early church. Julia Staton concludes:

> The female Christians were expected to participate as full members of the church's ministry (Rom 12:3-8; Eph 4:6-16, note

the use of the word "all"). They would have participated in the church's activities of teaching, fellowship, prayer, breaking of bread, taking meals together, selling possessions, and sharing their wealth (Acts 2:42-47; 4:34-37; 5:1).[3]

Before concluding this section dealing with Biblical examples of women in leadership, we would be remiss if we failed to note, however, the rather conspicuous absence of any mention of women in reference to the eldership of the churches. If there were those women who served in this way, they are simply not identified as such. Is this silence a prohibition, or simply an omission of any example?

Qualifications for Leadership

It would logically follow that the same qualifications of Christ-like maturity would be required of women as would be expected of their male counterparts. Jesus becomes the Yardstick by which everyone is to be measured. The same fruit of the Spirit described in Galatians 5:22-23 apply to women, as well as to men. The admonition in the verses following is also applicable:

> Those who belong to Christ have crucified the sinful nature with its passions and desires. Since we live by the Spirit, let us keep in step with the Spirit. Let us not become conceited, provoking and envying each other (Gal 5:24-26).

God has established no double standards. There will, however, be specific application of His uniform standards of Christ-likeness to each of us, according to the abilities and roles He has assigned us. In the home, for example, He has ordained a workable plan. It is summed up in Ephesians 5:21,

3. Staton, p. 117.

"Submit to one another out of reverence for Christ." This rule for Christians, both male and female, is to be applied in the church, in the home and at work. We see Paul develop the concept to include the various contexts in which Christians must exist in relationship to other people (Eph 5:22—6:9). This section of Scripture must be understood as one connected block of teaching, developing the key concept of accountability and submission to one another for Christ's sake. The concept of submission as required of all Christians, both male and female, is further developed in Romans 13:1-6; I Corinthians 16:15-18; Colossians 3:18—4:1; Hebrews 12:7-15; 13:17; James 4:7-12; I Peter 2:13—3:9; 4:7-11. When one has thoroughly studied these passages, he is ready to understand God's plan for the home. Suffice it to say, that the concept of submission is foundational for every relationship the Christian is to share—submission first to others, and ultimately to Christ.

In the passage cited (Eph 5:22—6:9), husbands are the ones made ultimately responsible to Christ for the home. As Christ is Head of the church, so the husband is made the head of the home. The parallel does not end there. The husband is expected to be as devoted and as self-sacrificing to his wife and children as Jesus has been to His church. What a standard by which to be measured! Husbands are to "love their wives as their own bodies" (v. 28). This requires growing up, leaving parents, and making a completely new home. They are to be united to their wives in such a complete way that they become as one flesh (v. 31). Paul says, "This is a profound mystery—but I am talking about Christ and the church. However, each one of you must love his wife as he loves himself, and the wife must respect her husband" (vs. 32-33). Paul is obviously talking about a man having to submit himself to Christ and devote himself to the needs of his wife and family. They come first!

A wife, then, is expected to respect and submit herself to her husband, since God has given him the ultimate responsibility for the home. Nothing can have two heads without becoming a monster! This does not mean in any way that the wife is to be trampled upon, or that her opinions will not be sought. They are to be a partnership, each contributing to the building and functioning of the marriage. There must be a tremendous amount of give and take from each side to make a marriage work. This is God's point. He is in no way talking about superiority of one sex over the other. They are not the same, for He created them differently. Nevertheless, they stand as equals in His sight. Husbands and wives are called to demonstrate a mutual respect for each other and to function harmoniously, with the abilities of one complementing those of the other. Together they are to build the marriage.

Children fit into the picture also. They are required to submit to their parents. Paul points out that, as Deuteronomy 5:16 says, it is to their benefit. Their lives will be better, happier and longer if they hear and heed the lessons their parents have learned from their parents and their own experience. Again, Paul hastens to add the reciprocal responsibility of the parents to their children in the sense that they are to consider their feelings and their best interests. Parents, with fathers in the lead, are to "bring them up in the training and instruction of the Lord" (6:4). The task is not to be left to the church or the school. Parents have the primary responsibility. What a sobering responsibility that is!

How many youth have married someone in order to escape their home requirements and to gain their freedom? It does not take long to discover that in marriage, freedom is not free! Neither marriages nor families can work when each person is insisting upon having his own way. As in all relationships, there must be a leader, and there must be mutual responsibility required of all parties involved. In no other way can the home succeed or survive. God knew this, so He designed a workable plan with submission required of everyone.

When we talk about qualifications of women for church leadership, if they are married, the way they function in their married roles as wives and mothers is definitely a factor to be considered—just as the way a man functions as a husband and father is to be considered in his selection for leadership (I Tim 3:4-5). They play different roles, but the standard is administered equally. Women who are not conscientiously caring for their responsibilities can get into trouble. Paul notes in I Timothy 5:13, "Besides, they get into the habit of being idle and going from house to house. And not only do they become idlers, but also gossips and busybodies, saying things they ought not to." Psychologically, it has been asserted that women have a greater inherent need to talk than do men. As James points out to both men and women, however:

> Likewise the tongue is a small part of the body, but it makes great boasts. Consider what a great forest is set on fire by a small spark. The tongue is also a fire, a world of evil among the parts of the body. It corrupts the whole person, sets the whole course of his life on fire, and is itself set on fire by hell.
>
> All kinds of animals, birds, reptiles of the sea are being tamed and have been tamed by man, but no man can tame the tongue. It is a restless evil, full of deadly poison.

> With the tongue we praise our Lord and Father, and with it we curse men, who have been made in God's likeness. Out of the same mouth come praise and cursing. My brothers, this should not be. Can both fresh water and salt water flow from the same spring? My brothers, can a fig tree bear olives, or a grapevine bear figs? Neither can a salt spring produce fresh water (James 3:5-12).

Consequently, when Paul describes the qualifications for women who are to serve in church leadership in I Timothy 3:11, he says: "In the same way, the women are to be women worthy of respect, not malicious talkers but temperate and trustworthy in everything." Their lives, including their speech, are to exhibit the kind of Spirit-controlled, fruit-bearing behavior which will earn them the respect of those within and without the church. The same "worthy of respect" (*semnas*) required of men is required of the women (vs. 8, 11). As with the men, we would note that this earnest respect is a prerequisite for selection to serve in leadership, rather than an automatic right to be expected and accorded with a position. The word used concerning their speech is, interestingly enough, the same word (*diabolos*) used to describe the devil, or "the slanderer."[4] They are to be the kind of women who control their tongues, deliberately refraining from intentional or unintentional slander of anyone. They are to be temperate, as is required of those who are to be overseers (v. 2). The word deals with maintaining a balance, or being self-controlled.[5] Finally, the last requirement has to do with faithfulness or reliability.

---

4. William F. Arndt and F. Wilbur Gingrich, *A Greek-English Lexicon of the New Testament and Other Early Christian Literature* (Chicago: The University of Chicago Press, 1952), p. 181.

5. Arndt and Gingrich, p. 668.

The Problem With Paul

Much has been made of Paul's comments in I Corinthians 14:33-36 concerning the necessity of the silence of women in the churches, and his note in I Timothy 2:11-15 concerning women learning in silence. On the surface, considering the way these verses have been translated, there appears to be a real problem here. He seems to be contradicting what he has said in commendation of women who served with him in church leadership. Julia Staton sums up a number of views when she says:

> Many scholars and women think Paul was a male chauvinist. . . . They feel that Paul showed in his teaching that he thought women were inferior, were to be put down and held down, and should be restricted in their activities simply because of their sex. Some say that Paul did not have a full understanding of Christ's desire to eliminate the prejudice against women and his eyes were clouded by the trends of his culture. Others say he was often confused about the role of women and thus changed his mind about them often—perhaps because he was single and not experienced with women's ways. Others say he did not completely set aside his Pharisaical upbringing so that his old views and patterns of thought about women crept into his teaching from time to time. I feel all these views could be summed up in one word—hogwash![6]

The point is that Paul wrote under the inspiration of the Holy Spirit, just as did the other Bible writers. The Holy Spirit is not inconsistent or contradictory in that which He causes to be written. When problems appear to exist between passages, they generally turn out to be man-made. Translators

---

6. Staton, pp. 120-121.

or interpreters have usually forced a particular understanding of the passages in question, or have erroneously translated a word. As we have already seen in our study of the Biblical blueprint for church leaders, there are numerous examples of this having occurred, generally due to the translators' cultural or theological bias.

Let us examine more closely the "problem passages." The answer to the dilemma is relatively easy to discover. If there are two possible interpretations for the same word, it is illogical to select the one meaning which is out of place and at odds with what has been said elsewhere on the subject. Our English language is full of examples of words which are used to describe two or more different subjects. We usually have little difficulty selecting the proper meaning, considering the context. When we do occasionally miss in our selection of the correct meaning, we can come up with some pretty strange and perplexing ideas. "Grass," for example, can mean the green vegetation comprising our lawns, or it can represent marijuana. "Gay" can mean being happy or homosexual. Our language continues to change, and the examples are endless.

The ancient Greek language also had its words which possessed double meanings. As we have previously noted, *gyné* was the Greek word for both woman and wife. This is the first key to unraveling the problem with Paul. We have already noted that some of the early Christian churches met in the synagogues. Murch, among others, has commented about the practice of Jewish Christians continuing to worship in the synagogue on Saturday, and then remaining after sundown (the beginning of the 1st day of the week, according to Jewish reckoning) to observe the Lord's Supper, sing Christian hymns, join in common worship and listen to a Christian sermon.[7]

Some understanding of the synagogue is necessary, therefore, for us to be able to accurately picture the setting of the Christian worship. The following descriptive account may be helpful:

> Between the end of the Old Testament and the beginning of the New there was considerable development in the formal religious life of the Jews. Regular worship now took place in the local synagogue—a practice evolved from the days in exile when there was no temple. Only the men took an active part in the synagogue service, the women and children being separated from them in a gallery. In charge was the Ruler of the synagogue—elected by the village elders. The service followed a pattern with creed, prayers and readings from the Law and Prophets. This was followed by a sermon and a time when the men could question the minister. Behind the pulpit, a curtained alcove contained the "ark" of sacred scrolls, which only the doctors of law might open. Between the alcove and pulpit, the readers sat facing the congregation, together with the chief teachers, who sat on raised seats known as Moses' seats.[8]

The context of I Corinthians 14:34-35 is Paul's discussion of problems in worship which were creating disorder. After pointing out that "God is not a God of disorder but of peace," (v. 33) he speaks concerning women. If the Corinthian church followed the practice of the synagogue, the point becomes quite clear. With the wives and children seated

---

7. James DeForest Murch, *The Free Church* (n.c.: Restoration Press, 1966), pp. 15-16.

8. David Alexander, *Eerdman's Handbook of the Bible* (New York: Guideposts, 1983), p. 96.

separately from the men in a gallery, for any wife to ask her husband something during a worship service would definitely be disruptive. She would have to shout across the room to be heard. Paul says that this kind of disorder should not be permitted. Julia Staton provides further clarification:

> The Greek for "keep silent" (*sigao*) means to act quietly. It is not the word (*phimoo*) which means to muzzle, to shut up, to silence. "It is improper for a wife to speak in church," v. 35. The Greek word for "speak" (*laleo*) can mean arguing, chattering or questioning, which fits the context of this passage. The wives were (in this context) evidently chattering or asking questions during the service, adding to the confusion. Paul was simply saying, "Don't disturb the worship service; ask your husband at home your questions about what was said."[9]

This is certainly a reasonable interpretation of this "problem" passage, and it fits with what we have recorded about New Testament practices. With such a logical explanation at hand, why should this passage be forced into a prohibition of women from ever being able to speak or teach in the church? Such a forced interpretation is clearly straining this text and would appear to be totally out of context.

The second passage, I Timothy 2:11-15, is the more difficult of the two. Considering the context, Paul is again speaking about conduct in worship. The fact that he is particularly addressing married women is apparent from his comment in verse 15 concerning childbearing. The passage actually begins with verse 9, where Paul admonishes women to dress with modesty, decency and propriety, so as not to

9. Staton, p. 129.

call attention to themselves and to detract from the worship. Showy hair styles and gaudy jewelry cause the wrong kind of impressions to be formed about a woman's values. Paul calls for an emphasis by women upon their inner worth, rather than a dependence upon outward display. As Guthrie says, "It reflects a right attitude of mind, for Paul was shrewd enough to know that a woman's dress is a mirror of her mind. Outward ostentation is not in keeping with a prayerful and devout approach."[10] While Paul is not calling for drabness or lack of attention to appearance, he is definitely encouraging the exercise of good taste. He is saying that misplaced values are often reflected in a need to display possessions and to call attention to appearances. Paul points out that good deeds are more appropriate adornment for women than fancy trappings (v. 10). Peter wrote in a similar fashion in I Peter 3:3-5.

Paul says in verse 11, "A woman (wife) should learn in quietness and full submission." This NIV translation is far better than others, which would appear to command absolute silence in the churches from women. Quietness (*hésychia*) has reference to undisturbed life, quiet and rest.[11] In other words, women are to learn without creating a disturbance. This along with the reference to being in submission to their husbands, appears to be reflective of the I Corinthians 14:34-35 passages which we have just considered.

Verse 12 is translated, "I do not permit a women to teach or have authority over a man; she must be silent." To begin with, the word translated "be silent" is the same Greek word

---

10. Donald Guthrie, *The Pastoral Epistles* (Grand Rapids: Wm. B. Eerdmans Publishing Company, 1957), pp. 74-75.

11. Arndt and Gingrich, p. 350.

we just discussed in verse 11. It can be not to create a disturbance. It is possible that Paul is still talking about the marital relationship in public worship, and the two things Paul prohibits are logically and grammatically linked together. The word translated "to teach" means to instruct, direct or admonish.[12] The word rendered "have authority" actually means to domineer over someone.[13]

Considering these alternatives, is it not possible that Paul is attempting to deal with a very common problem we have all experienced? Is there anything more uncomfortable or disconcerting than to be subjected to the company of a married couple, where the wife is continually correcting, contradicting and admonishing her husband? Such a domineering, disrespectful woman is publicly denying her God-given role as a wife. It seems that every church has women like this, who are more concerned about winning arguments, proving points and having the last word than they are about any need to publicly support their husbands and to treat them with respect. Such wives are a reproach to any church and an unmistakable contradiction of its teachings. Paul simply did not permit this kind of behavior by wives in any church.

Then in verses 13-14 he reminds wives of the trouble Eve caused both Adam and herself when she sought to take the lead in that relationship, and led Him into the sin which resulted in their banishment from the Garden of Eden. It is a solemn warning to any wife who may be tempted to egotistically publicly upstage her husband, seeking to make herself look superior by teaching him and putting him down. The consequences can be far-reaching and extremely costly.

---

12. Zondervan, *The Analytical Greek Lexicon* (Grand Rapids: Zondervan Publishing House, 1977), p. 98.

13. Arndt and Gingrich, p. 120.

Finally, in verse 15 Paul says, "But women will be kept safe through childbirth, if they continue in faith, love, and holiness with propriety." Again, the NIV is a preferable translation to most, which tend to translate this verse in such a way as to imply that a woman's salvation depends upon her ability to bear children. How many childless women have been put through anguish by these translators? Guthrie comments that Paul's statement here "must be among the most difficult expressions in the whole of the Pastorals."[14] It is important to remember, however, that Paul has just used the sin of Eve and its consequences as an example in the two preceding verses. He is continuing with that point. One of the consequences of her sin, according to Genesis 3:16, was the tremendous pain that women would have to endure in childbirth. The other consequence mentioned in that verse is that wives would be required to be in submission to their husbands.

Paul appears to be saying here in verse 15 that, even though the painful consequence of Eve's sin may seem unbearable at times to women who are going through the childbirth process, they will be able to make it through that ordeal safely, with all of its pain and difficulties, if their attitude and Christian conduct are what they ought to be. Paul prescribes faith, love and consecration (holiness), along with exercising good judgment. The latter word, incidentally, has to do with soundness of mind, being reasonable or sensible, keeping one's head, or being self-controlled. As applied to women in early Christian literature, it also came to mean "virtuous."[15] This verse appears to be Paul's word

14. Guthrie, p. 77.
15. Arndt and Gingrich, pp. 809-810.

of encouragement to women. Even though they have to suffer some painful consequences of Eve's sin, if they have their roles in proper perspective, they will be able to clear that hurdle and to move on far beyond it with God's help. Otherwise, self-centered women can wind up blaming God, hating childbearing and even hating their husbands and children for the ordeal they were forced to endure during their labor. Some remain selfish and bitter for a lifetime.

It should be added that Paul is not dealing here with the fact that some women will actually die during childbirth, due to complications and physical limitations. Some may conclude that he is blaming such deaths on lack of faith or goodness. This is not the issue. Paul is talking about the basic attitude of wives, whether it is to be self-centered or Christ-centered. He is challenging women to become all they are capable of being by looking beyond themselves and the gratification of their feelings. He is calling them to maturity and Christ-likeness. That is definitely in context with the following verses, which discuss the qualification of church leaders.

Cultural Limitations on Leadership

Every missionary is keenly aware of the ways in which different cultures dictate how they will be able to proceed with their work of evangelizing. More than the written laws of the country, each culture has its mores and taboos, along with its expectations which must be met by anyone who would successfully communicate the gospel.

Some of these cultural limits relate to dress. In some churches, a woman would not be permitted to wear slacks, shorts or swimwear, while in other cultures she would be considered an oddity and being judgmental if she did not. The length and style of her hair is construed in some cultures to designate her as single or married, virtuous or promiscuous. This is the point Paul is making in I Corinthians 11:3-15, where some Christian women were evidently disregarding the accepted standards of their culture, and were going about in such a way as to be regarded as immoral women. They were, therefore, a reproach to both the church and to their husbands.

Cultures have their established and accepted limits in relationship to physical contact, eye contact and acceptable distances. Touching and embracing are signs of sincerity and caring in some cultures, while they are interpreted as offenses or sexual advances in others. In many cultures, maintaining eye contact in a personal exchange is also an important sign of sincerity; but to an Indian tribe in Arizona, it is regarded as a sign of insincerity.

There are cultures which are patriarchal and those which are matriarchal. Those who would carry the gospel to them must be willing to recognize that a man will be accorded more respect in the one, and a woman in the other. In another Arizona Indian tribe, for example, it would be impossible for any man to be as successful in impacting the tribe with the gospel as could a capable and committed woman. That has been damaging to some male egos, but it is an inescapable fact. The tribe is matriarchal.

It must be admitted that the New Testament's cultural setting in Palestine was strongly patriarchal. With the structure and customs of the synagogues, as we have discussed, with women and children seated in a separate gallery, it would have been unthinkable to the Jews to have included women among their elders. This was obviously reflected in the Christian churches, who sometimes used those same worship facilities. Christian women were urged to work within the cultural limitations they encountered in order to be effective for Christ, and to refrain from being a reproach to the church. Flexibility and a willingness to adapt for the sake of Christ are the keys.

Whether one is male or female, there must be an honest desire to serve in whatever way God and the culture permit, recognizing that some cultures will not permit one to serve in certain capacities. A male gynecologist friend not long ago was forced to change his plans for missionary service, for the people to which he planned to minister would not accept a male gynecologist. He looked for and found another open door to serve in a different culture where his talents and gender were accepted. This was the attitude typified in the Apostle Paul. He concludes that tremendous section of chapter 9 in I Corinthians, which deals with freedom and personal rights, with this great personal affirmation: "I have become all things to all men so that by all possible means I might save some. I do all this for the sake of the gospel, that I may share in its blessings" (I Cor 9:22b-23).

Leadership by Women in the Restoration Movement

The Christian Churches have often been identified by others as "the church with the women preachers." To most members of the churches today, that accusation comes as such a shock that it is vehemently denied. It is, in fact, true. The Restoration Movement was probably the first to have women serving as ordained ministers. While they were always a rare minority, they served in this capacity relatively early in the history of the movement. Deborah Casey cites research which refers to women who may have been ordained by a Christian Church as early as the 1850's.[16]

H. Eugene Johnson records the fact that Melissa Garrett Timmons Terrell was ordained by the Deer Creek Conference of the Christian Churches in Ohio in 1867 at the age of thirty-three. He also refers to Clara Celestea Hale-Babcock who was ordained in 1867. Serving in Illinois and North Dakota, she was credited with 1,502 baptisms during her ministry. He goes on to tell the interesting story of perhaps the most successful woman preacher in the movement's history:

> Another early Disciples woman preacher was Sara McCoy Crank, born in 1863 and ordained in 1892. Her husband, J. R. Crank, was also a preacher. She was ordained by J. S. Clements, general evangelist for the American Christian Missionary Society. When the Cranks moved to Pargould, Arkansas, in 1906, the church board forbade her to preach. She pitched a tent nearby and held a revival meeting. *The Christian-Evangelist* (Nov. 24, 1948) carried her obituary, and the write-up credited to her ministry more than one thousand funerals, 761 weddings, and more than five thousand baptisms.[17]

The development of women in the pulpit of the Christian Churches was one which came into existence in spite of its male leadership, rather than with their support. The early

16. Deborah Casey, "Heritage and History: Hand in Hand," *Discipliana*, Summer, 1978, p. 20.

17. H. Eugene Johnson, *Duly and Scripturally Qualified* (Cincinnati: The Standard Publishing Company, 1975), p. 159.

Restoration Movement leaders were all unanimously opposed to women preaching or even teaching men. Alexander Campbell, when addressing the Henry Female Seminary of Newcastle, New York, in 1856 had this to say on the subject of "Woman and Her Mission":

> Yours is a beautiful mission, viewed in its entire aptitude; and in reference to it all your studies should be prosecuted, and all the virtues of Christian excellencies cherished in your hearts and practiced in your lives. The treasures of learning and science should be mastered, and every literary and scientific study be prosecuted with a vigorous diligence, in order to your successfully entering upon a career of usefulness so pregnant with enduring blessings to yourselves, so full of promise of laurels that which will never wither, of pleasures that will never cloy, and of a reward from the right hand of the Arbiter of the destinies of the world, richer far than all the treasures of the earth, and as enduring as the throne of God and the ages of eternity. There is no necessity to mount the rostrums to stand up in public assemblies, to address mixed auditories of both sexes, of all classes and orders of society, in order to fill up the duties of your mission. If Paul would not have a woman to pray unveiled in a Christian church, and if he made long hair a glory to her, because it veiled her beauty and protected her eyes from the gaze of staring sensualists, think you he would have sent her out on a missionary tour, or placed her on a rostrum, surrounded with ogling-glasses in the hands, not of old men and women of dim vision, but of green striplings of pert impertinence? Be assured, not one word of such import ever fell from the lips of prophets or apostles.[18]

---

18. Alexander Campbell, *Popular Lectures and Addresses* (Cincinnati: The Standard Publishing Company, 1863), p. 228.

Campbell's message was clearly a "No" to any woman aspiring to the pulpit. In spite of this kind of opposition to the leadership of women in the church, there was a strong support in the movement for the education of women. More than forty of these female seminaries were begun, enabling many women to have access to an education who otherwise would have been denied one.[19] With the increased educational opportunities, with women beginning to enter industry, and with the equal role women had so often occupied with men in America from the colonial days to the frontier era, the cultural pressures to give women leadership roles in the church were great.

Whether they occupied visible or recognized leadership positions or not, it was apparent that American women were at least "the power behind the throne" in the churches. Seth Wilson, commenting on the tendencies of churches to pattern their polity after their national government, referred —with tongue in cheek—to the elders being the Senate, the deacons the House of Representatives, the preacher the President, and, "I guess the ladies aid group is the Supreme Court, in that case. Sometimes you'll find it operates that way, too."[20]

Within the local church women often began to fill certain capacities of leadership as the Restoration Movement developed. Sometimes their leadership was, admittedly, due to a lack of available manpower. In other cases, it was simply a recognition of their abilities and willingness to serve. Sometimes they were elected deaconesses or members of the church board, while others organized groups, served on committees or taught classes.

---

19. Johnson, p. 157.

20. Seth Wilson, *Elders and Deacons According to the Bible* (Dallas: Bible Book Store, 1965), p. 42.

With the encouragement of a number of the men in the leadership of the movement at the time, the Christian Women's Board of Missions came into existence in Cincinnati in October, 1874, with Mrs. Maria Jameson as its president. Enos Dowling says of it:

> The organization of local and state societies was encouraged, each to be subject to the parent society. New life was infused into the missionary work of the churches. Missions were sustained both at home and abroad, and an educational program in mountain areas and among the Negroes was established.[21]

This endeavor enjoyed widespread support and, as Casey notes, even Mrs. Alexander Campbell was a member of it. She did make it known, however, that she would go no further than that: "It is predicted by some that our sisterhood's Missionary Society is but a 'stepping stone' to get to the pulpit. If I thought so I would immediately sever myself from it."[22]

Credit must be given the women of these local, state and national women's missionary societies. It was through their primary efforts that the Christian Churches began to develop a conscience for missions. Many of the missionaries were initially sent by these groups. Many new churches were begun, ethnic groups reached, benevolent and educational projects undertaken and Christian camps established. These women became known and respected for their ability to get the job done.

It would be derelict of us to fail to mention as well the unique leadership of Carrie Nation (1846-1911), the great

21. Enos E. Dowling, *The Restoration Movement* (Cincinnati: The Standard Publishing Company, 1964), p. 80.

22. Casey, p. 21.

temperance crusader. Either alone or with other hymn-singing sisters, she would invade the Kansas saloons, preach, pray and smash both the stock and the fixtures with hatchets. Becoming famous for her crusades, she lectured in numerous states, in Canada and in Europe. She was known as a devout member of the Christian Churches. W. H. Boles recounts a stay in her home:

> I never met a more godly, consecrated woman. I never was on my knees so much during 5 weeks as in the Nation home. . . . She fears no man, counts no cost, asks no quarter, and gives none to friend or foe. Always in a good humor, never unhinged, non-plussed. She relies on God for strength, has no plans or schemes, simple as a child, yet well educated and thoroughly posted in the Bible and almost all questions of the day.[23]

In Summary

Throughout the Old Testament women are mentioned who distinguished themselves in leadership of God's people. The examples selected demonstrate that God has sometimes used women both as His approved spokesmen and as leaders of men and women. In the New Testament women are mentioned even more frequently. Both Jesus and His apostles spent time teaching them and encouraged them to serve. It is perhaps significant that God used both a man and a woman to announce the significance of the birth of His Son in the temple at Jerusalem. Women are mentioned in a variety of leadership roles in the church, including teaching and serving as deacons. They are not mentioned

---

23. W. H. Boles, "Mrs. Carrie Nation," *The Christian Messenger*, March 22, 1901, p. 1.

as elders. Paul makes a special point in his letters to commend the leadership of numerous women, and to call for their acceptance and assistance for them by those who did not yet know them.

Since Christ-likeness is the standard of maturity for all Christians, both male and female candidates for roles of leadership should be evaluated by this standard. While men and women have different roles within a marriage and family, they should be evaluated by the way in which they fulfill their God-given roles. Neither is to be considered superior to the other, even though a husband is to be the head of the home; for both fall under the rules of mutual submission, and ultimate submission to Christ.

The two "problem passages" penned by Paul need to first be considered in light of other Scripture on the subject. Secondly, their immediate context must be regarded. Thirdly, logical alternate translations of the Greek texts ought to be evaluated, rather than the traditional anti-feminist interpretations of the passages. Close scrutiny does reveal at least the possibility of legitimate alternate readings which are consistent with other New Testament teachings concerning women in church leadership.

For both men and women cultural limits do affect the ways in which one can function in leadership in a particular setting. These limits must be understood and observed in order for a leader to be effective. A spirit of willingness to serve in whatever way necessary must characterize the Christian leader. Along with the proper motives, flexibility and adaptability are keys to successful leadership.

Finally, we noted a number of examples of the leadership of women in the Restoration Movement. These included frontier evangelists, teachers, misisonary society leaders and temperance movement leaders. With the exception of the encouragement given the women to form missionary societies, most other leadership by women emerged in spite of the concerted opposition by the male leaders of the movement.

9

A CHILD SHALL LEAD THEM

A Functioning Body

The Apostle Paul wrote to the Corinthians concerning the church: "The body is a unit, though it is made up of many parts; and though all its parts are many, they form one body. So it is with Christ" (I Cor 12:12). To the Ephesians he wrote, "Instead, speaking the truth in love, we will in all things grow up into Him who is the Head, that is, Christ. From Him the whole body, joined and held together by every supporting ligament, grows and builds itself up in love, as each part does its work" (Eph 4:15, 16).

Within that body are the young, the old and the in-between. All are intended to be functioning parts of a body that is growing up, in its entirety, into Christlikeness. The concluding phrase, "as each part does its work," implies that every portion of the body is expected to be involved in doing something productive as a part of the total ministry of the church. No part seems to be excluded, regardless of age.

Even in a relatively youth-oriented society, it is rather interesting that this point has largely escaped the notice of the church. In the midst of the Messianic prophecy of Isaiah is the fascinating line, "The wolf will live with the lamb, the leopard will lie down with the goat, the calf and the lion and the yearling together; and a little child will lead them" (Isa 11:6). While the message is clothed in symbolism, the basic meaning is quite clear: things would definitely be different in the kingdom of Christ.

The apostles were among those who had some difficulty understanding those differences. They were concerned one day about which of them would be declared the greatest in the kingdom of heaven. Matthew records the response of Jesus:

> He called a little child and had him stand among them. And He said: "I tell you the truth, unless you change and become like little children, you will never enter the kingdom of heaven. Therefore, whoever humbles himself like this child is the greatest in the kingdom of heaven. And whoever welcomes a little child like this in My name welcomes Me. But if anyone causes one of these little ones who believe in Me to sin, it would be better for him to have a large millstone hung around his neck and be drowned in the depths of the sea. . . . See that you do not look down on these little ones. For I tell you that their angels in heaven always see the face of my Father in heaven" (Matt 18:2-6, 10).

Then Jesus proceeded to tell His disciples the parable of the lost sheep. He described the shepherd's greater delight over finding the one sheep which had strayed than he had with the ninety-nine sheep who had remained safely in the fold. He concluded, "In the same way your Father is not willing that any of these little ones should be lost" (Matt 18:14).

In the next chapter Matthew also records another incident which involved a misunderstanding about the importance of children in Jesus' ministry. Little children were being brought to Jesus for Him to place His hands on them and to pray for them. The disciples, however, rebuked those who brought the children, undoubtedly feeling that such an activity was wasting the time of our Lord. Jesus responded, "Let the little children come to me, and do not hinder them, for the kingdom of heaven belongs to such as these" (Matt 19:14).

Jesus obviously valued the roles children and youth can play in the church. Luke records the only account we have of the boyhood of Jesus:

> And the child grew and became strong; He was filled with wisdom, and the grace of God was upon Him. Every year His parents went to Jerusalem for the Feast of the Passover. When He was twelve years old, they went up to the Feast, according to the custom. After the Feast was over, while His parents were returning home, the boy Jesus stayed behind in Jerusalem, but they were unaware of it. Thinking He was in their company, they traveled on for a day. Then they began looking for Him among their relatives and friends. When they did not find Him, they went back to Jerusalem to look for Him. After three days they found Him in the temple courts, sitting among the teachers, listening to them and asking them questions. Everyone who heard Him was amazed at His understanding and His answers. When His parents saw Him, they were astonished. His mother said to Him "Son, why have you treated us like this? Your father and I have been anxiously searching for you." "Why were

> you searching for Me?" He asked. "Didn't you know I had to be in my Father's house?" But they did not understand.
>
> Then He went down to Nazareth with them and was obedient to them. But His mother treasured all these things in her heart. And Jesus grew is wisdom and stature, and in favor with God and men (Luke 2:40-52).

This brief episode in Luke's gospel reveals that Jesus did not wait until He reached adulthood to begin assuming responsibility for functioning in ministry. His parents did not understand, but He felt compelled to be in His Father's house and about His Father's business, even at the age of twelve.

Another lad of undisclosed age played a key role in one of the most spectacular miracles of our Lord's ministry. He often escapes our notice, but his contribution was essential. John records the story of the crowd of thousands who had followed Jesus to the far side of the Sea of Galilee, and who sat upon the hillside and listened to Him teach. When Jesus asked Philip where they could purchase food for the people to eat, he replied incredously, "Eight months' wages would not buy enough bread for each one to have a bite!" It was Andrew, however, who reported to Jesus that a boy had offered five small barley loaves and two small fish (John 6:5-9). Though Andrew did not comprehend how so small an offering of food could be any answer at all, that boy's contribution offered in faith, when blessed and multiplied by the Lord, fed over 5,000, with twelve baskets of pieces from the barley loaves left over. How true were Isaiah's words, "A little child will lead them."

In Matthew 11:25-26 Jesus prayed: "I praise you, Father, Lord of heaven and earth, because you have hidden these things from the wise and the learned, and revealed them to little children. Yes, Father, for this was your good pleasure." Again in Matthew 21:15-16 we find another rather interesting encounter Jesus had with the religious leaders of that day, which related to the leadership of children:

> But when the chief priests and teachers of the law saw the wonderful things He did and the children shouting in the temple area, "Hosanna to the Son of David," they were indignant. "Did you hear what these children are saying?" they asked Him. "Yes," replied Jesus, "have you never read, 'From the lips of children and infants You have ordained praise'?"

Finally, it is significant that the Apostle Peter quotes the prophecy of Joel in his sermon on the Day of Pentecost, which heralded the birth of the church. That prophecy speaks of ways in which God intends to use youth in the ministry and leadership of the church:

> "In the last days," God says, "I will pour out my Spirit on all people. Your sons and daughters will prophesy, your young men will see visions, your old men will dream dreams" (Acts 2:17; Joel 2:28).

By way of fulfillment, Acts 21:8 tells of the visit to Philip the evangelist at Caesarea by Paul and his companions. Luke notes that Philip had four unmarried daughters who prophesied. While we are not given specific examples of others who may have been leaders in the church who had visions or prophesied, the prophecy undoubtedly had its fulfillment in cases which are not documented for us. We have already called attention to the youthful leaders who were trained by the Apostle Paul, and to John Mark, who was taken under the wing of Barnabas, and who was later inspired by God to pen one of the Gospels.

The fact that youth were to be given a part in the leadership and ministry of the New Testament church should not be too great a surprise to us. Other youth played key leadership roles in the accomplishment of God's purposes in the Old Testament. One thinks, for example, of Samuel, "the boy who ministered before the Lord under Eli" (I Sam 3:1). Then there was David, who dared to go up against the giant Goliath. As his nation stood paralyzed with fear of the giant and the Philistines, the boy David took the lead, trusting in the power of God. It was the mighty King Saul who objected, "You are not able to go out against this Philistine and fight him; you are only a boy, and he has been a fighting man from his youth" (I Sam 17:33). A boy with faith and courage, however, was used by God to eliminate that giant and to break the Philistine grip. As in so many cases, the adult leadership of the nation had lost the vision and the faith, and they had ceased to lead. They had calculated all the risks, and they could list all the reasons why every plan of action would fail. Consequently they cowered before the enemy, for they had forgotten the power of the God they claimed to serve. It took the faith and the commitment of a youth to lead them and to get the job done.

In addition to David's continuing leadership, which eventually led to his being chosen as king, two of Israel's finest kings actually began their reigns as boys:

> Joash was seven years old when he became King, and he reigned forty years. His mother's name was Zibiah; she was from Beersheba. Joash did what was right in the eyes of the Lord all the years of Jehoida the priest" (II Chron 24:1-2).

Of all the many kings listed, there were few who were credited with doing what was right in the eyes of the Lord.

Most of them abandoned God's purposes and sought to carry out their own self-serving agenda. There was, however, another boy king:

> Josiah was eight years old when he became the king, and he reigned in Jerusalem thirty-one years. He did what was right in the eyes of the Lord and walked in the ways of his father David, not turning aside to the right or to the left. In the eighth year of his reign, while he was still young, he began to seek the God of his father David. In his twelfth year he began to purge Judah and Jerusalem of high places, Asherah poles, carved idols and cast images (II Chron 34:1-3).

The account goes on to catalogue an impressive number of accomplishments of this young king, including the restoration of the temple, the rediscovery of the Book of the Law and the leading of the people of that nation in the renewal of their covenant with the Lord (II Chron 34:4-33). Again, it took a youth to lead the people of God, who had strayed from their commitment to Him.

While numerous other examples could be cited, it is sufficient to close our Old Testament survey with a reminder of the leadership of Daniel and his three young friends, Hananiah, Mishael and Azariah. Though taken captive by the Babylonians, these young men held fast to their convictions and dared to take their stand (Dan 1:3-21). Even when faced with the fates of a fiery furnace and a den of lions, they refused to renounce their faith or to alter their practice of it. As a result of their firm stands, both Nebuchadnezzar, King of Babylon, and Darius, King of the Persians were led to praise their God and to promote them to leadership (Dan 3:8-30; 6:15-28). The leadership example of these young men has served as an inspiration to both the youth and the people of God of all ages.

The Church and the Home

Throughout the Old Testament we find an emphasis placed upon the importance of the home also, and the responsibility of parents to rear children with a knowledge and a respect for the commandments of God. Deuteronomy 6:7 says, "Impress them on your children. Talk about them when you sit at home and when you walk along the road, when you lie down and when you get up." Proverbs 22:6 says, "Train up a child in the way he should go, and when he is old he will not turn from it."

In the New Testament we have already noted several passages which deal with parental responsibilities concerning their children. Ephesians 6:4 says, "Fathers, do not exasperate your children; instead, bring them up in the training and instruction of the Lord." Colossians 3:21 says, "Fathers, do not embitter your children, or they will become discouraged." I Timothy 3:4-5, 12 requires both prospective elders and deacons to manage well their homes and families. Paul comments to Timothy, "I have been reminded of your sincere faith, which first lived in your grandmother Lois and in your mother Eunice and, I am persuaded, now lives in you also" (II Tim 1:5). Again in II Timothy 3:14-15 he writes:

> But as for you, continue in what you have learned and have become convinced of, because you know those from whom you learned it, and how from infancy you have known the holy Scriptures, which are able to make you wise for salvation through faith in Christ Jesus."

Timothy grew up in the city of Lystra, according to Acts 16:1-2. His mother and grandmother were Jewish believers, while his father was a Greek, and was evidently not a believer.

In spite of having a father who did not contribute to his spiritual upbringing, Timothy was obviously the successful product of the faith and teaching of his mother and grandmother, who took their responsibilities seriously. When Paul arrived at Lystra, he found a young man of whom all the leaders spoke highly. Upon their recommendations, Paul selected Timothy to serve with him in a special kind of educational and intern experience which would equip him for ministry as a pastor and an evangelist (Acts 16:1-5).

From the earliest days of the church we see the important roles that Christian homes played in the ministry of the church. Acts 2:46-47 testifies concerning the first Christians:

> "Every day they continued to meet together in the temple courts. They broke bread in their homes and ate together with glad and sincere hearts, praising God and enjoying the favor of all the people. And the Lord added to their number daily those who were being saved."

The homes of the Christians were a place for gathering, for sharing and for praising God. It was considered to be the normal thing in the first church to make one's home available for ministry, however it might be needed, and to involve the family in welcoming and ministering to others of the church family.

Lydia felt it would be a privilege to have her home used to begin the church at Philippi (Acts 16:15). Both Acts 18:26 and Romans 16:5 speak of the uses which Priscilla and Aquila made of their homes. In the first instance, the couple used their home in Corinth to accommodate a home Bible study, teaching Apollos more completely the way of the Lord. In the second reference, they have a church meeting in their home in Rome. Far earlier than these instances,

Jesus taught a little man by the name of Zacchaeus that salvation could come to a house when its hospitality is offered to the Lord (Luke 19:9). In fact, the Apostle Paul makes the practice of hospitality a requirement for anyone who would be selected to lead the church as an elder.

The use of the home as a part of the ministry of the church has a profound impact upon the youth who are growing up in that home. They witness their parents actually modelling before them the practice of offering their homes for the Lord's use, and they as youth have the opportunity to share in that offering as they help to get everything ready. The privilege of being able to host a visiting missionary, speaker or part of a travelling music team is a special treat for youth in the home. Parents often overlook this. At a Thanksgiving service in which church family members were encouraged to express something for which they were most thankful during the past year, one young man surprised his parents and the church by declaring that the experience which had meant the most to him that year had been sharing his bedroom and home with a visiting missionary. There is much to be learned and treasured for a lifetime from such experiences. Both parents and children can grow through the exercise of Christian hospitality. Failure to use the home in this way both robs youth of their opportunity to learn and share, and teaches a very clear negative lesson about excluding their home from the lordship of Christ.

It is important to acknowledge that significant changes have occurred in the structure and the function of the family, many of them due to industrialization. Benson and Wolfe note that the modern church has often been confused about how to approach anything except the "ideal family . . . a home-based mother, a working father and a nice batch of homebred children." While they comment that this is a fine arrangement, "it is no longer the pattern in the United States. Only 15 percent of the households in America now are patterned like the nuclear family. Whether this is good or bad is not really the point."[1] With the prevalence of divorce, a growing number of youth are living with a single parent, and perhaps even with siblings from another family. Those who do live with both natural parents now generally have both parents working. Life together as a family has taken on vastly different dimensions.

In spite of a great deal of sermonizing and wishful thinking about restoring the "ideal family," as it has been defined and generally perceived, the church must be willing to come to grips with reality and to face the family as it exists today. The church must learn to help it, to strengthen it and to discover new ways to minister in and through the home. The acknowledgment of changes in the family structure does not excuse the modern home from being expected to implement the concepts of ministry taught in the New Testament. The fact of the matter is that few—if any—of the homes mentioned in the New Testament met these qualifications of being "ideal families." Yet, the Lord was able to work in and through them.

Gerald Tiffin discusses some of the changes which have taken place and identifies some of the ways in which industrialization impacts family and parent-child relationships in the home:

> The family no longer worked together, resulting in many hours spend apart from each other. . . . Industrialization

---

1. Dennis C. Benson and Bill Wolfe, *The Basic Encyclopedia For Youth Ministry* (Loveland: Group Books, 1981), p. 138.

> often forced youth to spend excessive idle time at home—usually until marriage. This extended time, coupled with frustration regarding work and economic security, tended to heighten generational distance and conflict because intimate daily interactions with parents led to arguments and conflict over freedom, money and leisure—issues that normally don't emerge in rural societies—as roles and life situations developed more naturally and earlier in the life cycle. The time of study and rhythmic movement from childhood to adulthood thus ended with the coming of industrial society.[2]

Tiffin also points out that industrialization breeds adolescence through its delay in granting adult status. Jobs become more specialized and require more education and maturity. Consequently, youth are often "put on hold" for a period of several years, until they are old enough, or educationally prepared enough, to enter the job market. With this, then, has come the creation of many kinds of youth sub-cultures, which help to meet some of the needs youth feel at various stages. These sub-cultures provide a way of gaining acceptance, status, and recognition. Obviously, many of these groups thus formed will have some very negative and destructive effects on both the youth and upon society when they have no Christian orientation. The violence of inner city gangs, the prevalence of drug and alcohol abuse among youth of all ages, increasing sexual promiscuity and peer pressures to conform to other anti-Christian codes of conduct and dress in order to gain acceptance are a few of the negative effects we would cite. Tiffin comments:

> Christian youth can live as part of loving, sympathetic Christian families and still experience generational conflict,

2. Gerald C. Tiffin, "Youth Culture Today: Backgrounds and Prospects," *Ministering to Youth*, David Roadcup, ed., (Cincinnati: Standard Publishing, 1980), p. 16.

> identity crisis, and role confusion. This occurs because Christian youth are not immune to environmental and peer influence. Christian leaders must learn that delayed adulthood, generational conflict, identity formation problems, and role confusion do not invalidate faith. Such problems are typical developmental problems common to all youth.[3]

Many opportunities in life are lost because they are viewed only as problems. It is a temptation to become discouraged and to give up in the face of that which may seem to many to be chaos in the family. There is, however, a tremendous challenge here before the church to use its resources to work with both parents and youth to reclaim the home for the Lord, and to develop it as a center for ministry. Exciting things can happen, for example, when a family of apartment dwellers view their location as an opportunity to reach their complex from the inside with a Bible study and fellowship ministry. Neighborhood cell groups and backyard Bible clubs are succeeding in reaching many other people who are reluctant to "go to church." The changes in the family structure, as we have said, do not in any way negate the principle of using the home for ministry. They simply challenge the church to change and to become more innovative in adapting its ministry to new circumstances.

Obviously, part of the church's ministry needs to be directed to the youth in helping them to understand themselves and their relationship to God's will for their lives. The church ought to be concerned about helping them to work successfully through their stages of development toward adulthood and Christian maturity. The church certainly has the resources and potential to do this and more. We will discuss the goals of youth ministry a little further along.

3. Tiffin, p. 34.

Before leaving the ministry of the home, though, it is important to note that parents also need some help from the church; and the church and the home need to be regarded as a team ministry, rather than exclusive endeavors on separate tracks. John Miller suggests the church can help by organizing such things as parents' support teams, beginning a parents' newsletter, offering parents' workshops, planning parent/teen socials and retreats, scheduling mother/daughter, mother/son, father/son and father/daughter banquets and other events, organizing parents' fellowships, visiting parents in their homes, establishing an open-door policy with parents and publicly acknowledging parents' involvement.[4] These are excellent suggestions. The last thing any church should attempt to do is to become a substitute for the function of parents or the ministry of the home.

Youth Ministry in the Church

This brings us rather naturally to our next point. What should be the goal of the youth ministry of the church? In far too many cases, youth ministry amounts to a frenzied, activity-centered program designed to involve and entertain youth in record numbers. Fantastic budgets are required to maintain these non-stop extravaganzas, which are designed to compete with television, school activities, rock concerts, and especially with the spectacular menu being offered by the competitor church down the street. Success is largely judged by which program out-draws the other, and by who is able to maintain the greatest numbers. Youth ministers have become expert promoters and entertainers, but where

4. John Miller, "The Parent Factor," *Working with Youth*, Ray Willey, ed., (Wheaton: Victor Books, 1982), pp. 48-49.

is the ministry? In what ways are the real needs of youth being met by these churches?

The New Testament picture of the church, as found in Ephesians 4 and I Corinthians 12, is that of a functioning body, with each part being expected to have some function, to be growing, and to be involved in some way in the total ministry of the body, the church. The problem with many youth ministries is the basic conception and exclusive expectation that we adults are to do something for the kids. In other words, we have fallen into the performer-spectator trap again, assuming that children and youth have to be ministered to, and are incapable of accomplishing any ministry themselves at their age. If we expect that they should not minister, they will not. They will sit back and let the adults perform. Watch out, though! They will become critics of those performances and will demand more and more of the spectacular to hold their attention and to maintain their allegiance. A bigger and better show will be required every week, month and year to keep the crowd.

This kind of program may develop into a successful competitor to the entertainment industry, and it may help to keep youth off the streets and away from some of the negative influences they face in our society; but it is not the kind of youth ministry found in the New Testament. It ignores most of the principles and objectives described there. Dennis Miller contends that "the primary objective of youth ministry is to develop discipled students—students brought to maturity in Jesus Christ." We are reminded that this is really the objective of the church in reaching and ministering to people of every age. This, he says, can be accomplished with youth by having youth workers who model spiritual truth, who lead as co-learners, who are involved in aggressive evangelism and who are committed to a multiplication ministry (with one student being trained to reach another).[5] This is indeed part of the New Testament concept of youth leadership. As in the case of adults, youth need to be both evangelized and to be trained to become evangelists in turn. Youth who have been reached for Christ can, and should, be expected to reach other youth. They will be more effective, in fact, in reaching their peers than will adult Christians. Miller is right, also, in pointing out that the spoken concepts will not be accepted by the youth, however well they are delivered, unless those youth see them being modelled by their adult leaders. They can handle the fact that these adults will not be perfect, but they expect them to be honest, open and growing with them into Christlikeness and spiritual maturity. They do not expect or really want their adult leaders to do everything for them, but they require them to lead the way as spiritual guides.

Certainly this represents a major part of the New Testament picture, but not all of it. Dick Alexander says concerning the goal of youth ministry:

> To say the goal of the church is evangelism is roughly akin to saying the mark of good parenting is having babies. The task is not merely to proliferate newborns who will be left un-nourished, but to develop growing, dynamic, maturing youth who share Christ from the fullness of their lives. If evangelism is the natural, inevitable overflow of a Christ-filled life, could it be that part of the reason for the current lack of evangelism in many circles is that we're asking the starving to give bread? Conversion is a step on the road to Christlikeness, but only one of many.[6]

5. Dennis Miller, "A Philosophy of Youth Ministry," *Working with Youth*, Ray Willey, ed. (Wheaton: Victor Books, 1982), pp. 12-14.

6. Dick Alexander, "The Goal of Youth Ministry," *Ministering to Youth*, David Roadcup, ed. (Cincinnati: Standard Publishing, 1980), pp. 44-45.

"Asking the starving to give bread" may be an apt description of many youth programs. A heavy emphasis is placed upon accepting Jesus as Savior and Lord; and much time and effort is spent in training and encouraging youth to go out and recruit their peers for Jesus. On the other hand, minimal attention is given to the development of a balanced diet which will adequately feed the developing young Christians, or to any kind of spiritual exercise which will help them to flex their muscles and to develop any expertise in ministering to others as a part of the body. Both food and exercise are required by every part of the body. Any portion which is denied one or the other, or both, will begin to wither and soon be rendered useless.

Les Christie speaks to this point when he describes the objectives of his ministry to youth:

> My ultimate goal as a youth minister is to bring youth to maturity in Christ; to prepare, disciple, and train them to serve God. The best way to motivate youth to serve in the local congregation is to give them real responsibility when they are young. This is not a new idea. The Bible says, "It is good for a man that he should bear the yoke in his youth" (Lam 3:27). Young people must learn to handle burdens and responsibilities.[7]

YOUTH ARE CAPABLE OF MINISTRY! They need to be involved in the exercise of ministry if they are to grow. They will not learn to minister, however, in an adult-centered program which is designed to entertain them or to simply minister to them. Certainly it is a lot easier to design and conduct a youth program which consists of a designated

---

7. Les Christie, "Developing Leadership In Youth," *Ministering to Youth*, David Roadcup, ed. (Cincinnati: Standard Publishing, 1980), p. 131.

youth meeting time, with an adult leader who stands up and gives a prepared lesson, and a monthly social event. Most churches do well to get even this far with a youth program for each age division. This is not enough! It is even easier to produce and perpetuate the super-spectacular extravaganza-type program for youth than it is to develop a responsible, fruitful, New Testament-style ministry with youth. Youth who grow up under these other types of youth ministry, however, will either leave the church as soon as they are able to decide for themselves, or they will remain to be the next generation of spectators in the church pews.

Even small children can be taught to serve the Lord and to use their talents in ministry. There are no more natural or effective areas for children and youth to minister than through music and drama. Whose heart and attention is not captured by the sight and sound of youthful musicians or dramatists who have been challenged to serve the Lord with their abilities, and who have diligently worked to prepare their service as an offering to God and a ministry to others? Any church failing to recognize the potential for both ministry by youth and for its outreach into our society to minister to family and friends is blind to one of the greatest opportunities God has given the church! Like most opportunities, however, it appears as a tremendous amount of work and requires the investment of the lives of a number of people, not to mention some expense.

Every church should develop a graded choir program and an instrumental music program which are designed, not simply to teach music or to make musicians, but to provide an opportunity for youth to minister. Drama is also an exceptionally effective vehicle for communicating a message and for giving youth another avenue for ministry. Rather than emphasizing the production of performances, all youth choirs, instrumentalists, ensembles and dramatists need to be taught and continually encouraged to view their musical or dramatic offerings as a valuable part of their ministry. To emphasize this point and to expand the scope of their ministry, they need to be given opportunities to minister outside the church building, as well as inside. Their ministries can be carried to shut-ins, nursing homes, shopping centers, schools and wherever God opens the doors for them to serve. Once there is a commitment and a willingness to go, both the youth and their leaders will be amazed at the doors God will open!

The Christian Minstrels, a youth music ministry begun with six high school youth in one church, grew and lasted for twelve years, eventually involving hundreds of young singers and instrumentalists. Through this ministry these youth helped to begin new churches, provided music for revivals and programs at home and in other churches, ministered to nursing homes and hospitals, sang for youth rallies and conventions, did benefit concerts for disaster victims, and travelled extensively in Mexico, assisting missionaries with their bi-lingual music ministry. Auditoriums, community concert halls and churches in Mexico would be packed with standing room only to hear this group, and even Communist-dominated universities opened their doors to welcome them on campus. Orphanages thrilled to hear their programs, and missionaries utilized the community exposure and penetration into the universities to distribute Bibles and literature, to attract prospects for their churches and to begin Bible study groups on the university campuses. One missionary testified to the Minstrels' home church "These young people you have sent can do more in opening doors with one evening's program than I can do in ten years of knocking on doors." The Christian Minstrels committed hundreds of hours to rehearsal and the learning of music in two languages, along with setting aside two weeks out of each summer for travel and ministry. In the twelve years of their existence, the group embarked on eight concert tours in Mexico. Twice they were featured at the National Christian Youth Convention of Mexico. Their appearances there served as a catalyst to encourage the development of similar musical ministries among the youth of the Mexican churches.

For fifteen years high school and college youth from California and Arizona participated in Youth Service Trips to Mexico. Organized to give youth the opportunity to both view missions first-hand and to give them the chance to personally minister through work projects, hundreds of youth eventually travelled in groups of 25-50 to Rancho de los Ninos, an orphanage in Baja California, Mexico, to offer their time, abilities and labor. They painted buildings, repaired and replaced roofs, worked on plumbing, built outhouses, put up fences, dug a well, dug ditches and laid a water line, dug garbage pits, set power poles and strung wire, and participated in countless other essential and meaningful projects at the orphanage. The relationships which developed between these youth and those Mexican orphans were something to see! In an outdoor chapel service during a work break on each trip the youth and their leaders were reminded from God's Word that their travel and labors constituted real worship. They came to find a personal meaning in the words of James 1:26-27. In every case, they returned home appreciating more what they had, and feeling good about themselves and the service they had rendered.

They had exercised their faith, and they had grown through ministry.

Many other instances could be cited of youth who have been challenged to develop and use their talents in ministry and Christian leadership. One church has developed a vital ministry through Christian athletics. One girl found a very needed ministry when she was taken by her youth minister to a nursing home and was introduced to an elderly lady whose arthritic hands no longer permitted her to communicate with her family or friends. The girl began to go each week on her own to take dictation and to write the letters for that woman which renewed her relationships with family and friends. What a meaningful personal ministry! Many such projects on behalf of the elderly and the incapacitated can be undertaken by youth, either as individuals or as groups.

Youth can minister, but they must be challenged. The biggest problem is that most churches fail to believe in their youth or in their potential for ministry, and they offer no challenges to them. The fact is that youth will respond to difficult challenges more readily than most adults. They tend to have more faith and optimism. They are more ready to give something new a try. They offer far fewer excuses as to why a ministry cannot succeed. They are far less worried about taking risks and about possible dangers or liability problems which may be encountered. Consequently, they are able to maintain a greater sense of purpose. If the Lord wants it done and has opened the door, let's get on with it! They trust *Him* to deal with the problems if they are faithfully doing their part. Youth are also generally more flexible and adjust to necessary changes more easily than do adults. There are simply many areas of ministry where youth can do a better job than adults, and others where they, in fact, have to lead adults with their faith and enthusiasm.

Solomon said to his son, "Remember your Creator in the days of your youth, before the days of trouble come and the years approach when you will say, I find no pleasure in them'" (Eccl 12:1). That wise old king knew whereof he spoke! In the language of youth ministry it says, "We use them, or we lose them!" God never intended youth to sit on the sidelines and to watch ministry being performed for them, just soaking it up like soggy, inert sponges. He never intended that they should be forced to wait until they reached adulthood before they could participate. It was His design for the church that youth should be vital functioning parts of the ministering body—members of the priesthood of all believers (I Peter 2:5, 9).

Qualifications for Ministry

When we speak of youth ministry, it must then be recognized that it is essential to consider both the adult leadership for that ministry and the youth who serve as a part of it as well. We will examine the qualifications for adults who would lead the youth of the church a little later. First, let us take a look at the youth themselves.

We have established the fact that youth were intended by God to be ministering parts of the body, and that they are capable of providing valuable leadership for the church. The New Testament does, however, make some requirements of youth who would lead in the church. The Apostle Paul wrote to the youthful Timothy,

> Command and teach these things. Don't let anyone look down on you because you are young, but set an example for

the believers in speech, in life, in love, in faith, and in purity. Until I come, devote yourself to the public reading of Scripture, to preaching and teaching. Do not neglect your gift, which was given you through a prophetic message when the body of elders laid their hands on you" (I Tim 4:11-14).

One thing is very clear from what Paul says: youthfulness itself should not disqualify one from ministry and leadership in the church. On the other hand, neither does it automatically qualify one to minister or lead, any more than does the chronological age of an adult. Secondly, Paul points out that youth—like adults—must exhibit the kind of Christian lifestyle which would enable them to lead through their example. Even as Paul addresses those who would lead as elders and deacons in the church in I Timothy 3:1-13, citing areas of their lives which should be exemplary, so Paul makes similar requirements in this passage for youth who would lead in ministry in the church. Youth are to provide for the church an example in what they say, how they conduct themselves, in demonstrating genuine Christian love, in exercising faith and in keeping their lives morally straight. Certainly one who demonstrates this kind of commitment to the Lordship of Christ in his life is fit to lead in the church, even though he be a youth.

It has been argued that Timothy was perhaps 35-40 years of age when Paul sent this letter to him, since Jews regarded a man as a youth until he had reached the age of forty.[8] The fact that this was the Jewish viewpoint about designating youthfulness does not necessarily force us, however, to assume that Timothy was therefore pushing forty. At any

8. R. C. H. Lenski, *The Interpretation of St. Paul's Epistles to the Colossians, to the Thessalonians, to Timothy, to Titus and to Philemon* (Columbus: The Wartburg Press, 1946), p. 640.

rate, the point is irrelevant; for Paul's admonition could apply to youth of any age.

In Timothy's particular case, he was to lead through the public reading of Scripture, in preaching and in teaching. Furthermore, he was also admonished to utilize the special gift he had received from God when the elders had set him apart for ministry. What was this gift? Lenski contends:

> Timothy's charisma was his ability to understand the true gospel teaching over against spurious and false teachings. He had the gift of prophecy (Rom 12:6; I Cor 12:10) and of discerning spirits (I Cor 12:10), i.e., seeing through all false teaching. He could properly transmit the true Word of God, could also teach and expound it, and could detect what deviated from it.[9]

There is a good probability that Lenski is correct, although the text itself does not specify what that gift was. The application of this for all youth is that they are to serve in whatever way God has gifted them, and in any situation which affords them the opportunity.

Out of every group of Christian youth should be developed a core group of leaders—that group described by Les Christie as "the inner circle into whose lives we as youth ministers will flow." He goes on to say, "I am convinced . . . that kids want tasks that will stretch them (the tougher the better) and place real responsibility on them to fail or succeed." He describes this inner core of specially selected leaders as "servant leaders" whose "main task is to flow into the lives of the fringe kids as well as the other leaders."[10]

Obviously, an adult-centered youth program which puts on its spectaculars and weekly performances will have little

9. Lenski, p. 644.
10. Christie, pp. 132-133.

time or use for selecting and developing such an inner core of leaders from among the youth. A youth ministry which has New Testament goals and style, however, will seek to develop leadership from within every group. Some will call them officers (unfortunately), but this sets up all kinds of negative connotations from our culture and difficulties in understanding Christain leadership. The Lord neither ordained officers for youth nor adults in the church. He intended to be, as we have seen, its only Officer. Some churches call them discipleship group leaders, or simply group leaders. In any case, special training and expectations are given to this core group in preparation for their ministries as leaders.

To each leader is assigned a group of his peers, along with an adult coach or sponsor. Together the youthful leader and the coach minister to their "flock" and seek to strengthen and multiply it. Together as a team the youth leaders, adult coaches and youth minister develop goals, plans, programs and projects for the total group. Since they "own the agenda," these youth leaders have no qualms about selling it to their followers.

How are such core leaders to be selected? Some youth ministers and coaches simply pick them from the group, based upon their observed leadership potential and spiritual growth. Christie, on the other hand, has his groups elect their own leaders—with some limitations. He does not permit non-Christians to vote. He distributes an alphabetical-order list of all of the members of the group and instructs each voter to circle the nominees he thinks God would want to have leading the group. He gives them Scriptures which help them understand the characteristics required of Christian leaders. Then he has the ballots tabulated by the youth minister and the adult sponsors, who are given veto power if they find someone has been chosen who is not qualified to serve. After that, before the youth are notified of their selection, the youth minister calls the parents to explain the position their youth will hold and what it will require, seeking the parents' approval. If they approve, then the youth are notified and begin their preparations for service.[11] If an election is to be held, this plan certainly does much to teach youth about the selection of youth and church leadership!

Now what kind of adults should be selected to work with youth? Phil Kennemer says they ought to be F.A.T.—"faithful, available and teachable."[12] Obviously they should be people of faith and compassion for youth. In addition, they must have a sufficient degree of Christian maturity to be able to model the Christian lifestyle, as well as to teach its principles. The warnings of Jesus in such passages as Matthew 18:6-10 are a sobering reminder of the tremendous responsibility one assumes when he agrees to lead youth for Christ.

Many youth leaders are convinced that a good canned curriculum is the key to successful youth ministry, if not the answer to its every problem. Publishing companies peddle a lot of paper to those who buy this concept. Don Hinkle, however, accurately observes, "The most important factor in youth work . . . is who you are as a person. That takes precedence over any method or program. You soon discover you cannot build a program without committed people."[13] Amen!!

---

11. Christie, pp. 132-133.

12. Phil D. Kennemer, "Recruiting Youth Sponsors," *Working With Youth*, Ray Willey, ed. (Wheaton: Victor Books, 1982), p. 27.

13. Don Hinkle, "The Person of the Youth Minister," *Ministering to Youth*, David Roadcup, ed. (Cincinnati: Standard Publishing, 1980), p. 38.

People are indeed the key to successful youth ministry—committed Christians who are willing to open and expend their lives in order to lead youth to discover Christ and to grow through Him into spiritual maturity and fruitful ministry. It must be added that these people who are selected to lead must be willing to serve as coaches. They must believe in the youth enough to allow them, and to help them, play the game. Star performers among the adult coaches are not needed! They will only rob the youth of their opportunities to minister and to grow.

Those who would serve as youth ministers also need to see their role as that of equipping and administering these adult coaches, along with the core youth leaders. Here again, star performers are not needed! Neither can the church afford to call a youth minister as a sponsor for a single group. In far too many cases, this is exactly what happens. The youth minister prefers a particular age group—usually the senior high—for whom he becomes the adult sponsor. This role so consumes his time and energies that the rest of the youth program either limps along on its own or collapses from neglect. Youth ministers—like all paid ministers—can justify their existence ONLY if they become equippers and coordinators of others in the leadership of the total youth ministry. To do less is to cheat the church and to rob its members of their opportunity to be equipped and to successfully serve as leaders in the youth ministry of the church. Again we would note: no church can afford enough paid performers to do its ministry for it.

Both the youth minister and the adult youth coaches must possess an enthusiasm for youth work and a belief in the youth themselves. Their abiding confidence in the value and potential of each youth, along with their faith in the power of God to change and empower their lives, are absolutely crucial to the success of their ministry with youth. Their positive reinforcement and constant encouragement are desperately needed by each young person. The fact that their leaders love them, respect them and believe in them can make all the difference in the world—and in eternity—for them.

Finally, the personal, growing relationship with God of each person involved in youth leadership is vitally important. Don't try to kid the kids! They can spot a phony a mile away. They will not go where their leaders are unwilling to personally lead them by their example. As a youth coach, your group will walk in your footsteps; and, like it or not, they will soon become the extension of your own shadow. This is an inescapable fact of youth leadership.

Functions of Youth Ministry

We spoke earlier of the changes which had come from industrialization, and about their impact upon youth and families. Rather than viewing those consequences as insurmountable problems facing our society, the church needs to recognize the tremendous opportunity God has given it to meet real needs with a vital youth ministry. An age-graded program, which is geared to the needs of each group, can help provide the peer group acceptance, the essential sense of identity and the required opportunities for achievement. Most of the youth today do not have to work. They have time. While that can be a tremendous problem if the youth fall in with the wrong crowd, it is a golden opportunity for the church to utilize that time to minister to them and their families.

Every youth has some basic needs, regardless of his age. They include:

1. *The need for security:* to feel wanted, to be loved and to belong to something bigger than himself.
2. *The need for recognition:* to be recognized as an individual with a name, and identity and personal worth.
3. *The need for new experience:* to be able to do and to think the new and the untried, which are essential to maturing and growth.
4. *The need for achievement:* to invest himself in something of value in which he can be a winner and can establish a sense of self-worth.
5. *The need for Jesus as Lord and Savior:* to experience His forgiveness and to commit his life to the control of Christ.
6. *The need to know the will of God:* to be able to understand God's purposes for human existence, and particularly their application to his life.
7. *The need to be involved in ministry:* to develop and to utilize his own God-given abilities to serve the Lord and to minister to others.

Every youth ministry ought to be committed to meeting these needs. There are, of course, other specific needs experienced by each age group. They also should be recognized and met with an effective ministry. These basic needs, however, must be dealt with at every level.

In order to successfully accomplish this goal, a youth ministry requires the following three elements:

1. *Bible Study:* where the Bible's message and meaning can be understood and applied as the foundation for building lives. It is a sin to bore youth with the gospel!! Inadequate preparation and second-rate presentations

are inexcusable. If youth are to be captured by its message, the Bible must be presented in exciting and creative ways. Nothing less than our best effort is acceptable to God, for we have the opportunity to reach and develop youth for Christ. Neither we nor anyone else may get another chance to reach them if we turn them off.

2. *Social Functions:* where youth can learn that Christians can and do have fun together, and where they can find acceptance and build friendships. Much can be accomplished to meet real and important needs through group social activities. They do not have to turn into Bible studies to have a legitimate function as a part of the youth ministry.
3. *Ministry Projects:* where youth are challenged and given opportunities to use their time and talents in actual ministry to others. Service projects of many kinds can be designed for both groups and individuals. In addition, ministry groups in music, drama, puppets and other such on-going ministries can provide continuing opportunities to develop talents and to serve.

These three basic elements are each essential to balance any youth program. The omission of any one of them cripples a youth ministry. They are foundational for all else that may be done.

In addition to the church and home-based programs, youth ministries also need to include the valuable resources of retreats and Christian camping. In these settings, away from the church, home and other involvements, perhaps more can be accomplished in an effective discipling ministry with youth than at any other time or through any other method. In these extended experiences together leaders can be particularly effective in modelling the Christian lifestyle and in engaging the youth in actually experiencing that lifestyle in a controlled setting for several days or more at a time. In addition, concentrated teaching can be done with a minimum of distraction and time pressures. Relations can be built between youth and with the leaders which are sometimes impossible to build at home or at church.

The effects of retreats and Christian camping experiences can be dramatic. It is often in these settings that youth develop their closest personal relationships with God and make the most important decisions of their lives. It is important to caution, however, about the great temptation to become manipulative with youth in these settings. Manipulation should be avoided at all costs! The Holy Spirit is still capable of convicting through the inspired Word without our devices (John 16:7-11). The God who took the risk of giving each of us a free will has not licensed youth leaders to over-ride that freedom of choice by manipulating youth to get desired results. Their decisions must remain their own decisions, or they will not stick with them. Youth need to be exposed to God's Word in the most attractive ways, and they must be given opportunities to understand, to consider and to respond to God's will for their lives. They need to be encouraged; but they must make their own decisions, rather than our making them for them.

In Summary

The body of Christ has been designed to grow up in its entirety into Christlikeness and to function in ministry. Youth are not excluded from either the need to spiritually grow or to be involved in ministry. Ample examples exist in both the Old and the New Testaments of youth who also served in leadership among God's people.

God also intended for the home to be a seat of ministry and to be a partner with the church in its youth ministry.

While significant changes have taken place in the family structure since industrialization, these changes have not altered God's expectations for its functions or given the church the responsibility for becoming its substitute.

The goal of youth ministry should be to develop disciples for Christ and to involve them in both evangelism and ministry. Youth of all ages are capable of successful and effective ministry and should be so challenged and given opportunities to minister.

Youth are expected by God to minister and to lead, but He has set qualifications for their leadership, similar to the qualifications He has set for other church leaders. A leadership core needs to be developed in each youth group, recognizing these standards. Adult youth coaches should be recruited and trained to work with these core leaders. Youth ministers must essentially be equippers and coordinators of these core leaders and adult coaches, rather than star performers.

Youth ministry should be designed to meet the basic needs which all youth have for security, recognition, new experiences, achievement, accepting Jesus as Savior and Lord, knowing the will of God and being involved in ministry. In order to accomplish this, Bible study, social functions and ministry projects are the foundational elements required in every youth ministry. Retreats and Christian camping experiences can help to accomplish these functions.

10

AUTONOMY OR FELLOWSHIP?

The Struggle to Be Free

We traced in a brief fashion in chapter 1 the evolution of the church hierarchy and again made reference to that progression in our discussion of the eldership. When one begins with the premise that the church has been given offices and officers, and then concludes that authority is vested in those offices, a hierarchy of some sort is the inevitable consequence. In some cases that hierarchy will be limited to the local church. In most cases, however, it has developed into a superstructure of authority over a number of churches.

When such authority is claimed and granted, it also seems inevitable that it will eventually be corrupted and abused. We have cited numerous incidences of this in the development of the Roman Catholic hierarchy, and we also pointed out examples of this tendency in the Free Church Movement as well. When the oppressed gain power and authority over others, they in turn become the oppressors. The cycle has been repeated over and again in church history. Harrold McFarland writes:

> It is the struggle to be free. The human desire to build organizations is always a threat to the simple church of the New Testament. Nothing in the Scriptures indicates that additional organization above and beyond the local church is necessary. Yet men who chafe at the neglect and indifference, and lack of concern of individuals and local churches, still seek by any means to get the work done. In this, they often forget that God's ways are not men's ways and that He said, "not by might or by power, but by my Spirit" (Zech 4:6).[1]

That struggle to be free of oppressive, and often persecuting, superstructures of church officers and councils has prompted each new development in the Free Church Movement, including the Restoration Movement in America. Enos Dowling says, "In breaking away from the established ecclesiastical order of their day, the early leaders in the Restoration Movement renounced the jurisdiction and questioned the legitimacy of authoritative religious organizations outside the local congregation."[2] In 1824 Alexander Campbell wrote:

> An individual church or congregation of Christ's disciples is the only ecclesiastical body recognized on earth. . . . Whether such an alliance of priests and the nobles of the

1. Harrold McFarland, *The Struggle to Be Free* (Joliet: Mission Services Press, 1960), p. 10.
2. Enos E. Dowling, *The Restoration Movement* (Cincinnati: The Standard Publishing Company, 1966), p. 73.

> kirk be called a session, a presbytery, a synod, a general assembly, a convention, a conference, an association, or an annual meeting, its tendency and result are the same. Whenever and wherever such a meeting either legislates, decrees, rules, directs or controls, or assumes the character of a representative body in religious concerns, it essentially becomes "the man of sin and the son of perdition. . . ."
>
> There is not the least intimation in any part of the New Testament of a representative government. Nothing is said about a number of church lords being selected as an ecclesiastical council over a number of individual churches. When the inspired writers speak of a single assembly of a number of churches, or the churches of a province or district, they do not call them a church, but churches.[3]

This noted leader of the Restoration Movement makes several significant points. First of all, there is nothing wrong with an association of Christians or churches called together for a purpose, unless they yield to the tendency and temptation to regard themselves as a representative body with the authority to legislate for other Christians or for the churches. Herein lies the problem. As long as they have gathered for mutual edification from the Word of God, for cooperation in ministry or for strengthening the fellowship of the saints, there is not any conflict with the Word of God, and the results will be positive.

Secondly, Campbell's point about the nature of the church is well-taken. While the term "church" is used on a number of occasions to describe the church universal, as we have seen earlier, the only other New Testament usage of the term is applied to the local assembly of believers in a given

---

3. Alexander Campbell, "Essays on Ecclesiastical Characters, Councils, Creeds and Sects, No. III," *The Christian Baptist*, July, 1824, p. 228.

place. Paul's letters, for example, are addressed to the "church" at Corinth, Ephesus, etc., but to the "churches" of the geographical region of Galatia. There is ample evidence of communication and cooperation between the churches in that first century, but there is never any hint of any supra-congregational structure or authority being approved or established, beyond the authority of Jesus and that delegated to His apostles. It should be noted, however, that this does not imply that there was no supra-congregational leadership. That subject will be addressed in the next chapter. We are discussing here an authoritarian structure over the church. In an 1898 editorial Isaac Errett wrote:

> The autonomy of the church, or its congregational government, throws a certain responsibility upon each member of it; at the same time it brings him into friendly counsels with all other members, thus cultivating within him a due regard for others, side by side with his own manly independence. The apostles assumed at least the potential manliness and brotherliness of Christians and directed their polity accordingly. An aristocratic polity, on the other hand, not only seems foreign to the spirit of Jesus and the teaching of the New Testament, but assumes that church "laymen" are an inferior sort of beings, fit only to be managed and rod-ruled by their superiors.[4]

It is interesting to note the cultural and political overtones present in both Campbell's and Errett's statements. There is, in addition to their Scriptural exegesis, a definite reflection in their writings of the American spirit of independence and the reaction to the aristocracy and European

---

4. Isaac Errett, "Ecclesiastical Democracy," *Christian Standard*, November 12, 1898, p. 1480.

political constraints against which the American Colonies had fought. Beyond these overtones, however, Errett is right on target when he points out that workability of the autonomy of the local church depends upon each member fulfilling his personal responsibilities for involvement in ministry and in selecting capable and qualified leadership for the church. As McFarland called to our attention, it is when the members of the local body become indifferent and irresponsible that the accomplishment of ministry begins to bog down, and leaders begin to seek other devices to make it happen.

Again, the key focus must be directed to the character and the mission of the church. What are its primary purposes and functions in any period of history? The New Testament, as we have seen, does give some definite guidelines. According to the Great Commission given by Jesus in Matthew 28:18-20, upon the basis of His exclusive authority in heaven and on earth, the agenda for the church is that of making disciples for Him, baptizing them in testimony to their acceptance of His Lordship and for the forgiveness of their sins (Acts 2:38), and instructing them in everything He taught us. In short, the church is under a mandate to evangelize the world and to edify the body. For this purpose the church was given leadership "to prepare God's people for works of service, so that the body of Christ may be built up until all reach unity in the faith and in the knowledge of the Son of God and become mature, attaining to the whole measure of the fullness of Christ" (Eph 4:12-13).

There is a definite implication from this passage in Ephesians, along with the one concerning the functioning body in I Corinthians 12:12-31, in addition to the pictures of the church given in Ephesians 2:19-22 and I Peter 2:5, 9, that each church body is sufficiently endowed by God to be able to function as an entity of its own, being capable of growing up into maturity and accomplishing ministry. Many churches spend their time gazing enviously at their sister churches, excusing their own inaction and lack of productivity in ministry and growth on the basis of their insufficiency. "If only we had ______________ we would grow and produce." You can fill in the blank with names, abilities, property, buildings, equipment and a variety of excuses. The problem is that churches fail to realize their resources and their potential, and they forget the power of God to multiply and make effective that which He has given them in order to accomplish His purposes.

God expects each church to develop and to utilize what He has given it. When its leadership and members do that, more will be given. Until then, God is waiting for them to prove their faith and their commitment. This is the point of Matthew 6:33-34; 21:43-44; John 15:1-16 and the Parable of the Talents (Matt 25:14-30). Certainly the small church will not, and cannot, function in the same way or offer the same scope of ministry as a large church. That does not excuse the small church, however, from functioning and producing to the best of its ability. The message is clear: God requires a return on His investment in each church body. He expects them to function and produce, or they will be cut off. Neither wishing nor worrying ever gets the job done. Again, God never does for man that which he can do for himself. When the church begins to do what it is capable of doing—whatever its size—God will bless and multiply that effort.

The Problems of Local Autonomy

As we have noted, Christ has established the agenda for the church. He has endowed it to be able to accomplish this agenda, not one which its leaders or members choose to substitute. When the church adheres to this agenda, God's purposes are accomplished. When its leaders lose sight of this agenda, however, the church can get into trouble and rapidly become side-tracked from the accomplishment of God's goals. One of the most common pitfalls a church can encounter is an obsession with its independence and its assumed rights. In the struggle to be free from oppression and from the dictatorship of any authority above the local church, the pendulum often swings in reaction to the opposite extreme. Thus is born the concept of the total autonomy of the local church.

The first problem with the concept of the local autonomy for the congregation is that it lacks Scriptural support. The words "autonomous" and "autonomy" never appear anywhere in the New Testament. They, like many other concepts relating to church leadership, have been imported from our culture and its politics. They have now been around long enough that most church members and leaders within the Restoration Movement of Christian Churches have come to accept them as being Biblical. They are not. To many, this may again appear to simply be a matter of semantics. We find a concept in the Scripture and then borrow a term from our culture or politics which is similar, and apply it. The problem is that we too often forget that the word is only similar, and that it may carry a lot of connotations which will then color our perspective of the scriptural teachings, and cause us to read in elements which were never intended.

In 1901, for example, R. H. Bolton, applying the concept of local autonomy for the church, cited three principles in Scriptures regarding the New Testament church:

1. The governmental power of each church is vested in the hands of its members, including its officials—the pastor, elders and deacons.
2. A majority of the members of the church have a right to rule (II Cor 2:6).
3. The action of the church is final, and not transferable (Matt 18:15-17).

Based on these premises, he reasoned that each church is: (1) Independent; (2) Competent to select its own officers and to handle its own affairs; (3) Its elders can form a board of elders; (4) It has the right to employ its own pastor; (5) It has the right to ordain men to the ministry; and (6) It has the right to associate and cooperate with what other churches it pleases.[5]

Now regardless of the merits of some of his conclusions, a quick examination of the Scriptures cited in support of Bolton's principles reveal how shaky the foundation really is which he sought to use in undergirding the structure he was building on them. It is difficult to understand how these verses could be construed to either state or imply the principles he presumably derived from them. This provides us with an excellent example, however, of the kind of proof-texting which can occur when we first adopt a thesis, and then go to the Bible in search of supporting texts to legitimize it. Support is claimed through some vague connection, even though verses must be lifted completely from their context,

---

5. R. H. Bolton, "Churches of Christ—Officers and Governments," *Christian Standard*, May 25, 1901, pp. 652-653.

and twisted, strained and stretched to serve our purposes. Needless to say, the rest of the conclusions based upon these dubious premises are nothing more than pure fabrication. Unfortunately, much of the theology relating to the principle, application and extension of the concept of church autonomy rests upon such weak exegesis.

We have discovered that there is at least the strong implication that each congregation is sufficiently endowed by God to be able to grow toward maturity and to accomplish ministry, without requiring any hierarchy above it. Murch contends, "Congregational autonomy makes it possible to transact all essential business of a Christian Church, settle all questions of expediency, choose all necessary officers possessing scriptural qualifications and deposing them if they become disqualified."[6]

It would appear from a study of the practices of the churches noted in *Acts* and from the teaching directed to them in the Epistles, his contention is basically accurate (Rom 14:1—15:7; 16:17-19; I Cor 1:10-17; 12:1-31; II Cor 6:14-17; Gal 1:6-9; 6:1-10; Eph 4:1-16; Phil 4:1-19; Col 2:6-8; I Thess 1:2-10; II Thess 3:14-15; I Tim 3:1-9; Titus 3:9-11; Heb 13:9; I Peter 5:8-9; II Peter 3:17; I John 4:1-6; Jude 17-23; Rev 2:14-16, 20-25). We would, of course, take exception to his unfortunate use of the word "officers" instead of "leaders."

The leadership meeting in Jerusalem recorded in Acts 15, concerning the issue of the terms for Gentile acceptance by the church, has often been cited as a valid precedent for a representative legislative council above the local churches. Those who take such a position are again reading

6. James DeForest Murch, *The Free Church* (n.c.: Restoration Press, 1966), p. 21.

too much into the text. It was a conference of leaders to consider the issue at hand in light of the apostolic testimony. When that testimony had been heard, the issue was already decided. Their only course was to accept it. The church has always been obligated to consider all issues in the light of the teachings of Jesus and the apostolic doctrine, and to regard them as the authoritative rule for faith and practice. Beyond the authority of Jesus and His apostles, no further legislative position of judicial authority was ever delegated or authorized by the New Testament. Murch concludes:

> Two principles are evident here: the New Testament is the only rule of faith and practice to the exclusion of all human creeds, canons, traditions and philosophies; and private judgment or interpretation is the right and duty of all. The Christian is thus freed from all human authority in religion and is bound only by divine authority. It rescues him from clerical interpretation and fully recognizes his personal responsibility to God. Emphasis on the New Testament does not in any way repudiate the validity of the Old Testament as the Word of God, but it makes the New the only law of the Christian Church. It abolishes Jewish rites and ceremonies that were a "shadow of things to come." It retains all the enduring principles of God's moral government which are the same in all ages.[7]

Each church, therefore, is capable of examining the New Testament and applying its message and guidelines in its particular situation. No "official position of the church" needs to be sought from any other authority. Indeed, God recognizes no other authority. It is under the singular authority of Jesus that the church is to function and to grow, including the selection of its leadership.

---

7. Murch, p. 20.

Herein may lie the greatest safeguard built into the New Testament design for the church. With the rise of the hierarchy, as we have seen, the leadership evolved into positions of authority so removed from any control by the local church that these offices and their occupants become "untouchables." They were beyond the reach of any effective measures to hold them accountable to the body or to discipline them if they ignored the authority or the agenda of Christ for His church. The authority they proclaimed to be vested in their offices, either by virtue of apostolic appointment or succession, insulated them from any action which might be taken to correct or remove them. It is true that leadership can become corrupt and unfaithful at any level, but to elevate it to positions created out of reach of the church is both unscriptural and extremely dangerous. The New Testament recognizes no such offices or authority. It maintains the right and responsibility of each church to select and to hold responsible and faithful its leadership. It also requires them to follow that leadership when they are responsible and faithful (I Thess 5:12-14).

This brings us to our second problem with the concept of total local autonomy. What happens when a church fails to select Scripturally qualified leaders or refuses to hold them responsible when they fail to lead? A church may exist for a hundred years or more under a concept of leadership which is foreign to the New Testament. It may continue its existence from year to year, but never really accomplish anything listed on the divine agenda for it. It may acquire a dictatorial, representative or performance style of leadership which prevents growth and defeats ministry. It may even develop a power-hungry leadership which is bent on splitting the church and driving away any other potential leaders in order to protect its exclusive control over the church. Rather than being hypothetical possibilities, examples of these kinds of problems in churches exist all around us today. If the thesis of total autonomy for the local church is maintained, how will these churches ever be changed? That premise is effectively protecting and perpetuating the status quo in each of these churches.

Thirdly, and related to this, is the problem which exists when a church and its leadership have rejected the authority of Christ, His teachings and His agenda for the church revealed in the New Testament. Does the autonomous church have the right to the protection of its total autonomy, and its implied prohibition of any "outside" intervention, when it ceases to be a New Testament Church in its teachings and practice? Again, this is no hypothetical example. Churches have actually been permitted to evolve into totally different organizations operating under their own guidelines and goals, instead of those of the New Testament, while other churches have stood by bound to inaction and non-intervention by their creed of total autonomy for the church. Must we continue to lose churches because we refuse to release our grip on this concept, or has the time come for a more reasoned and New Testament approach?

The fourth problem with the concept of local autonomy is its tendency to isolate a congregation from the larger fellowship of the church universal, and even from sister congregations around it. As each autonomous church concentrates its attentions, energies and resources upon its own kingdom-building, the vision and scope of its ministry is often limited to immediate local goals and to the traditions and methods owned by that church. "We have never done it that way before," is the resistant cry which wards off any changes, however meritorious they may be. In addition, there is a limited concern for the welfare of the brethren in the other churches, and a lack of any sense of responsibility for extending the ministry or resources of the one church to help the others. "Charity begins at home," both members and leaders will object, as they channel everything they can get into finishing the immediate local project. This spirit is certainly foreign to the teaching of the Apostle Paul in II Corinthians 8:1-15! Much re-study of the New Testament needs to be done in this area. Our independent, autonomous, isolated kingdoms are not representative of the New Testament church.

Finally, there is a protectivism which develops as a part of the kingdom building within the autonomous church. The leaders tend to intentionally isolate and insulate their members from other ministries, both of individual churches and cooperative endeavors, for fear that they will draw them or their resources away from their allegiance to the local church. Autonomy becomes a convenient and effective theology to excuse and disguise the obsession by leaders to control, along with their paranoid fear of losing control over the church. Members are literally robbed of fellowship and equipping experiences which could strengthen them and the ministry of their church, due to the arbitrary decisions of ministers, elders and boards to toss in the wastebasket notices of such opportunities, rather than announcing them and encouraging their members to take advantage of them.

A mentality exists among leadership which says, "We cannot schedule or support everything, so we will choose that which will be done, and we will all do it together." Such a concept immediately binds and limits the scope of the church's vision, its growth and its ministry to a tragically small circle. Excluded are all of those whose interests, abilities and concerns do not match those of their leaders. Such a policy effectively guarantees that a church will always remain substantially as it is and as the exact reflection of its current leadership. The church of Christ was intended to be and to accomplish far more than is happening in these tightly-controlled autonomous kingdoms.

The Larger Fellowship

There is indeed a fellowship of believers beyond the local church! Unfortunately, many who are members of churches who preach the doctrine of local autonomy may have no personal acquaintance whatsoever with this larger fellowship. The local leadership so effectively keeps their noses to the grindstone that they never have the opportunity to look up and beyond their immediate context and project to ever catch the vision of the larger fellowship or its potential. What a tragedy this is, and what a perversion of the New Testament church! Many who are brought up in this tradition assume that theirs is the only "pure" practice of New Testament Christianity, and that the fellowship is limited to their small group who have pledged allegiance to the ministry, leadership and goals of their congregation.

One of the greatest tragedies resulting from this perversion of the gospel is the plight of the church member who is transferred from that community of believers to another city or another country. A high percentage of these members are lost to the church. After checking out the groups meeting in the new location, and finding them "different" from the church back home, they decide to stay away from the church, rather than "compromise their beliefs" and to adjust to the differences, which are generally matters of methodology, rather than differences in basic doctrine. The end result is inevitable when any member is cut off from that body. That member dies. Who is responsible for these spiritual deaths? That question may have to be answered in Judgment.

In our examination of the Biblical blueprint in chapter 2, a study of the word *koinonia,* or fellowship, was involved in our gaining an understanding of the essence of the church. It was pointed out that it is primarily a word of relationship. I Corinthians 1:9 speaks of that relationship with God's Son, while II Corinthians 13:13 describes our relationship with the Holy Spirit. Particular attention was paid to the passage found in I John 1:3-7, in which the Apostle employs this word no less than four times in the four verses. It was obviously a vitally important concept to John and to the Holy Spirit who inspired his writing. In fact, this concept was developed as the foundation upon which John was to build the rest of his instructions to the church in that epistle.

John emphasizes that there is no fellowship (or any church) apart from the primary relationship to the Father through His Son Jesus. We have no fellowship with each other—whether it be local or larger—unless that primary relationship with Christ exists. When we have accepted him personally as Lord and Savior, we automatically come into relationship with everyone else who has so accepted Him. Through the one Lord, one faith and one baptism we become a part of the one body and one Spirit, and are born into the family of the one God and Father of us all (Eph 4:4-6). Whether we recognize it, agree with it, or like it, we consequently automatically inherit brothers and sisters all over the world.

As Peter says, "Once you were not a people, but now you are the people of God; once you had not received mercy, but now you have received mercy" (I Peter 2:10).

In addition to the concept of relationship, however, John also emphasizes the aspect of participation in the common growth and ministry experience. "If we claim to have fellowship with Him yet walk in the darkness, we lie and do not live by the truth. But if we walk in the light as He is in the light, we have fellowship with one another, and the blood of Jesus, His Son, purifies us from all sin" (I John 1:6-7). There is activity and growth required to remain a part of the fellowship. I Corinthians 10:16 speaks of our fellowship in participating in the Lord's Supper. Philippians 3:10 describes our need to share with others in the fellowship of suffering. II Corinthians 8:4 interprets fellowship as participation in helping fellow Christians who are in physical need. We conclude that "fellowship" is a very active term which requires our involvement in many kinds of ministry and in exercises leading to spiritual growth.

It is impossible to study the New Testament concept of the fellowship of the saints and to maintain the doctrine of total autonomy for the local church. There is simply a larger fellowship to be considered which is not limited to the provincial vision and concerns of any isolated, autonomous body. There was in the early church a vision and compassion which stretched far beyond the local boundaries drawn by any church leadership. Consider, for example, the church at Antioch. Even though suspect by some of the Jerusalem church members and leaders for their practices, when they heard of a coming famine which would affect that area, "The disciples, each according to his ability, decided to provide help for the brothers living in Judea. This they did, sending their gift to the elders by Barnabas and Saul" (Acts 11:29-30). Their vision did not end there, however, for we have already seen how it eventually resulted in the establishment of churches all over the known world.

The Antioch church was not alone in its vision and concern about the larger fellowship. Paul's letters to the church at Corinth (I Cor 16:1-4; II Cor 8:1—9:15) help to document the vision and generosity of the Macedonian churches and that which he was encouraging among the Corinthian brethren as well. Among the closing verses of I Corinthians we also find a typical reflection of Paul's encouragement to each of the churches to be aware of each other and the larger fellowship they shared:

> The churches in the province of Asia send you greetings. Aquila and Priscilla greet you warmly in the Lord, and so does the church that meets in their house. All the brothers here send you greetings. Greet one another with a holy kiss (I Cor 16:19, 20).

Shared Leadership

We have commented concerning the awareness by the Antioch church of its relationship to the larger fellowship and to its sense of responsibility toward those who already were a part of that fellowship. More than simply praying for the needs of others within that fellowship, they recognized that they must become personally involved in allowing God to use them in helping to meet those needs. Did that church not have needs of its own and its own program to support? Certainly it had every excuse for ducking responsibility which is cited by churches today. They refused to compromise their ministry, however, with selfish or short-sighted concerns.

They were committed to being a part of the implementation of the Great Commission (Matt 28:18-20) on the world-wide basis which Jesus had commanded, rather than within a limited circle drawn by faithless and self-serving leadership.

The vision of the Antioch church also stretched to those who were not yet a part of their larger fellowship, but who needed to become members of the body of Christ by accepting Him as Lord and Saviour. They recognized, as Paul affirmed, that:

> Everyone who calls upon the name of the Lord will be saved. How, then, can they call upon the One they have not believed in? And how can they believe in the One of whom they have not heard? And how can they hear without someone preaching to them? And how can they preach unless they be sent? As it is written, "How beautiful are the feet of those who bring good news!" (Rom 10:13-15).

How difficult a decision it would be for a church today to take its very best and most effective leadership and to send it off to begin some new churches! Was it any less difficult for the Antioch church to do that? When a church is blessed with men of the stature of Paul and Barnabas as its leaders, would it not be extremely hard to keep from thinking protectively about the impact upon the continued growth of the local church of a decision to send them away to begin new works? How do you replace a Paul or a Barnabas? Was there no concern about the danger of losing relatively new members who had come into the fellowship of the church due to the influence of these men, and who were still closely tied to them in their spiritual infancy?

We would be extremely naive to assume that these were not concerns of Antioch church leaders and members, just as they would be of those of churches today. Yet, the Antioch Christians were committed to their responsibilities to be a part of the cultivation and expansion of that larger fellowship. That commitment surpassed provincial concerns, for *they were convinced that the local body would continue to be built up through its involvement in extending the larger fellowship of the body of Christ.* This is a key concept. Solomon once wrote: "Cast your bread upon the waters, for after many days you will find it again" (Eccl 11:1). This is akin to the words of Jesus: "But seek first His kingdom and His righteousness, and all these things will be given to you as well" (Matt 6:33). The application of that admonition and promise was not limited to an independent, autonomous kingdom being built in Hometown, USA. Jesus said to the church, as well as to individuals, "Whoever finds his life will lose it, and whoever loses his life for My sake will find it" (Matt 10:39).

The eternal paradox of the kingdom of God is that one receives most by giving away the most! This is true of individual Christians and of local churches. The minute we begin to become protective of that which is "ours," we begin to lose ground and to rob ourselves of experiencing the full potential of the ways in which God can use us and work through us.

Certainly this principle can be mis-applied. There are churches who pride themselves in giving 20% to 50% of their income to missions, but who are using that as an excuse for pitifully under-paying their preacher and neglecting their responsibility to invest in a productive program or facilities which could build up and expand the local body to the extent that it could have a significant ministry both at home and away. The relatively insignificant sum given to missions by such churches could be multiplied many times over if they removed this prideful excuse for their refusal to be a viable, growing and functioning body. The only way such mission contributions can be viewed is as "conscience money." Paul wrote:

> Carry each other's burdens, and in this way you will fulfill the law of Christ. If anyone thinks he is something when he is nothing, he deceives himself. Each one should test his own actions. Then he can take pride in himself, without comparing himself to someone else, for each one should carry his own load. Anyone who receives instruction in the Word must share all good things with his instructor. Do not be deceived: God cannot be mocked. A man reaps what he sows. The one who sows to please his sinful nature, from that nature will reap destruction; the one who sows to please the spirit, from the spirit will reap eternal life. Let us not become weary in doing good, for at the proper time we will reap a harvest if we do not give up. Therefore, as we have opportunity, let us do good to all people, especially to those who belong to the family of believers (Gal 6:2-10).

Yes, this has application to individual Christians. Let us remember, though, that it was written to "the churches of Galatia" (Gal 1:2). Therefore its application to the local church needs to be equally considered, however uncomfortable its indictment may be.

The Antioch church did not attempt to duck its responsibilities for helping to cultivate and expand the larger fellowship by sending conscience money. They shared their leadership. In so doing, they became personally interested and involved in that larger fellowship. Vitally important parts of their body had been donated to help give life to other bodies within that larger fellowship. We who have become excited about the potential of organ transplants in the field of medicine in recent years need to be reminded that the concept of organ transplanting is as old as the practice of the first churches.

The sharing of leadership to help begin new churches has application today. There is no more effective way to begin new churches than for one church to give birth to another. The mother church needs to help parent it in its infancy and to share its leadership with its offspring until it can grow leadership of its own. There are so many areas in which the resources of an established congregation can be used to benefit a new congregation until it can get on its feet and stand on its own. This can happen, though, only when the leadership and membership of a church understands and is committed to its responsibility to the larger fellowship.

Finally, the sharing of leadership is also needed to help existing congregations who are struggling, failing to produce, wandering off course or who are having a variety of problems. We have too long sanctified the non-scriptural notion of total autonomy and its corollary of non-intervention! The apostles shared no such notion. They continually encouraged a utilization and exchange of leadership among the churches. Note, for example, the extensive list in Romans 16:1-16. These leaders all had something to offer the Roman church. Paul encouraged them to accept them and to utilize them. Paul had no qualms about intervening in the problems he saw developing in the churches (I Cor 1:10-17; 4:14-21). With his first letter to the Corinthian church he sent Timothy "to remind you of my way of life in Christ Jesus, which agrees with what I teach in every church" (4:17b). If that did not work, he was concerned enough to personally come and intervene "with a whip" (4:21). That is pretty strong language! Yet, Paul employed it to emphasize the point that *the autonomy of the local church ends when it ceases to function under the Lordship of Christ.*

As an apostle, Paul felt a responsibility toward all the church to see that the authority and teachings of Christ were maintained as the only rule of faith and practice for the church in any location. Let us consider the context of his intervention. Here was a church which was coming apart at the seams due to a leadership struggle:

> You are still worldly. For since there is jealousy and quarreling among you, are you not worldly? Are you not acting like mere men? For when one says, "I follow Paul," and another, "I follow Apollos," are you not mere men? (I Cor 3:3-4).

Under the pretext of upholding the teachings of Paul, Apollos, Peter or Christ (1:12), four distinct and warring segments had emerged in the congregation, each led by leaders who were seeking to gain control of the church and to have the preeminence. Were there actual doctrinal differences between Paul, Apollos, Peter or Christ? Of course not! The Holy Spirit guided the others to accurately convey the message of Christ. Were there differences in appearance, personality, presentation and methodology between the four? Certainly! These, however, could be used only as a pretext for dividing the church in a leadership struggle, for they were unrelated and non-essential aspects of the presentation of the gospel. The issue was a power struggle over who would control the church at Corinth.

It is interesting that these leaders at Corinth also felt themselves to be protected in their struggle by their autonomy.

> Some of you have become arrogant, as if I were not coming to you. But I will come to you very soon, if the Lord is willing,

> and then I will find out not only how these arrogant people are talking, but what power they have. For the kingdom of God is not a matter of talk but of power. What do you prefer? Shall I come to you with a whip, or in love and with a gentle spirit? (I Cor 4:18-21).

Paul dispelled any doubts in their minds about his intention to cross any presumed protective boundaries of their autonomy in order to intervene. He would not tolerate their arrogant power play, which would destroy the church. They thought they possessed power, but they deceived themselves. The church possesses ample power, but it all belongs to Christ (Matt 28:18). The best these leaders could do was to manipulate people with their talk. It is obvious from the remainder of the letter that they were so obsessed with the question of who would be in control of the church that they were seriously neglecting their leadership responsibilities. He immediately proceeds to indict them in chapters 5 and 6, for example, for failing to act in matters of immorality and lawsuits within the congregation. If they were going to be church leaders, they would have to lead the church as Christ intended, or they would be replaced. Paul would see to it!

Now it may be argued that Paul was an apostle, and that he was only exercising an apostolic prerogative to intervene in the affairs of this church. He had begun the church, as well, and he had a continuing responsibility and right to step in as needed. Common sense, however, would tell us that someone had to do something, or the church would be destroyed. In Revelation 1:17—3:14 John is instructed by the Lord to write letters to seven churches to tell them to shape up their acts, or they would face His condemnation in Judgment. In the case of the church at Pergamum, Jesus indicates that He would soon "come to you and fight against them with the sword of My mouth" (Rev 2:16) if they did not repent and change their ways. The leaders of that church were permitting teachings and practices which were definitely contrary to the Word of God.

It is interesting to note, as we did in our earlier chapters, how the fathers of the Restoration Movement, such as Alexander Campbell, also felt compelled to intervene in church affairs to help straighten out problems with leaders. This they did, even though they had personally struggled in their own experience against the denominational stranglehold placed on churches and their leadership. This they did, even though they had fiercely defended the concept of local autonomy for the churches. *They intervened because common sense told them that total autonomy was an indefensible and unworkable idea, and that the success of any church's autonomy depended upon both members and leaders who were willing to accept their responsibilities under the Lordship of Christ.* They saw the evidence of this in the New Testament's accounts of the first churches, and they witnessed ample evidence of this in the churches of their day.

Who, then, should intervene when a church is struggling with unresolved internal problems? We have no apostles among us. We do, however, have the larger fellowship of the church. Not long ago, a church which was about to lose everything as a result of its leadership problems approached a strong, healthy sister church and asked for guidance from her elders. They agreed, and after months of consultation and restructuring, that church is now healthy and growing. Other churches, realizing their failure to grow or to accomplish ministry as they should, have brought in capable, knowledgeable church leaders to consult with them and to guide them in a restructuring of their leadership and their church's ministry. The churches who have conscientiously worked with these consultants have been able to turn their ministries around and to experience new life and growth within the church. Those churches who have only listened, and then ignored the consultant's recommendations, have continued to flounder, doing things the ways they have always done them, and with the same results. Some of those churches have even died. In other words, calling in a consultant will be a waste of time, effort and money unless there is a commitment on the part of the church to work with him.

In these cases cited, the intervention has been by invitation of the church—either by its leaders or its members as a whole. Obviously, this is the most desirable and the most productive solution to problems which may exist. A growing number of churches are recognizing their need for this kind of help and are seeking it. What about the church which does not seek help, however, but desperately needs it? Is there not a responsibility within the larger fellowship of the other churches to intervene?

Intervention in a church's internal affairs should, obviously, be approached very carefully and prayerfully. The leadership of one or more sister congregations should request a meeting with the leaders and/or members of that church, at which time they should offer their assistance. If that assistance is refused, perhaps they should next offer to help bring in some consultant whose guidance would be accepted by that church. In the case of a church whose leaders have actually led it away from the teachings of the New Testament and who have rejected the authority of Jesus and His apostles, the leadership of those churches may even need to take legal action to regain for faithful members the property and facilities of that church, and to begin anew with a responsible and committed leadership. Such action should definitely be a last resort when all other measures have first been attempted and have failed.

Cooperative Ministries

Within the larger fellowship of the church are possibilities and a potential for accomplishing ministry which often does not exist within any local church. For example, which single church could have met the need for providing financial relief for the brethren in Judea? These victims of famine and persecution numbered thousands. We witnessed how the Antioch church immediately responded with assistance in Acts 11:29, but that was not sufficient to handle the size of the problem in Acts 20:1 (cf. II Cor 8:1—9:15). Paul sought help from all of the churches, including those as far away as Macedonia and Greece.

There are many essential ministries today which cannot be handled by a single church, or which could be accomplished better by a united and cooperative effort of several or more churches. Major relief efforts are certainly one example of this. Catastrophic events, persecution, famine and other such hardships being experienced by fellow Christians, even in other remote parts of the world, should still concern the church today and elicit its unified financial aid.

In addition, preparation of competent, professional leadership for the church is another area in which cooperative action and a pooling of resources is needed. Certainly it is possible for some capable pastors to invest their time in training such leadership in their churches. If a pastor invests his time in this way, however, it will be to the neglect of other leadership responsibilities he has toward his church. Certainly such an investment should be made for a period of time with qualified and prepared interns, but to saddle the pastor or other church staff with the total educational preparation of a person for professional church leadership is to require too much. In addition, few churches possess the library resources or the facilities which would be needed to support an adequate education.

Education in preparation for professional ministry within the confines of a single church also deprives the person being educated of the breadth of curriculum, perspective and experience he needs for leadership in ministry today. This can be provided only through the combining of the resources of numerous churches to develop an educational institution committed to the purpose of equipping a trained leadership for the church. In such institutions can be pooled the library resources needed, the most talented and knowledgeable specialists in the various fields of study and the financial aid required by many students. Here also an evironment of fellowship in learning can be created, along with the development of consistent standards for the composition and the quality of the educational elements and experiences needed to adequately equip qualified leaders. This can obviously only be delivered, however, through a cooperative ministry of numerous churches. Education of this caliber, along with the essential supporting facilities, is more costly than any single church can afford.

Christian camping is another area of ministry in which the cooperative efforts of the churches of an area are required. It would be both economically unfeasible and extremely wasteful, from a stewardship standpoint, for each church to attempt to build and support its own camp. Certainly there is a great need for developing this kind of ministry. Outside the Christian home, Christian camping probably provides the church with its greatest discipling opportunity. Here, in a 24-hour per day controlled environment, Christian principles can be taught and modelled by the faculty and actually experienced by the campers. A significant number of youth each year make their first commitment to Christ as a result of their encounter with the Word and their experiences at these camps. Here, too, is the church's prime recruiting ground for tomorrow's church leadership. It is estimated that 80% to 90% of the ministers and missionaries now serving the churches initially made their decisions to prepare for specialized Christian ministry at a Christian camp.

We have already mentioned the tremendous value of retreats in fostering spiritual growth and developing relationships when working with youth. The value of retreats with adults and families also needs to be recognized. Planning retreats can be invaluable in helping church leaders to develop goals and plans for their churches. The Christian camp can be the ideal location for all of these retreats, and the camp's staff can help churches in planning successful growth experiences for their people.

Here in the Christian camp setting is also the ideal opportunity for churches to develop a primary equipping center for adult church leadership. While few church members will ever be able to go away to a Christian college for extensive preparation for their ministry responsibilities within the church, most of them are able to attend weekend conferences designed to challenge and equip them for being Bible school teachers, youth coaches, church music directors, leaders of singles' ministries, Vacation Bible School directors, etc. Again, in such a cooperative ministry it is possible to pool the finest resources and personnel available to do a better job of equipping for ministry than any single church is capable of doing on its own.

We have noted also that many missionary and new church planting ventures require the resources of more than one church. It is certainly the best plan from many aspects for a single church to undertake the total support for a missionary or to establish a new congregation. Larger congregations should definitely do both on their own. Many churches, however, will never get around to doing either if they have to wait until they are able to support such a venture by themselves. If they cannot, they should look for one or more partner churches to share in the ministry with them.

We have experienced in recent generations a tremendous extension in life expectancy. People are living longer, but with the growing number of older people comes an increased responsibility for the church to help care for their needs. Christian retirement and nursing facilities are definitely needed, but few churches are able to build and maintain these as individual congregations. Like colleges and camps, they are expensive. The larger fellowship, however, possesses the combined resources to meet these needs by providing for them through cooperative ministries.

Cooperative efforts are also needed in the areas of research and development of more effective methods of evangelism and ministry in the inner city, on mission fields and in changing cultures. United endeavors are required in the area of Christian publishing. Conventions and conferences designed to encourage and further equip church members and leaders also require the participation of many churches to be successful.

In each of these cooperative ministries cited within the larger fellowship of the church, there exists the potential for accomplishing much good. If participation by the associated churches remains voluntary, and if those churches involved retain the right to collectively decide the course of each venture to which they have committed their resources, these ministries can be successful and effective. On the other hand, within each of these ministries lies the potential for the development of a hierarchy of authority over the churches. If those churches participating in them relinquish responsibility for their direction and for requiring their accomplishment of the purposes for which they were brought into being, hierarchies will inevitably emerge which will seek to dictate to the churches. Accountability to the participating churches is the key. It must be required.

In Summary

We have witnessed how oppressive and persecuting church hierarchies have prompted each struggle to be free and how they have given birth to new groups which have at least initially taken some positions more out of reaction against the excesses of the regimes from which they broke away than from any clear directive from the Scriptures. Within the Restoration Movement there has from the beginning been an emphasis upon the autonomy of the local church. We have seen how the church described in the New Testament was, in most cases, defined as a group of Christians who gathered as a fellowship in a particular city. It is also clear that no authoritarian super-structure of leadership existed over the local church in the New Testament. In addition to this, it is also apparent that each church is given the right and responsibility to select its own leadership, and that each church is endowed by God with sufficient resources to be able to accomplish that which God expects of it, if it is functioning as God intended. Restoration leaders chose to borrow the term "autonomy" from our culture, therefore, to describe the church as it should be, and to distinguish it from the denominations and the control exercised by their hierarchies over their local churches.

Unfortunately, the concept of autonomy carries from our culture the idea of total independence and isolation. In embracing these notions along with the Word, church leaders have sought to read them into the Scriptures; but they are not to be found there. The concept of total autonomy for the local church is both unscriptural and unworkable. If a church fails to select qualified leaders, refuses to hold them accountable for failing to implement Christ's agenda for the church, or rejects the authority of Christ and His teachings, it would appear from the New Testament that they have forfeited any presumed rights to their autonomy. Someone must intervene to bring the church back to the Biblical blueprint, or it will cease to be Christ's church.

Each Christian and each church are, in fact, a part of a larger fellowship which finds its identity through Jesus in a common Father. We all have become a part of the family of God, and each part is intended to share both concern and some responsibility for the others. This concern should prompt each local church to be willing to share its leadership, both in the beginning of new congregations and in assisting those who are having problems, rather than concentrating solely on building a large, isolated and independent kingdom for itself. It is always best when such shared leadership is requested by churches who are experiencing problems.

In the event help is not sought, however, sister congregations should not sit idly by without intervening in some way to help that troubled part of the body. They should offer to share their leadership, or to help bring in other consultants whose guidance would be accepted by the church. If the authority and teachings of Christ have been abandoned by the church, sister congregations should consider legal remedies to recover the property and buildings, and help re-establish the congregation with qualified and responsible leadership.

Within the larger fellowship of the church are also a number of needs which can only be met through the combined resources of two or more churches. These cooperative ministries may include major relief efforts, educational preparation for professional church leaders, Christian camping ministries, missionary and church planting ventures, facilities to care for the aged, research and development of effective evangelistic and missionary methods to meet changing cultures, Christian publishing endeavors and conventions and conferences. These cooperative ministries must, however, remain accountable and responsive to the participating churches, or they have the potential of developing into hierarchies over those churches.

11

SUPRA-CONGREGATIONAL LEADERSHIP

Apostolic Precedent

It would, of course, be folly to maintain that the leadership of each church mentioned in the New Testament was completely independent, and that no church leadership existed outside the autonomous confines of the individual congregations. The preponderance of evidence which exists is to the contrary. It is true, as we have already seen, that each church existed as an entity of its own, and that each church was responsible for the selection of its own leadership and for growing and functioning together to accomplish God's purposes. Each church was also capable of accomplishing God's mission for them by using the abilities and opportunities God gave them.

That was the ideal. It was possible. That ideal did not always materialize, however. Sometimes congregations did not understand or take seriously their responsibility to select spiritually qualified leaders, while others refused to follow the leaders they had selected. Some leaders used their positions as an opportunity to take advantage of the people they led, and some refused to accept the lordship of Christ or His agenda for the church. In such cases, intervention and other measures were necessary. On the island of Crete, for example, Paul did not instruct the young churches there to select their own leadership. Instead, Paul writes to Titus: "The reason I left you in Crete was that you might straighten out what was left unfinished and appoint elders in every town, as I directed you" (Titus 1:5). Why was the Jerusalem church permitted to select its own leaders (Acts 6:1-7), and yet the Cretans were not? Paul gives us the answer to that in Titus 1:10-14:

> For there are many rebellious people, mere talkers and deceivers, especially those of the circumcision group. They must be silenced, because they are ruining whole households by teaching things they ought not to teach—and that for the sake of dishonest gain. Even one of their own prophets has said, "Cretans are always liars, evil brutes, lazy gluttons." This testimony is true. Therefore, rebuke them sharply, so that they will be sound in the faith and will pay no attention to Jewish myths or to the commands of those who reject the truth.

That was obviously not an ideal situation at Crete. Leadership for the churches was essential, but it would have to be selected carefully and upon the right basis (Titus 1:6-9). The church members there were being too easily influenced by false teachers. They could not be trusted to select the kind of leaders the church needed, and that selection was too important to be left to chance. Consequently, the apostle authorized a supra-congregational leader, Titus, to appoint the leaders.

One does not have to read very far in the New Testament before coming to the realization that there was indeed an interrelationship which existed between these visible representations of Christ's body. There was a larger fellowship created through their common Lord, their common faith, and their common new birth into the family of God (Eph 4:5). As we have seen, they cared about each other. The huge relief effort on behalf of the Judean Christians is an excellent example of this interaction between churches (Acts 11:27-30; I Cor 16:1-4; II Cor 8:1-15).

With that relationship which existed among the churches also came some interdependence upon church leadership. II Corinthians 8:16-24 gives us an excellent example of this:

> I thank God, who put into the heart of Titus the same concern I have for you. For Titus not only welcomed our appeal, but he is coming to you with much enthusiasm and on his own initiative. And we are sending along with him the brother who is praised by all the churches for his service to the gospel. What is more, he was chosen by the churches to accompany us as we carry the offering, which we administer in order to honor the Lord Himself and to show our eagerness to help. We want to avoid any criticism of the way we administer this generous gift. For we are taking pains to do what is right, not only in the eyes of the Lord, but also in the eyes of men.
>
> In addition, we are sending with them our brother who has often proved to us in many ways that he is zealous, and now even more so because of his great confidence in you.

> As for Titus, he is my partner and fellow worker among you; as for our brothers, they are representatives of the churches and an honor to Christ. Therefore show these men the proof of your love and the reason for our pride in you, so that the churches can see it.

The Corinthian church had struggled with many internal problems. Its leadership and membership has been divided (I Cor 1:10-17; 3:1-23). In addition, the leadership had failed to deal with problems in the church of immorality, lawsuits between the members, disruption of the worship, competition over spiritual gifts and other matters which had prompted Paul's first letter. In that first epistle Paul indicates that, in addition to the letter of correction, he would be sending Timothy and Apollos to work with that church in resolving its difficulties (I Cor 16:10-12). In fact, the situation which existed in the Corinthian church was so bad that Paul was obviously having difficulty persuading Apollos to go as a supra-congregational leader to work with them (v. 12).

It is apparent from Paul's second letter to the church that much progress had been made. There was still, however, need for more improvement. Paul speaks of his intent to visit them a third time (II Cor 12:11; 13:1). He writes the letter to warn and to instruct them, so he would not be forced to act harshly with them in correcting them when he came to visit. Along with this letter he is again sending some leaders, including Titus, "my partner and fellow worker among you" (II Cor 8:23). The primary mission of these leaders was to work with them on their stewardship (vs. 6-17). Along with Titus the apostle was sending another unidentified "brother who is praised by all the churches for his service to the gospel" (v. 18) and who had been chosen by the churches to accompany Paul and his companions in carrying the offering for the Judean Christians (v. 19). A second leader is mentioned later in verse 22.

Who are these church leaders whom Paul commends so highly to the Corinthians? McGarvey and Pendleton are convinced that this first leader was Luke, based upon his apparent presence with Paul on that journey (Acts 20:2-6).[1] Johnson also notes the possibility of Luke as that leader, but points out that three other Macedonian church leaders are cited in Acts 20:4-6 as accompanying Paul and Luke on the journey to Jerusalem. These included Sopater, son of Pyrrhus, from Berea; Aristarchus from Thessalonica; and Gaius from Derbe. The party also included Tychicus and Trophimus from Asia, along with Timothy. Johnson favors two of these Macedonian leaders as the probable ones being sent with Titus to Corinth.[2] The second leader is described as "our brother who has often proved to us in many ways that he is zealous, and now even more so because of his great confidence in you" (v. 22). Commentators have proposed a great variety of possible identities for both of these men. The fact remains, however, that Paul does not tell us; and we do not know.

The point is that the church at Corinth did not exist in isolation. It was not permitted to destroy itself with its problems, while others stood idly by, bound to inaction by some concept of total autonomy or by prohibition of intervention. The Apostle Paul, who had begun the church at Corinth,

---

1. J. W. McGarvey and Philip Y. Pendleton, *Thessalonians, Corinthians, Galatians and Romans* (Cincinnati: The Standard Publishing Company, n.d.), p. 214.

2. B. W. Johnson, *The Peoples' New Testament* (Nashville: Gospel Advocate Company, n.d.), pp. 149-150.

addressed at least two letters to correct those problems and to guide the church. I Corinthians 5:9 is interpreted by most commentators as referring to still a third letter which Paul had sent prior to I Corinthians.[3] In addition to these letters, Paul had personally made a return visit to work with the church, and was planning yet another such visit when he wrote II Corinthians. Assuming that Timothy and Apollos actually served there for periods of time, Paul also now sends Titus and two other leaders to them. He was obviously determined to see that this church shaped up and realized its potential! *If it had not been for the intervention of this massive dose of supra-congregational leadership, the church at Corinth would have, in all likelihood, destroyed itself.*

One other element is involved here in this passage which we should not overlook. Paul notes that these leaders he is sending are "representatives of the churches and an honor to Christ" (v. 23). Then in verse 24 he says to the church, "Therefore show these men the proof of your love and the reason for our pride in you, so that the other churches can see it." There is here a subtle, but positive, pressure applied to the church to comply with Paul's requests. Representatives of the other churches who were a part of the larger fellowship would be coming, and they would be reporting to those churches concerning the performance of the Corinthian church and its leaders. Not only was Paul concerned about this church; so were the other churches!

On the heels of this announcement of the impending visit by these leaders, Paul devotes the next fifteen verses of chapter nine to further developing this awareness of their responsibility to set an example before the other churches.

---

3. T. R. Applebury, *Studies in First Corinthians* (Joplin: College Press Publishing Company, 1963), p. 92.

Note the comment in verse 4: "For if any Macedonians come with me and find you unprepared, we—not to say anything about you—would be ashamed of having been so confident." We would call this a utilization of "peer pressure" today. The leaders are being sent to help them look good in the eyes of the other churches (vs. 3, 5). Paul is a real master at applying this kind of pressure. In verse 2 he lets them know that he had already used them as an example to inspire others, and predicts in verse 13 that "men will praise God for the confession of the gospel of Christ, and for your generosity in sharing with them and with everyone else." That is good psychology! It is also excellent leadership. As Blanchard and Johnson note: "If you are first tough on the behavior, and then supportive of the person, it works."[4]

There is an important principle of leadership here to be remembered. Correction and discipline, whether they be by congregational or supra-congregational leadership, must concentrate on the problem behavior, rather than attacking, degrading or humiliating the person. This distinction is overlooked by many church leaders and by entire churches. We are not called to condemn and destroy the person who sins, but to condemn the sin itself. In far too many cases there is a kind of self-righteous vengeance wreaked upon the individual by both the leaders and the brethren. In most instances, the person is then lost—if not driven out—from the fellowship of the church. In direct contrast to this is the apostolic directive in Galatians 6:1-5:

> Brothers, if someone is caught in a sin, you who are spiritual should restore him gently. But watch yourself, or you may

4. Kenneth Blanchard and Spencer Johnson, *The One Minute Manager* (New York: Berkley Books, 1984), p. 89.

also be tempted. Carry each other's burdens, and in this way you will fulfill the law of Christ. If anyone thinks he is something when he is nothing, he deceives himself. Each one should test his own actions. Then he can take pride in himself, without comparing himself to someone else, for each one should carry his own load.

The emphasis here is upon gentle restoration of the person who has sinned, rather than upon condemning him or driving him out of the fellowship. The attitude of those who are to deal with the person, then, is very important. The spiritually immature or self-righteous have no business handling such matters. Only those who have the humility and spiritual maturity to be able to see beyond the sin, to value the person and to be able to gently restore him in his walk with the Lord should work with such a situation.

That which is true of leading and restoring individual Christians who have sinned is also true of supra-congregational leadership of churches. Note Paul's comment regarding Titus, who was being sent to the Corinthians: "I thank God, who put in the heart of Titus the same concern I have for you" (II Cor 8:16). Paul was not sending some leader who was seeking an opportunity to inflict his wrath or who was coming to satisfy some personal vendetta. He was sending a leader who really cared about them. He was also sending one who believed in them and who was enthused about the opportunity to work with them (v. 17). This was vitally important. The supra-congregational leader who does not value the leaders and the church members with whom he must work, or who approaches the opportunity with pessimism and a lack of enthusiasm, will find it impossible to succeed in his task. His attitude will alienate and destroy, rather than restoring and building up the body.

There are numerous other examples of the apostolic precedent set in the matter of supra-congregational leadership. We would conclude this review, however, by examining the way in which Paul ministered to the Colossian church. Tychicus was chosen as the supra-congregational leader to deal, in this instance, with a very delicate situation which could have thrown the church at Colosse into turmoil (Col 4:7). Paul recognized the problem before it directly affected the church, and he chose to act decisively and to intervene through correspondence and Tychicus. Actually Tychicus was commissioned by Paul to carry three letters: one to the church at Ephesus (Eph 6:21) and two to the church at Colosse (Colossians and Philemon).

The background of the problem which would develop at Colosse was the fact that Onesimus, a slave, had run away from his master, Philemon. It was in this same Philemon's house that the Colossian church met (Phile 2). Paul had encouraged this slave in Rome and had converted him, That, of course, had changed the man's life. Paul then convinced him that he should return to Colosse and to Philemon.

How, though, would a returning slave be received and treated by Philemon or by the church? Would he simply be regarded as disobedient property to be punished, or would he be received as a brother in Christ who had returned to right a wrong? As a runaway slave, Onesimus was, by law, a fugitive. He could be arrested and returned in bonds to his master for punishment. If Philemon decided to exercise his right to punish the man, however, what would that do to his Christian commitment or his need for fellowship within a church family? How could the church extend to Onesimus a hand of fellowship in opposition to his status with their host?

Tychicus was chosen by Paul to help work through this situation and to accompany Onesimus back to Colosse as his protector during the journey. Note how he is described and commended to the brethren as "a dear brother, a faithful minister and fellow servant in the Lord" (Col 4:7). Paul obviously did not send a novice. He says to the Colossian Christians: "I am sending him to you that you may know our circumstances and that he may encourage your hearts" (v. 8).

It is interesting that Paul does not specifically tell the Colossian church what to do with this returned slave. He does, however, give a subtle hint in the letter by the way in which he mentions him. Paul says: "He (Tychicus) is coming with Onesimus, our faithful and dear brother, who is one of you. They will tell you everything that is happening here" (Col 4:9). Lenski comments:

> The implication that the Colossians will receive Onesimus as a brother lies in the last brief addition: "They shall make known to you everything here," a quiet but significant plural. Onesimus is to help Tychicus tell what the congregation will want to know. They will receive him in the congregation, will accept him as a brother, one of Paul's own converts who was brought to Christ in a strange way. Paul dictates and commands nothing; he has the fullest confidence in the Colossians. Their hearts will tell them what to do. Let your imagination picture the scene when Tychicus brought Onesimus back to Colosse, when the remarkable news spread, when Philemon had his slave back with a special letter from Paul, when the congregation met, heard Paul's letter to them, etc. Wonderful, indeed! the whole of it exceedingly fine.[5]

---

5. R. C. H. Lenski, *The Interpretation of St. Paul's Epistles to the Colossians, to the Thessalonians, to Timothy, to Titus and to Philemon* (Columbus: The Wartburg Press, 1946), p. 197.

Paul's letter to Philemon, like his letter to the Colossian church, again expresses confidence in him and the church that they will be able and willing to do that which is right (Phile 7, 21; Col 1:2-9). Note that he addresses the letter "To Philemon our dear friend and fellow worker, to Apphia our sister, to Archippus our fellow soldier and to the church that meets in your home (Col 1:1-2). It was basically a personal letter to Philemon, but again Paul employs some peer pressure on him to perform honorably, as he includes the others in the letter's address, in addition to his sending a second letter specifically addressed to the church. He is more explicit in Philemon's letter about his expectations concerning the treatment which should be given Onesimus:

> Therefore, although in Christ I could be bold and order you to do what you ought to do, yet I appeal to you on the basis of love. I then as Paul—an old man and now also a prisoner of Christ Jesus—I appeal to you for my son Onesimus, who became my son while I was in chains. Formerly he was useless to you, but now he has become useful to both you and me.
>
> I am sending him—who is my very heart—back to you. I would have liked to keep him with me so that he could take your place in helping me while I am in chains for the gospel. But I did not want to do anything without your consent, so that any favor you do will be spontaneous and not forced. Perhaps the reason he was separated from you for a little while was that you might have him back for good—no longer as a slave, but better than a slave, as a dear brother. He is very dear to me but even dearer to you, both as a man and as a brother in the Lord.
>
> So if you consider me a partner, welcome him as you would welcome me. If he has done you any wrong or owes you anything, charge it to me. I, Paul, am writing this with my

> own hand. I will pay it back—not to mention that you owe me your very self. I do wish, brother, that I may have some benefit from you in the Lord; refresh my heart in Christ. Confident of your obedience, I write to you, knowing that you will do even more than I ask (Phile 8-21).

To say that Paul is applying some personal pressure as a supra-congregational leader would definitely be an understatement! He makes obedience an option for Philemon, but he does not give him much room to decide otherwise. The final note tacked on by Paul is the clincher: "And one thing more: Prepare a guest room for me, because I hope to be restored to you in answer to your prayers" (v. 22). Not only did Paul send another supra-congregational leader to assure the successful resolution of the problem, and address two letters to the church to help bring peer pressure to bear; now he informs Philemon and the church that he is also planning to come for a visit.

Our examination of these situations which set the apostolic precedent for supra-congregational leadership for the churches demonstrates that there are some constant elements which we should use as guidelines for any intervention by supra-congregational leaders:

1. Only the most spiritually mature leaders should be used for this work.
2. Only those leaders who are able to value the church leaders and members involved, and who can approach the situation with genuine care, optimism and enthusiasm should be utilized.
3. Letters from supra-congregational leaders can be effective tools in intervening in problem situations if they also reflect a genuine love and concern for the church, if they concentrate on correcting the problems rather than

humiliating the people, and if they express a confidence in the people to be able to succeed in overcoming the problem and continuing to be of value in Christ's kingdom.

4. Peer pressure can be applied effectively to accomplish needed changes, both from within the church and from the larger fellowship of churches.
5. The primary goals of such intervention must be those of correction, restoration and growth, rather than those of winning battles and defeating or destroying people in the process.
6. No authoritarian superstructure or regulatory agencies were created to deal with these problems in the churches, nor did the supra-congregational leaders who came to work with them remain to control the churches after their problems had been resolved.

It is true that supra-congregational leadership continued to exist and to be involved in numerous ways with the churches as needed. The various letters of the New Testament bear testimony to this. The apostolic precedent, however, does appear to set some relatively uniform limits upon the scope and character of their ministry.

Subsequent Problems

Even within the pages of the New Testament are a number of examples of supra-congregational leadership which created problems, rather than resolved them. Paul, writing to the churches of Galatia, asks: "You foolish Galatians! Who has bewitched you?" (Gal 3:1a). He also says: "I am astonished that you are so quickly deserting the one who called you by the grace of Christ and are turning to a different gospel—

which is really no gospel at all. Evidently some people are throwing you into confusion and are trying to pervert the gospel of Christ" (Gal 1:6-7). These leaders had come to the churches and challenged Paul's credentials, proclaiming instead their own concepts and persuading the churches to accept them as being superior to Paul's teachings. Paul is forced to defend his apostleship and his doctrine as being from Christ, rather than from men (Gal 1:10—2:10).

This was a constant problem Paul had to combat among the churches. There were those who saw in supra-congregational leadership an opportunity to rule and to establish their reputations as teachers. Paul comments to Timothy at one point: "For the time will come when men will not put up with sound doctrine. Instead, to suit their own desires, they will gather around them a great number of teachers to say what their itching ears want to hear. They will turn their ears away from the truth and turn aside to myths" (II Tim 4:3-4). Paul knew full well that there were those in the churches who, like the Athenians he had addressed at the Areopagus, liked nothing more than to hear something new (Acts 17:21-22). He further instructed Timothy:

> The Spirit clearly says that in later times some will abandon the faith and follow deceiving spirits and things taught by demons. Such teachings come through hypocritical liars, whose consciences have been seared as with a hot iron. They forbid people to marry and order them to abstain from certain foods, which God created to be received with thanksgiving by those who believe and who know the truth. . . . If you point these things out to the brothers, you will be a good minister of Christ Jesus, brought up in the truths of the faith and of the good teaching that you have followed (I Tim 4:1-3, 6).

These examples of apostolic comment, however, almost pale by comparison to those of Peter in II Peter 2 and 3. He says, in part:

> But there were also false prophets among the people, just as there will be false teachers among you. They will secretly introduce destructive heresies, even denying the sovereign Lord who bought them—bringing swift destruction on themselves. Many will follow their shameful ways and will bring the way of truth into disrepute. In their greed these teachers will exploit you with stories they have made up. Their condemnation has long been hanging over them, and their destruction has not been sleeping. . . .
>
> Bold and arrogant, these men are not afraid to slander celestial beings; yet even angels, although they are stronger and more powerful, do not bring slanderous accusations against such beings in the presence of the Lord. But these men blaspheme in matters they do not understand. They are like brute beasts, creatures of instinct, born only to be caught and destroyed, and like beasts they too will perish. They will be paid back with harm for the harm they have done. Their idea of pleasure is to carouse in broad daylight. They are blots and blemishes, reveling in their pleasures while they feast with you. With eyes full of adultery, they never stop sinning; they seduce the unstable; they are experts in greed—an accursed brood! They have left the straight way and wandered off to follow the way of Balaam, son of Beor, who loved the wages of wickedness (II Peter 2:1-3, 10b-15).

Given the perpetual presence of these unqualified opportunists who would lead both individual Christians and entire churches astray for personal gain or aggrandizement, what is the solution to this ever-present danger? Paul had the answer to that. When the church is functioning with responsible leadership according to the pattern he outlined for it in Ephesians 4:11-13, he says: "Then we will no longer be infants, tossed back and forth by the waves, and blown here and there by every wind of teaching and by the cunning and craftiness of men in their deceitful scheming" (Eph 4:14).

Here again, then, we must return to the New Testament concept of church leadership and ministry if we are to protect the church from the wolves which would devour it. God has given no other remedy. Those who would devise their protective and regulatory structures as the means for keeping the church pure are doomed to failure. Frustrated also will be those who would seek to preserve the purity of the church through isolation and monasticism. Only the healthy, growing and functioning body is capable of repelling the diseases which would attack it. Only those Christians who have been faithfully taught the Word of God, and have grown up on it as their constant diet, will be capable of making the distinction between true and false teaching. It will be recalled that the Great Commission (Matt 28:18-20) required teaching obedience to ALL that Jesus had commanded, not simply giving a capsulized inoculation of the truth. Paul admonished the Thessalonian Christians to "Test everything. Hold on to the good. Avoid every kind of evil" (I Thess 5:21-22). The Apostle John likewise cautioned the church:

> Dear friends, do not believe every spirit, but test the spirits to see whether they are from God, because many false prophets have gone out into the world. This is how you can recognize the Spirit of God: Every spirit that acknowledges that Jesus Christ has come in the flesh is from God, but every spirit that does not acknowledge Jesus is not from God. This is the spirit of the antichrist, which you

have heard is coming and even now is already in the world (I John 4:1-3).

The testing which was to occur involved a comparison of any new teachings with the teachings of Christ (Gal 1:8-9). Continually the apostles invited the churches to compare their teachings with God's Word and the Gospel as they had first received it (I Cor 15:1-2). Agreement with, and the acceptance of, the teachings of Jesus and His apostles comprised the acknowledgment of Jesus as Lord. John is not simply requiring a verbal affirmation of the existence of Jesus, or even of His Lordship. Matthew 7:21-23 demonstrates the folly of such empty declarations. The ability to test and distinguish the truth from that which was false was developed as the result of a committed life transformed by the reconditioning of the mind through the acceptance of these teachings. Paul said: "Do not conform any longer to the pattern of this world, but be transformed by the renewing of your mind. Then you will be able to test and approve what God's will is—His good, pleasing and perfect will" (Rom 12:2).

When the church functioned as it was intended; when its leaders led the rest of the members into spiritual maturity by their example, when they nurtured them as spiritual parents, when they equipped them for sharing in the ministry, and when they served and helped them find God's answers at the point of their needs, *the church produced the kind of members and leaders who were capable of both accomplishing the purposes of Christ, and of distinguishing and resisting false teachers.* When a church and its leaders failed to function as Christ intended, it became vulnerable to all of the vultures who would make it their prey.

We will not again retrace the emergence of the hierarchy in the early church or recount its atrocities over the centuries. It is sufficient to say that problems will always develop on the supra-congregational level if the churches fail to function as intended or are incapable of distinguishing between truth and error on the basis of God's Word. They will be led off into all kinds of dead-end alleys where they will be victimized. The supra-congregational leader who does not invite and welcome comparison of his teaching with that of God's Word should be immediately rejected before he is allowed to damage the church. To do anything else is to compromise the Lordship of Christ over His church.

Journalistic Leadership

Within the Restoration Movement there was, from the beginning, communication and cooperation between the churches of the movement. There was also leadership which existed beyond the level of the local church. Anyone who would deny the widespread influence of a number of these Restoration leaders would simply be ignoring the facts. It is true that no organizational or official superstructure existed, but there were indeed leaders whose influence extended far beyond their immediate local ministries. This was primarily due to a recognition of their personal spiritual maturity and leadership abilities, rather than by virtue of any office, as it had been in the New Testament. We have already noted how the area evangelists were both called upon and chose to intervene in the affairs of churches which needed their guidance.

W. T. Moore uses the intriguing expression, "government by journalism." He observes, "This government by journalism has perhaps been unavoidable in view of the fact that the Disciples have never had an organization of the churches which could speak for the whole brotherhood."[6] He wrote in 1909:

> To build up a newspaper to where it wields a decisive governmental influence is no easy task, but when it is fully established, it is equally a difficult task to break it down, or even to circumscribe its influence. The editor has the ear of his subscribers, and very generally these subscribers believe in him, and are therefore converts to the policy of the paper which he edits. He can, consequently, count upon their sympathy and support, even where there is strong opposition to his paper, by many who do not believe in what it advocates. These friends of the paper will be excited to work for its circulation by the very opposition which is manifested to it, and what the paper may lose in support, in any given case, will be more than made up by the new subscribers secured by the old friends. This fact alone makes a newspaper a great power, and the editor a great despot, if he chooses to exercise the authority of his position.[7]

Such was the supra-congregational leadership exercised by a number of the early Restoration leaders. H. Eugene Johnson observes, "When a preacher edited a paper or journal he, consciously or unconsciously, assumed the role of an area evangelist."[8]

Elias Smith was probably the first Restoration leader to realize the potential of leadership through journalism. A

---

6. W. T. Moore, *A Comprehensive History of the Disciples of Christ* (New York: Fleming H. Revell Co., 1909), p. 702.

7. Moore, p. 698.

8. H. Eugene Johnson, *Duly and Scripturally Qualified* (Cincinnati: The Standard Publishing Company, 1975), p. 47.

school teacher, doctor, preacher, author and editor, he was a remarkable man and one of the leaders of the New England Christians around 1800. The other key leader of that group was Abner Jones, also a school teacher, doctor and preacher. It was Smith's abilities as an author and editor which eventually made him most influential. He had authored a number of medical and religious books. In 1805 he began a quarterly, *The Christian's Magazine, Reviewer and Religious Intelligencer.* Then beginning in 1808 he published the first religious newspaper in America, *The Herald of Gospel Liberty,* which became the important link between Christians in the various parts of the country. For three years, beginning in 1829, he also edited *The Morning Star and City Watchman.*

We have quoted from some of the smaller papers published by a number of the Restoration leaders, along with most of the larger publications of the movement. The following list of those major journals may be helpful:

Christian Baptist (Monthly, 1823-1830), edited by Alexander Campbell.

Christian Messenger (Monthly, 1826-1845), edited by Barton W. Stone.

Millennial Harbinger (Monthly, 1830-1870), edited by Alexander Campbell. (1830-1865), and by W. K. Pendleton (1865-1870).

American Christian Review (Monthly, 1856-1857; Weekly, 1858-), edited first by Benjamin Franklin (also known at times as *Octographic Review* and as *Apostolic Review*).

Christian Standard (Weekly, 1866-), edited by Isaac Errett.

Gospel Advocate (Weekly, 1855-), edited by Tolbert Fanning and William Lipscomb.

The Christian (Weekly, 1882-), edited by J. H. Garrison and B. W. Johnson, formerly the *Christian Evangelist*.[9]

These, while the major editorial endeavors, are only a minute representation of the innumerable publications which came into existence in the brotherhood. Alexander Campbell complained in 1852:

> The unlicensed press of the present day, and especially in our department of reformation, is the most fearful omen on my horizon. . . . As a community we have been the most reckless in choosing our editors, our scribes, our elders and our preachers. . . . We have had a brood of periodicals the most voluntary and irresponsible that I have ever known.[10]

During the seven years of the *Christian Baptist*, Alexander Campbell was particularly writing in reaction to the clerical hierarchy. That his views were highly influential is testified by Abner W. Clopton who wrote in 1830: "Few men in this country, since the days of George Whitfield, have produced so much agitation in the religious community as Alexander Campbell of Brooke County, Virginia."[11] With the beginning of the *Millennial Harbinger*, his influence continued to spread, and he became the indisputable foremost leader of the movement. It was widely read throughout the growing brotherhood. It carried the news of the movement and overflowed with controversy. He carried both sides of correspondence and articles on the issues of the day. He

9. Enos E. Dowling, *The Restoration Movement* (Cincinnati: The Standard Publishing Company, 1964), pp. 96-100.

10. Alexander Campbell, "The Christian Magazine," *Millennial Harbinger*, July, 1852, pp. 390-391.

11. Abner W. Clopton, "The Sayings of A. Campbell Examined," *Millennial Harbinger*, March, 1830, p. 98.

proved himself to be a master with the argument and the pen. Campbell was heavily influenced by Locke, as we have noted. Harold L. Lunger comments:

> Campbell was sure that reason, properly used, points in the same direction as revelation. He once said that "man was created and made to walk by faith and reason, not separately but cojointly."[12]

Certainly no journal has been more influential in shaping the thinking of the Restoration Movement than the *Christian Standard,* which is still published weekly today. It remains the primary vehicle carrying the news and the views of the movement. M. M. Davis says of Isaac Errett, whose first edition of the *Christian Standard* carried Alexander Campbell's obituary:

> When Mr. Errett came into prominence, and went to the wheel, the sea was stormy, and there were dangers on every hand. But with a clear vision and a steady nerve, and with the spirit of a true pilot, he guided the ship safely to port. . . . His special mission was to maintain the integrity of the plea of the Campbell's, and hold the Restoration movement to its original purpose, and for a quarter of a century he did it most nobly.[13]

Along with the many journals, there were also a number of excellent Bible commentaries produced. Richard Koffarnus says of them:

> Isaiah Boone Grubbs, Moses E. Lard, and J. W. McGarvey each produced monumental works on the book of Romans. Robert Milligan wrote an exposition of Hebrews that still

---

12. Harold L. Lunger, *The Political Ethics of Alexander Campbell* (St. Louis: The Bethany Press, 1954), p. 123.

13. M. M. Davis, *The Restoration Movement of the Nineteenth Century* (Cincinnati: The Standard Publishing Company, 1913), p. 227.

ranks as a classic. It was McGarvey, though, who emerged as the foremost commentator of the brotherhood. Besides his work in Romans, he produced outstanding commentaries on the book of Acts, and on Thessalonians, Corinthians and Galatians. His *Fourfold Gospel* has been the basis for similar studies ever since its publication. Isaac Errett was another voluminous writer, whose major work was a three volume set, *Evenings With the Bible.*[14]

Other notable authors included Walter Scott, Barton W. Stone, Z. T. Sweeney and Benjamin Franklin. Unfortunately, however, the movement saw a decline in the publishing of major works after the turn of the century. Controversies over the musical instrument, liberalism and organization occupied the attention of the brotherhood. Koffarnus notes:

> The first Restorationist to introduce the organ into the worship service was reportedly L. L. Pinkerton, minister of the church at Midway, Kentucky, around 1859. An instant controversy raged that has continued for over a hundred years. As a result, the Movement suffered in three ways. First, its authors began to spend more and more time and print arguing the music question, and less and less time producing literature to reach the denominations. Second, the internal strife made the brotherhood look extremely hypocritical. Outsiders took a dim view of a movement claiming to promote Christian unity but unable to maintain internal peace. Third, and most decisive, the controversy came to a boil in 1906, with the permanent separation of the two factions.[15]

In more recent years Standard Publishing Company, of Cincinnati, Ohio, and College Press, of Joplin, Missouri,

---

14. Richard Koffarnus, "Whatever Happened to Restoration Writing?" *The Sentinel*, December, 1979, p. 2.

15. Koffarnus, p. 2.

have undertaken the task of encouraging and publishing the works of Restoration writers. These two companies serve as the major publishers for the movement today.

Educational Leadership

While the early leaders of the Restoration Movement were all well-educated men, this was not true of many of those who followed, especially those who served on the frontier. It was realized by a number of the leaders that educational institutions would have to be established in order to equip men to preach effectively. Enos Dowling comments:

> Leaders in the Restoration have been greatly concerned about education. This concern is shown by the great number of educational institutions that they started. One research worker has compiled a list of more than 250 schools established by those associated with this movement. Others have estimated the number at a much higher figure. These schools included institutes, academies, colleges and seminaries. An emphasis on education for women led to the foundation of a number of academies for women.[16]

Alexander Campbell particularly abhorred hearing any preacher who was incapable of using good grammar, or who attempted to attack the theologians without an adequate educational background to equip him. Such a public display of ignorance in either case he found inconsistent with the message which was to be delivered. Consequently, he led the way in educational ventures by opening Buffalo Seminary in his own home in 1818. He had two objectives: (1) to help

16. Dowling, p. 84.

educate some of the youth of that area who were lacking educational opportunities, and (2) to prepare some young men for the ministry of preaching. It was a coeducational institution, and he and his father operated it for four years. Failing to accomplish his second objective to the degree he had hoped, he closed the Seminary in 1822 and turned to other endeavors.[17]

A succession of other schools followed, including:

Bacon College (1836), Georgetown, Kentucky; Walter Scott, President.

Bethany College (1840), Bethany, Virginia; Alexander Campbell, President.

Hiram College (1849), Hiram, Ohio, (first known as Western Reserve Eclectic Institute); A. S. Hayden, President.

Butler University (1855), Indianapolis, Indiana, (first known as Northwestern Christian University); John Young, President.

College of the Bible (1865), Lexington, Kentucky, (first associated with the University of Kentucky); Robert Milligan, President.[18]

W. T. wrote at the turn of the century in reflection over the many educational ventures of the movement by that time:

> Doubtless some mistakes have been made with respect to the matter of education among the Disciples. The supreme independency which controlled in the organization of churches controlled also in the organization of colleges. . . . Every one was at liberty to start a college where he might choose to do so, and often a college was started at a particular place largely for the local influence it was supposed to

17. Dowling, p. 84.
18. Dowling, pp. 84-90.

exert upon the development of the town where it was located.[19]

Indeed, both the college and the president of the school did exert some degree of influence and leadership upon the churches of the area as well. Through the efforts of the president, faculty and students new churches were often begun and others sustained. None of these colleges were largely endowed, and that had both positive and negative effects. To make their continuing existence possible, the schools were consequently dependent upon the churches and individuals to help supplement the income from tuition. On the positive side, that did help to keep the colleges accountable, to some degree, to the churches, due to their financial dependency. One of Alexander Campbell's great fears of theological schools was that they would become liberal in their view of the Bible. As their dependence on the churches decreased, this did indeed become a real problem.

On the negative side, the poor geographical placement and the proliferation of colleges created the problem of insufficient financial support for many of them, and became the major cause of the demise of not a few. Adequate support from the churches has continued to be a problem for the colleges who have sought to remain primarily tied to and dependent upon the churches for their income. This has sometimes created an inadequate and inferior quality of education in these institutions, along with a grossly underpaid faculty who are forced to live at near-poverty level incomes in order to minister with these schools. Many of

19. Moore, p. 682.

their graduating students earn beginning salaries in the churches which exceed those of their professors. Most church leaders agree that the continued proliferation of colleges will perpetuate this condition, and that the only remedy is for a number of them to combine and to pool their resources and support.

One of the problems affecting support by the churches has been the fact that not all of the brethren have shared the enthusiasm for learning. One writer in *The Christian Evangelist* in 1892 characteristically wrote: "The God-fearing, Christ-loving illiterate preacher, intelligent in the Gospel, and zealous in the work, can make 10 converts in the Ozark Mountains to your D.D.'s one."[20] In this can be seen, in part, something of the fear of and reaction to an educated ministry. On the other hand, the writer was doubtless right about the Ozarks at that time.

Sectional differences and local culture should be considered in the selection of a pastor and the degree of education required to make him effective in that particular area. Within the urban setting there has always been a greater need for quality ministerial education, due to the higher educational level and expectations of the people. Churches which minister in cities to professional people will require higher educational qualifications for their pastors. On the other hand, that man who is highly educated and culturally oriented to the city would probably flounder and face suspicion and rejection in the Ozark Mountains. On the whole, however, as the general educational level in the country has increased, so has the need become more pressing for adequately educated pastors and other church leaders who are capable

20. Herman (pseud.), "Ministerial Education," *The Christian-Evangelist*, May 5, 1892, p. 277.

of effectively relating and communicating the gospel to educated people.

Still today, though, there has persisted within segments of the movement a nagging fear and distrust of accredited or quality ministerial education; and graduate theological training has been equated by many with certain liberalism. Part of this has been due to the fact that, following the Disciples-Independent split, the Independents had to leave with the Disciples all of the graduate seminaries, many of which had already become quite liberal. Consequently, they began Bible Colleges, which have been primarily four-year undergraduate schools with a solid Bible curriculum at their core, and majors mainly in either Bible or some ministerial specialty. The earlier description given by W. T. Moore has also characterized this Bible College movement, which has scattered colleges across the country. As we have seen earlier, the presidents of these colleges, too, have generally been looked to by the churches of their area for supra-congregational leadership and consultation.

Itinerant Leadership

In chapter one we examined at some length the role of the evangelist in the early days of the Restoration Movement. Leaders such as Alexander Campbell emphasized correctly that "A church set in order by an evangelist is not under him as an official."[21] Nevertheless, they envisioned a supra-congregational leadership role for him. We have seen how the churches became convinced that evangelists should be selected and employed by the churches of an area, and

21. Alexander Campbell, "Office of an Evangelist," *Millennial Harbinger*, June, 1858, p. 330.

how they were commissioned to evangelize and begin new churches within that designated area on behalf of those churches. Men like Walter Scott became well-known for their service as area evangelists.

In addition to their evangelizing, however, we also noted how these evangelists, based upon their identification with Timothy, Titus and others mentioned in the New Testament began to assume a kind of area superintendency over the churches they served in their district. Whenever one of those churches began to have unresolved problems, it was generally the area evangelist who stepped in to serve as counselor and mediator. He was also regarded as a sort of court of appeal for congregations or their members who questioned the decisions of their elders. At first Campbell protested this development in the role, but he soon changed his mind and began to function in this role himself. Johnson comments: "Campbell performed more as an evangelist than a congregation's elder in much of his ministry."[22]

Besides his influence on the movement as an author, editor and educator, he travelled, held protracted meetings and engaged in debates. Moore notes that Campbell was at first opposed to oral debates, which were popular among the politicians of the era. After seeing the interest generated by his first two experimental debates in 1820 and 1822, however, along with the fact that the texts of those debates were published and widely circulated, he decided that this was an excellent way to propagate his views.[23] He participated in five of these debates with the following:

1. John Walker, Presbyterian, (June 19-20, 1820, Mt. Pleasant, Ohio), concerning the mode and subjects of baptism.

---

22. H. Eugene Johnson, p. 45.
23. Moore, p. 164.

2. William L. MacCalla, Presbyterian, (October 15-21, 1823, at Washington, Kentucky), concerning the mode and subjects of baptism.
3. Robert Owen, skeptic, (April 13-21, 1829, at Cleveland, Ohio), concerning the evidences of Christianity.
4. John B. Purcell, Roman Catholic Bishop, (January 13-21, 1837, at Cincinnati, Ohio), concerning Roman Catholicism.
5. Nathan B. Rice, Presbyterian, (November 15 - December 1, 1843, at Lexington, Kentucky), concerning the mode, subjects and purpose of baptism; operation of the Holy Spirit; creeds; and Christian union.[24]

These debates drew great public attention and attendance, and the Restoration view, along with Campbell's name and reputation increasingly spread around the country through the news media coverage of these events. Campbell was as gifted a debater and speaker as he was a writer. He was in great demand as a speaker, and became highly respected even among the most influential leaders of the country. President James Madison once said of him:

> It is as a theologian that Mr. Campbell must be known. It was my pleasure to hear him very often, as a preacher of the gospel, and I regard him as the ablest and most original and powerful expounder of the Scriptures I have ever heard.[25]

In addition to this context, President Madison had also served with Alexander Campbell when they were both elected to the Virginia Constitutional Convention in 1829. It is obvious that Campbell did not view his leadership as

---

24. Dowling, p. 58.

25. William K. Pendleton, "Death of Alexander Campbell," *Millennial Harbinger*, March, 1866, p. 131.

limited to the confines of a local church. He became integrally involved with the leaders and the issues of his time. His pulpit was wherever an opportunity presented itself. Harold Lunger testifies concerning Campbell's growing influence throughout the nation and its capitol:

> Campbell's . . . prestige is seen in the fact that he was asked to preach before Congress on Sunday, June 2, 1850, to pray before the Indiana Constitutional Convention on November 11, 1850, and to address the Missouri Legislature in 1853. When he preached in the Baptist Church in Washington late in 1857, he was "honored with the presence of the President, and a majority of his Cabinet, and a good representation of both houses of Congress." Upon this occasion he reported enjoying "the generous hospitalities of Judge Black and family, now Attorney General of the Union." President James Buchanan also received him at the White House. Campbell counted among his close personal friends Henry Clay, Robert E. Lee, James A. Garfield and many others prominent in the political life of his time, many of whom visited his home in Bethany.[26]

Others also gained fame nationally and internationally through their debates and writing. Among them was J. W. McGarvey (1829-1911). He travelled widely, wrote numerous commentaries and books, penned a regular weekly column, "Biblical Criticism," in the *Christian Standard* from 1893-1911, and conducted at least five public debates. Between 1865-1895 he served as Professor of Sacred History at the College of the Bible in Lexington, Kentucky. Following that he served as its president until his death in 1911. The London *Times* said of him: "In all probability, John W. McGarvey is

26. Lunger, p. 149.

the ripest Bible scholar on earth."[27] Now that is really some kind of compliment! It is evident, though, that McGarvey was another whose leadership stretched far beyond the local congregation. In all probability, he and Campbell exercised the greatest influence of any two men within the Restoration Movement over the thinking and practices of churches across the country.

Throughout the history of the movement there have been those men and women whose leadership influence has been spread over a segment of the country, over the entire nation or around the world. It is important to note, however, that *their leadership has been so recognized on the basis of their personal abilities and stature, rather than due to an ecclesiastical office or position of authority.* This is an important distinction.

Conventions

Our study of supra-congregational leadership would certainly be incomplete if we did not include some mention of the church leadership exerted through conventions. From the beginning of the Restoration Movement there was an apparent need for cooperation between the growing number of autonomous churches across the country. The concern was, however, that coordination of efforts be achieved without sacrificing the freedom of the individual congregations. As early as 1804 churches in Kentucky began meeting and working together, with the churches in other states following their example. By 1820 a United States Christian Conference was organized, but with limited support. Alexander

27. David, pp. 231-233.

Campbell saw the value of such supra-congregational associations, but was concerned about their possible abuses, recalling his tragic experiences with the Presbyterians and Baptists. In 1842 he enumerated "Five Arguments for Church Organization," including more effective united efforts in Bible distribution, greater missionary activity, improving the ministry, protecting the churches from unqualified leadership and better stewardship of the total financial resources of the churches.[28]

Enos Dowling points out:

> Campbell found Scriptural precedent for the cooperation which reason suggested and justified. A group of churches could and must do what the individual congregations found impossible. References in the New Testament to the "Churches of Galatia," the "Churches of Macedonia" and similar expressions, were taken as illustrative of his contention that "the churches were districted in the age of the Apostles." The churches of Galatia and Achaia co-operated in raising money for the poor in Judea; churches united in choosing and appointing persons for certain religious purposes (II Cor 8:19). Those thus chosen, according to Campbell, were "the messengers of the churches" from the districts which chose them. As early as 1831 he proposed a widening circle of co-operation among the churches. Beginning with the county, co-operative organization would ascend through the districts and states to a national level."[29]

Numerous examples of organizational efforts could be cited, but in 1849 the first national Christian convention was held in Cincinnati, Ohio, coinciding with the formation

28. Alexander Campbell, "Five Arguments for Church Organization," *Millennial Harbinger*, November, 1842, p. 523.

29. Dowling, pp. 75-76.

of the American Christian Missionary Society, which sent missionaries to Jerusalem, Jamaica and Liberia. Alexander Campbell was elected President of both. He says of the meeting:

> Our expectations from the Convention have more than been realised. We are much pleased with the result, and regard it as a very happy pledge of good times to come. The unanimity, cordiality, and generous concurrence of the brethren in all the important subjects before them, were worthy of themselves and the great cause in which they are all enlisted. Enough was done in one session, and enough to occupy our best energies for some time to come. Bible distribution and evangelical labour—two transcendent objects of Christian effort most essential to the conversion of the world—deserve at our hand a very cordial and generous support. We may rationally anticipate, from the indications afforded during the session, that they will be liberally patronised and sustained by all the brotherhood. The suggestions deferentially submitted to all the brotherhood, for their concurrence and action in reference to the necessity and importance of periodically meeting, in given districts, large or small, as the case may be, for consultation and practical effort in the advocacy of the cause in all their localities, must, we think, meet the approbation of all the intelligent and zealous brethren and Churches everywhere; and, we doubt not, will give great efficiency to the labours of evangelists in those districts.[30]

To say that Campbell had high expectations for this joint venture would be something of an understatement. He was not alone in this reaction. Moore says: "The action of the Convention thrilled the churches everywhere with a new

30. Moore, pp. 446-447.

enthusiasm, and the great leaders of the movement returned to their fields of labour with new hopes as to the final outcome of the movement."[31] Some good things were indeed accomplished. Such conventions brought together the leaders of the churches and helped them to focus upon the purpose of the church. Great preaching was heard, which stirred everyone present. The gatherings also provided for a realization of the scope of the larger fellowship, and gave a vision of that which might be accomplished cooperatively. In fact, many very worthy ministries and united endeavors grew out of these gatherings including orphanages, hospitals, homes for the aged, mission projects around the world, ministerial relief, and many others.

In 1869, however, the "Louisville Plan" was introduced and adopted as an attempt to set up a delegate system of representation of churches in a General Christian Missionary Convention (two delegates per state, plus one delegate for every 5,000 members), with a formula for collection of funds through district, state and the national conventions. The purpose of this plan was to overcome the financial problem which the united missionary endeavor was experiencing. Churches simply were not sending enough funds to the national organization to get the job done. Unfortunately, the pendulum had swung too far. Many of the leaders had come to the conclusion that the only way to accomplish anything in missions was through a national, centralized effort. So they set up the kind of structure which would make the churches accountable to the national organization. Mission offerings collected on the local level would be turned over to the district. Half of the offerings would be

31. Moore, p. 448.

retained at that level, with the other half going to the state organization. The state level would retain half of that amount, sending the other half to the national. The plan did not work, but it was a significant organizational step. This was the beginning of a period of tremendous struggle, for many other leaders recognized in the "Louisville Plan" the beginnings of another structured denomination. Without delving into the developments of that period, suffice it to say that their fears were justified.

The General Christian Missionary Convention became the General Convention of Churches of Christ in 1912, The International Convention of Disciples of Christ in 1917, The International Convention of the Christian Churches (Disciples of Christ) in 1956, and finally has recently undergone the ambitious "Restructure," with the controls over the churches being strengthened at each step. The Committee on Brotherhood Restructure explains:

> The aim of brotherhood restructure is to develop an organization that expresses the organic wholeness of the church in all its parts. That there is more to the church than the local congregations—that agencies, institutions, associations and conventions are parts of the body of Christ and not detachable things like clothing—is a growing conviction among Disciples.[32]

That translates into "a unified structure—one body with many parts; congregational, regional and international—'manifestations' of the one church." The central organization has the exclusive right to ordain individuals to serve in its new orders of ministry, and to assume control over

32. Committee on Brotherhood Restructure, *The Direction in Brotherhood Restructure* (Indianapolis: International Convention of Christian Churches - Disciples of Christ, n.d.), p. 3.

the actions and the resources of all member congregations. One of the key motives for this restructure has been the desire to bring the churches into the kind of denominational structure which can be merged with one or more other denominations. Although the C.O.C.U. "super-church" merger failed, the Disciples leadership has continued to pursue some kind of merger, and a union with the United Church of Christ denomination is expected before the end of the decade. Along the way, there have also been some rather obvious theological shifts in this organization, moving increasingly toward liberal interpretations of the Scriptures and emphasizing social concerns more than restoration of Biblical principles.

A division finally came in 1927 with the establishment of the North American Christian Convention. With P. H. Welshimer serving as its president, the new convention was called into being in reaction to practices being condoned on mission fields and to the theological stance of the hierarchy which had evolved in the movement. Many of the churches and leaders had begun to fear the growing size and power of the organization, along with the control over the churches it was beginning to assume. Along with this was the growing frustration of the churches over the removal of the missionary ventures from the effective jurisdiction of the local congregations. Missionaries were now sent out by the hierarchy who operated the United Christian Missionary Society (a conglomerate of six mission agencies formed in 1919), and they were answerable only to them. The same was true of the other boards and agencies operating under the U.C.M.S. umbrella. The churches were required to funnel all funds through "headquarters," from which point they were divided and administered as that leadership saw best.

Reports began to filter back down to the churches about comity agreements made on the mission field, about open membership (not requiring baptism) being practiced there, and about the closing of some mission stations. Other reports came about waste, extravagance and indebtedness. Inquiries and appeals through the hierarchy of the U.C.M.S. brought no action. The churches were being required to support practices on the mission field which they could not justify by the Scriptures, and they witnessed the growth of an expensive, wasteful and unresponsive superstructure which demanded their money but failed to show the promised results. The letters "U.C.M.S." were commonly translated in many of these churches as "You see a mess!"

When veteran missionary Leslie Wolfe was recalled from the Philippines by the U.C.M.S. in 1925 for his opposition to the open membership practices there, the division in the movement was not long in coming. The practice of "direct support missions," sending missionaries out directly from the churches and eliminating the administrative hierarchy and its financial overhead, was reinstituted. The North American Christian Convention, which first met in Indianapolis October 12-16, 1927, was created as a non-delegate annual free fellowship of Christians and was, as Welshimer put it, "a clarion call back to the old paths."[33] Thirty-five hundred gathered in Cadle Tabernacle for the first North American to share in Christian fellowship and to be inspired by great preaching. A continuation committee was appointed to lay plans for another such meeting the next year. With few exceptions, the North American has continued to meet annually in various locations across the country and has

33. Harrold McFarland, *The Struggle to Be Free* (Joliet: Mission Service Press, 1960), p. 13.

become one of the largest religious conventions in the nation. It has continued to be characterized by great preaching, outstanding music, practical workshops in almost every area of ministry, and fellowship for church and missionary leaders from around the world. The development of sessions for children and youth has helped it to attract many Christian families who include the North American as an inspirational part of their vacations.

Another significant convention was born in March, 1948. Meeting in the Los Angeles home of John and Wahneta Chase, beloved veteran missionaries to Japan and Korea, Marian Schaefer and J. Russell Morse joined the Chases in laying the plans which developed into the National Missionary Convention. The new convention began as a one-day missionary rally prior to the North American in Springfield, Illinois, in April of 1948. By 1950, however, it had developed into a separate convention of its own. Its purposes were to provide a fellowship for both home and foreign missionaries, to encourage the churches to focus upon the missionary challenge, and to recruit Christians for missionary service. David Filbeck comments "The National Missionary Convention has been held annually since and has performed an important function in not only promoting missions but also galvanizing the Direct-Support method of the Christian Churches into a missionary movement."[34]

It is important to note that neither of these conventions was organized as, or allowed to become, a delegate convention. Neither was presumed to have any authority over the churches. Neither permitted the development of legislation for the churches. The only business conducted at

---

34. David Filbeck, *The First Fifty Years* (Joplin: College Press Publishing Company, 1980), p. 216.

either convention has been the appointment of those who would plan the next convention. Convention officers were given no authority or jurisdiction beyond tending to that task. Both conventions have continued to exist in dependence upon the churches for their financial support. Consequently, both have been held accountable to the churches as well.

Those who have been chosen to lead in planning the conventions, as well as those who have been selected as the spokesmen from the pulpit and in the workshop classrooms, have obviously influenced the churches of the movement with their supra-congregational leadership. They have had to do so, however, by appealing to their listeners to accept their messages on the basis of their reasonableness and upon an examination of the Scriptures. They could not command anyone to do anything by virtue of their position or authority. This same procedure has been successfully followed in numerous state and area Christian conventions, as well as specialized conferences or conventions of Christian writers, educators, youth leaders, ministers, etc. For the most part, leadership for these conventions has remained volunteer. The larger conventions now employ a paid staff, which is given the responsibility of handling the preparations and publicity for the gatherings from year to year. Even such paid staff members, however, are given no authority over the churches. Herein has been the key to their success. They exist to serve the churches, rather than to represent or to command them.

In Summary

There is a definite apostolic precedent set for roles of supra-congregational leadership for the churches. Whenever the church failed to function according to the divine expectations, guidelines and agenda set for it, supra-congregational leadership was needed to intervene and to restore it to its task. No church in the New Testament existed in isolation. Intervening leadership, however, must focus upon the problem behavior, rather than attacking the worth of the persons involved; and it must be committed to the task of restoring the church and those involved to productive growth and ministry for Christ. Only the most spiritually mature are to undertake such work, and they are not to develop any kind of permanent superstructure of control over the churches.

Since the early days of the church there have been those who have sought to become supra-congregational leaders without the proper qualifications and for purposes of ruling and victimizing the churches. The apostles had to deal with this problem continually. The most effective deterrant to such attempts to take over the churches is for them to become the healthy, growing, ministering bodies they were intended to be. They become susceptible to attack when they fail to function as designed, but they become strong and resistant to disease when they are healthy and functioning.

Following the apostolic precedent, we have witnessed the power of journalistic leadership in the Restoration Movement. A host of journals have emerged over the years, with their editors exercising to various degrees a supra-congregational leadership of the churches. Along with these religious newspapers and magazines have been produced a number of significant commentaries and other books. These have also helped to shape the thinking of the movement.

With the growth and expansion of the churches came a need for the education and preparation of competent, professional leadership for these churches. Numerous schools were begun for this purpose. Those who led and who taught in these schools also exercised, in a variety of ways, a supra-congregational leadership with the participating churches of their area. The tremendous multiplication of these educational endeavors, however, has left most of them relatively small in size, inadequate in educational resources and lacking sufficient financial support from the churches to effectively accomplish their mission. Mergers will be inevitable for survival.

Itinerant leadership in the persons of those who served in the capacity of area evangelists also played a key role of supra-congregational leadership in the Restoration Movement. Through their preaching, debates and utilization of other means of communicating, some of these leaders gained both national and international prominence. In each case, however, their leadership was sought and respected on the basis of their personal abilities and stature, rather than being due to any official position or power they held.

Finally, a recognition of a need for cooperative efforts among the churches in accomplishing some aspects of the mission of the church led to the formation of conventions. When these were allowed to develop into representative bodies with power to legislate and to control the churches, the result was the development of another ecclesiastical hierarchy and the formation of another denominational structure. When these were designed and maintained as servants of the churches without representative or governing powers, they have been able to accomplish much good. The leaders of the former type of convention became the authoritarian rulers of the churches, while the leaders of the latter type were forced to lead through appeals to reason and the Scriptures.

12

QUO VADIS?

The Validity of the Plea

It might well be asked, "Where do we go from here?" Has the Restoration Movement arrived? Is there nothing remaining to restore? This is apparently the practiced—if not the stated—conclusion of many who are the contemporary heirs to this noble endeavor. Carl Ketcherside cautions: "It is a little risky for any generation to assume that it has arrived while all others have departed."[1] The Restoration Movement may have indeed done some "arriving" in its restoration of New Testament doctrine. In view of the many problems and inconsistencies which we have discovered in

1. W. Carl Ketcherside, "Sources of Our Pattern," *Mission Messenger*, June, 1970, p. 85.

the areas of church leadership and church polity, however, it would appear that there is an urgent need for the movement to once again begin moving toward restoration in these crucial areas—and quickly!

The identification of errors is always considerably easier than the recommendation or implementation of workable solutions. Yet, it is the height of irresponsibility to criticize or to destroy that which one is either unwilling or incapable of rebuilding in a better form. It is the intent, then, of this final chapter to review some of the more workable and more scriptural alternatives to the present concepts of leadership, which appear to be preventing the churches from realizing their potential in accomplishing Christ's mission, and to propose ways in which they can be implemented.

Is the Restoration Plea still valid? Can the Great Commission ever be successfully accomplished? Can the church ever be reunited through a return to a Biblical faith and a restoration of Biblical principles and practices in order to cooperate in the accomplishment of the Great Commission? Is it essential that restoration include the rediscovery and implementation of New Testament principles for church leadership in order to accomplish that mission? The answer to all of these questions is a ringing affirmation!

It is reasonably evident that most of the problems encountered by the Restoration Movement in reaching its objectives have resulted either from ignorance of the Bible or from its desertion. God simply plans no failures! The Holy Spirit has not erred in conveying, by His inspiration, that message to men. We must necessarily then assume that the errors have been on our part. We have been overly influenced by our culture and we have over-reacted to the errors of others. Consequently we have failed to comprehend and to translate into practice that Message with its guaranteed plan for success.

Having affirmed this confidence in the validity of the Restoration Plea, however, it is essential that we once again re-state the key principles we have discovered before we proceed any further. These principles are foundational in our restoration of New Testament church leadership.

The church is a monarchy. Jesus said, "On this rock I will build my church" (Matt 16:18). He repeatedly refers to it as His kingdom (Luke 22:30; John 18:36), and He is described as the Eternal King, the King of kings and Lord of lords (I Tim 1:17; Rev 19:16). To Him has been given *all* authority in heaven and on earth (Matt 28:18). He is identified as the Head of the body, which is His church (Eph 4:15).

At the very root and core of many of our problems has been a basic misconception about the nature and ownership of the church. It is a monarchy with Jesus, the Christ, as its King. To Him was given exclusive authority, and He still has that authority. It has never been delegated or relinquished to the church or to any leaders of the church. Consequently, the church has never been—nor will it ever be—a democracy. To become such, it would have to overthrow the King and the form of government it already has. Neither can the church ever invest any position, person or group of officers it may create or elect with any authority which it does not itself possess. Being a monarchy, no decisions of any individual, congregation or council can over-rule the decrees of Jesus. The first and foremost important question for any church or any leader to ask must be "Has the Lord spoken about this subject?" On any issue where He has spoken, the matter is forever settled for all in His kingdom. Ours is neither to question, to argue nor to change His edict, but to learn it, to accept it and to obey it. He is both Lord and King, and we are His subjects.

Edwin Errett said it well some years ago "The theory that the church is a democracy has been used, not only to alter the organizational set-up of the church, but to change its doctrine and its ordinances." He notes that Jesus did give His apostles authority to "bind and loose" under the direction of the Holy Spirit, but that it was not transferred beyond them.[2] Harold W. Ford adds:

> Those charged with church leadership and responsibility . . . should forever remember that the identity of the church of Jesus Christ is determined by its express continuance in the faith and practice of the church in those times when it was under the apostolic leadership. . . . No man, however gifted or informed, has any right from the Lord or otherwise to make up the supposed deficiency he may think he sees in God's revelation by making laws for the church, where God has been silent.[3]

The leadership pattern is sketchy, but the principles are plain. Referring to the misapplications many have made of the fourth proposition of Thomas Campbell's "Declaration and Address" (that the Old and New Testaments alone contain the authoritative constitution for the church of Christ), James G. Van Buren cautions that, "The implication that the New Testament is to be used by the church today in the same way as the Old Testament was used in the Jewish community . . . is surely open to question."[4] In other words,

2. Edwin Errett, "Is the Church a Democracy?" *Christian Standard*, April 26, 1941.

3. Harold W. Ford, "The Validity of Restoration," *Chritian Standard*, September 30, 1979, pp. 879-880.

4. James G. Van Buren, "Reflections on the 'Restoration Plea,'" *Christian Standard*, July 12, 1970, p. 663.

the New Testament is not to be interpreted and applied legalistically. Carl Ketcherside sums up his conclusions:

> God has not imposed upon us a rigid and stereotyped pattern, but has given us guidelines within a historic situation. We must use these as a starting point. We must work toward maturity within their framework. . . . We are coming to see that, in many cases, the pattern we have espoused is not derived from the sacred scriptures at all. It is merely an unwritten creed, hallowed by usage and hardened by debate.[5]

Hoy Ledbetter concurs with this and goes a step further when he posts this warning to the church:

> A restoration which seeks to reproduce the exact forms employed by the early church is doomed to frustration and failure. The Bible leaves no doubt that certain tasks are to be performed, but by whom is often open to question, the ultimate answer to which must be left to the wisdom of the congregation concerned.[6]

So there is a difference between "patternism," or the legalistic reproduction of exact forms, and the implementation of Biblical principles. Some very clear guidelines and principles for church leadership do exist in the New Testament. We are not, however, given a detailed blueprint for the leadership of each church with the instruction to reproduce it in our church and in every other church. To have done so would have rendered the form inflexible and unworkable in the many different times and places and cultural settings in history. Principles are adaptable and can be applied; detailed patterns cannot. That which the Lord did,

---

5. Ketcherside, pp. 88-89.

6. Hoy Ledbetter, "The Paid Professional Preacher," *Integrity*, November, 1977, p. 87.

then, was to establish through His Word some brief, basic principles within which we are to work in devising workable and contemporary forms.

That which the Lord did not do in His Word, however, we have sought to do for Him by randomly collecting and discarding the bits and pieces of references, practices and instructions given, and have proceeded to fashion and permanently weld those which we have chosen into a fixed framework of elected officials and representative government for the church. In so doing we have almost completely lost sight of the New Testament's real emphasis regarding church leadership.

The emphasis is upon function in church leadership. As we have demonstrated in chapter two, the entire concept of an office or an officer in reference to church leadership is totally foreign to the New Testament. Jesus is the only Officer of the church. The emphasis is consistently upon the function and upon the selection of those who are best qualified by ability and spiritual maturity to function effectively in leadership. Four primary functions of leadership are described and required: (1) Leading by example; (2) Nurturing (parenting) the family of God; (3) Equipping God's people to be able to share in the ministry of the church; and (4) Serving—meeting people at the point of their needs with ministry and God's answers. Again, these four functions are discussed in detail in chapter two.

Two words are actually translated as "leadership" in the New International Version of the New Testament. The first of these, quoting Psalm 108:8 in Acts 1:20, speaks of the need to fill the vacant leadership position of Judas. The word used in that case in the Greek is the same one used for overseers (elders). The second word, *proistēmi,* appears in Romans 12:8, I Timothy 3:4; 5:17 and I Thessalonians 5:12. Variously translated as "lead," "manage" and "rule," it carries the idea of going ahead of, directing, managing, being concerned about, caring for and giving aid. It is an active word relating to responsible function on behalf of those being led. In particular it is applied to those who are preaching, teaching and admonishing those they lead. The passages point out that those who have this responsibility are to fulfill it with all diligence, and that they are to be accorded honor and respect by those they lead when they function faithfully.

Consequently, leaders in the church—whatever their titles—must necessarily be functioning in these ways, or they are not really New Testament church leaders. Neither election by a congregation nor occupying an office by appointment can qualify or make a person a leader. If that person is not leading, he is not a leader; for leadership is functional, rather than official. He is simply an official with, or without, the potential for leadership. Such officials inevitably create institutions, develop hierarchies and become more concerned about protecting their existence, forms, authority and control than about the accomplishment of the mission of the church. History is replete, as we have seen, with ample evidence of this oft-repeated evolutionary development. Gene Getz further notes:

> New Testament Christians did not consider certain forms and patterns and structures to be absolute. Rather, these were but means to carry out New Testament directives and reach New Testament objectives. When patterns do appear, they vary from situation to situation in the areas of both communication and organization and administration.[7]

---

7. Gene A. Getz, *Sharpening the Focus of the Church* (Chicago: Moody Press, 1974), p. 210.

As Getz implies, the New Testament church was characterized by a goal-orientation. Everything which was done in the church was done for a purpose, and the methods employed were selected to best accomplish that purpose. Purpose is not achieved, however, when the attention of the church is concentrated upon the development and preservation of forms, offices, titles and controls. There must be a restoration of a goal-orientation for both the church and its leadership; and for goals to be reached, there must be a concentration on the effective functioning of leadership.

A capable minister is needed to help provide expressive leadership. For too long the Restoration Movement has hallowed early "Campbellism" as its creed on this subject, refusing to acknowledge the pastoral role in church leadership and relegating him to a role similar to that of a hired hand. Every group of people will—and indeed must—have a visible leader. Some leader will as inevitably arise in any group as cream will rise to the top of fresh milk. Sherwood Evans has commented: "It is impossible to have a situation in which 'everyone acts middle.' Leaders will 'rise to the top' or 'take two steps forward' as you will."[8]

Yes, there will be a visible leader in every church. The problem is to make certain that it is the right leader. In the Old Testament Israel was perpetually following the wrong leaders. Then, when they found themselves suffering the worst possible consequences of their popular, but wrong choices, God would raise up for them a leader—one who would speak to them the Word of the Lord and lead them back to Godliness.

---

8. H. Sherwood Evans, "Who Runs the Church?" *The Restoration Herald*, October, 1979, p. 162.

We have noted in the New Testament that God gifted some to become pastors (Eph 4:11). These whom He gifted were then called to commit themselves to the ministry of the Word and to the leadership of God's people. For this ministry of expressive leadership they were to be both educationally and spiritually prepared. As expressive leadership specialists, they were to become the right kind of visible leaders for the church, working in cooperation with the eldership.

For too long the church has cast preachers and elders in mutually exclusive and adversary roles. This should not be. Besides being the pulpit spokesmen, along with the elders, pastors are to share in shepherding the flock of God, caring for their needs, leading them into spiritual growth and equipping them for participation in the ministry of the church. As Evans affirms: "You can have a preacher and a plurality of elders with no detriment to the scriptural role of either."[9] They are to supplement and to complement each other in sharing in the expressive leadership of the church. Neither is intended to be under the authority of the other, but all are under the authority of Christ. Both ministers and elders are obligated to see that His authority is maintained and that His will is accomplished in and through the church. In the event either strays from the Word, he is to be corrected and exhorted by the other. Grayson Ensign describes the elders as "coaches" and a pastor as a "specialty coach."[10] The coaching analogy is a good one, describing much of the function and reflecting the common relationship to the team; although a pastor might better be identified as a "head coach" in that analogy.

9. Evans, p. 162.

10. Grayson H. Ensign, "Restoring a Biblical Leadership," *The Restoration Herald*, October, 1979, p. 163.

By whatever name he is identified, this gifted specialist or "professional," is uniquely qualified to lead the church in the accomplishment of the will of the Lord. He should know the Word and be able to communicate it better than anyone else in the church. Recalling our basic premises, then, who would be better qualified to provide visible, expressive leadership for the church, or to lead it in the accomplishment of its God-given objectives? As God's spokesman, his charge is to:

> Preach the Word; be prepared in season and out of season; correct, rebuke and encourage—with great patience and careful instruction. For the time will come when men will not put up with sound doctrine. Instead, to suit their own desires, they will gather around them a great number of teachers to say what their itching ears want to hear. They will turn their ears away from the truth and turn aside to myths. But you, keep your head in all situations, endure hardship, do the work of an evangelist, discharge all the duties of your ministry (II Tim 4:2-5).

A pastor who is employed as a hired hand will never be able to fulfill this inspired commission. It is foolish to propose that any person who is gifted, prepared and called by God, and laid under such a charge, should be expected to take some sort of back seat and not assume the role of being the visible and vocal primary expressive leader of the church. Woe be unto him—and to the people of God—if he does not! If he does not assume this leadership, someone else will assume it who probably knows less of God's Word, and who may have a different set of priorities for the church which he will see substituted through his leadership. Such a leader will write his own agenda for the church and will "keep the preacher in line." The pulpit voice will be considered irrelevant and will either be ignored or silenced, depending on how much a pastor decides to "meddle."

Such has been the costly lesson we have had difficulty learning in the Restoration Movement. We have bemoaned the escalating exodus of the frustrated "men in the preaching ministry who are leaving it to enter secular vocations," the increasing "number of congregations seeking preachers for their pulpits," the prevalence of brief, unproductive ministries and the vast majority of churches who are showing little or no net growth each year. As Alvin Tiffin continues to attest:

> These men entered the labor with high hopes and dreams of real ministry for our Lord. Many of these people entered the labor desperately wanting to be significantly used of God in His kingdom. There are two vital factors in the causation of this terrible attrition. First, is the inadequate preparation of workers to meet the needs and pressures of the modern located ministry. . . . A second factor . . . lies in the relationships between the preacher and the congregations that are served . . . leaders and members of the flock are not understanding of the preacher's or their own role in ministry as they labor together.[11]

It is the unanimous testimony of the church growth experts that the minister is the key to the growth of any church. If he is capable, committed, fits the congregation, is supported by the members and the other leadership and is permitted to lead for a long enough period of time, almost any church can grow. Brief ministries of three years or less seldom accomplish anything. Most of those who have spent years

---

11. Alvin L. Tiffin, "A Matter of Concern," *Gospel Log*, November, 1979, p. 2.

studying thousands of churches claim that the most productive years of a pastor's ministry seldom begin before the fourth, fifth or sixth year of his leadership with a church.[12] Prior to that time, he is building the relationships, earning the confidence and laying the groundwork necessary to lead the church into a period of significant growth.

Rather than adversary roles, ministers and elders need to adopt and cultivate a sense of mutuality in their shared leadership, and to conscientiously support each other in leadership. Dennis Fulton insists upon a commitment of *loyalty* to all other leadership and of *confidentiality* from all who would serve as leaders at Chapel Rock Christian Church in Indianapolis. He points to disloyalty and to breaches of confidence as being the causes of most leadership problems in churches.[13] He is right! The vow required by Chapel Rock should be required by every church who wants to keep its pastor or any of its other leaders.

Neither ministers nor elders should seek to control every ministry in the church. Neither should they permit themselves to become the "dumping ground" for all of the unwanted responsibilities of the members or the other leaders. As expressive leaders, they must concentrate on the functions of expressive leadership, equipping and delegating to others the tasks of implementive leadership. Joe Ellis reminds us:

> Expressive operations are those that create and maintain in a body of people a vital commitment to a clear and shared purpose. These operations point the way, guide, motivate,

---

12. C. Peter Wagner, *Leading Your Church to Growth* (Ventura: Regal Books, 1984), p. 69.

13. Dennis Fulton, "Essentials for Church Leaders," *Christian Standard*, March 17, 1985, pp. 8-9.

> challenge, inspire, devise and execute plans, instruct, enable people to function well, and keep the vision clear. They center on stating, re-stating, reminding, and clarifying purpose. They interpret actions and efforts in terms of how they contribute to achieving purpose. They serve as the "eyes" for the body to see where it is and where it is going. . . . The major functions of expressive servant-leaders include: (1) exhorting, encouraging, or urging people toward the goal; and (2) correcting, reproving, rebuking, and exhorting people back on the track to the goal when they have deflected. Expressive concerns focus in the general oversight tasks and communication functions such as preaching and teaching.[14]

A qualified and functioning eldership is absolutely essential. Lyle Schaller notes that the most significant question which can be asked of a church is, "Who is really in charge here?"[15] The answer to that question should be, as we have seen, "Jesus!" But is He? If He can be overruled in practice by the by-laws, by the elders, a pastor, the church board or by the vote of a congregational meeting, He is not really in charge. Our concept of leadership, along with our concept of the eldership, must first and foremost assure the Lordship of Jesus over His church. It must guarantee, as much as possible, that His purposes and agenda will be accomplished in and through the church.

To accomplish this, the most Christ-like and spiritually mature men in the church are to be appointed to the serious responsibilities of overseeing, shepherding and leading the

---

14. Joe S. Ellis, *The Church on Purpose* (Cincinnati: Standard Publishing Company, 1982), pp. 133-134.

15. Lyle E. Schaller, *The Decision Makers* (Nashville: Abingdon Press, 1974), p. 179.

flock of God's people who are placed in their charge. They, along with ministers, are given the task of providing the expressive leadership for the church. It is not a matter of authority, but one of responsibility. The only authority involved is that of Christ, whose authority must be honored in the lives of both elders and congregation. Consequently, elders are in no position to "lord it over the flock." The standard of qualifications for elders is set so high that they must continually be pressing on toward the mark (Phil 3:12-14). They are not permitted to measure their spirituality in comparison to other Christians, but are required to measure it in comparison to Christ. With the humility which this breeds, acknowledging their own failings and shortcomings, along with recognizing their need to keep growing, the elders can then say to the flock, "Follow us as we grow together."

This kind of elder views himself as neither legislator nor judge. His primary concern is that of seeing the revealed Word of God honored and incorporated into the lives of the members of the body. His secondary concern is to assure that neither he nor anyone else is permitted to "speak in the silences" of the Bible, or to bind opinions or pronouncements upon the church which has been placed in his care. Neither as an individual nor as a group of elders will he create additional laws or render authoritative any interpretations of the law of Christ to bind upon the members.

This kind of elder does not view himself as simply being a member of a board, conceiving his duties to have been fulfilled by attending a meeting and casting a vote. Larry Richards, decrying elders who only perceive themselves as "board members," comments:

> In our culture "board members" set policy, control, and make decisions for those "under" them. . . . Biblical elders

> serve *among* the Body, and their function is to disciple, mature, teach, encourage and guide members of the Body to freedom and responsibility to Christ, who is the sole head of the Church. Thus the decisions made by consensus by the elders will relate to *their* ministry in and to the Body. But their decisions should not be made *for* groups, teams, or agencies of the Body. To begin to make decisions . . . for others is to violate Peter's warning against "lording it over those entrusted to you" (I Peter 5:3).[16]

Therefore, the eldership which leads the church into maturity and ministry will not be an authoritarian body of officials at the top of a hierarchical power pyramid, but will be in name and function those who are shepherds to the flock and under-shepherds to the Lord, "the Chief Shepherd" (I Peter 5:1-4). To them, because of their great and grave responsibility to the Lord for those in their charge, is due:

1. *Submission* (I Peter 5:5; Heb 13:17) - even as we are called to be subject to one another in the kingdom of Christ.
2. *Honor and high esteem* (I Tim 5:17; I Thess 5:13) - when they actually function in leading.
3. *Confidence* (I Tim 5:19) - disallowance of vindictive charges brought against them, unless such charges are substantiated by two or three witnesses.
4. *Imitation* (Heb 12:7) - of their faith and their lifestyle.

Capable and qualified deacons are essential to the church. Rather than being ill-defined and nondescript officers and board members, however, deacons need to be selected as implementers to lead in the organization and accomplishment of specific areas of ministry for the church. Whether

16. Larry Richards, "Consensus: The Answer?" *Newsbrief,* Fall, 1979, p. 5.

they be men or women, deacons should be chosen on the basis of their spiritual maturity and their special abilities to handle a particular task. As the best qualified persons to get the job done, they should be allowed to do it without interference and with the necessary financial and other resources supplied. Church budgets should be planned in such a way as to provide these resources.

The relationship between expressive and implementive leadership can be illustrated by the roles of the symphony conductor and the section leaders of an orchestra. While the conductor coordinates and gives expression to the total effort, the section leaders are responsible for rehearsing and helping their sections to each do their part in producing the over-all effect desired from the orchestra. It requires completely different musical abilities to play the instruments in each section, and none of the parts sound exactly alike when played alone. Some of them, in fact, may seem unimportant when heard alone, but each is essential to the performance of the composition. The section leaders are the most capable people available to organize and develop their own sections in producing their essential parts. They are the implementive leaders of the symphony.

The roles of deacons in providing implementive leadership, however, will vary from congregation to congregation and from time to time in each church, depending upon the tasks which need to be done. Deacons must be in tune with —and committed to—the same mission, principles and goals for the church as the elders. Without this unanimity among the expressive and implementive leaders, the church will inevitably struggle and have great difficulty in reaching its goals.

Church boards need to be replaced. They are the products of our culture and often operate in opposition to scriptural principles of church leadership. In its present stage of evolution, the typical church board is both unscriptural and anti-scriptural. It is an unworkable combination of both democratic representative government and the corporate business structure.

Church boards too often spend their time asking and trying to answer all of the wrong questions: "What do *we* want to do?" "How does *the church* feel on this issue?" "Do *we* want to spend any money for this ministry?" "Do *we* feel that anything should be done in this area—now or ever?" These questions usurp the authority and Lordship of Jesus. They reflect the fact that the board is serving as the representative weather vane of the prevailing winds blowing in the congregation. In short, they reflect treason! The primary questions should be, "What does the Lord want done," and "How are we going to get it accomplished?"

Lest we throw out the baby with the bath water, however, we would note that there is a need for coordination, sharing and planning among the leaders of the church. If the church board can be re-defined, cease to act as a board in the policy setting and church running sense, and can become instead a coordinating and implementing council or fellowship of the church leaders, it could serve a useful purpose. Few boards have this capacity, though. Many need to be executed and buried, and a fresh start needs to be made under a new name and format.

Church leadership must be followed. C. Peter Wagner, church growth expert, has coined the word "followership" and devotes an entire chapter of one of his books to the importance of congregations learning to follow leadership if they are to grow. He says:

> There seems to be a curious assumption that while leaders need special instruction in exercising their role, followers need no such instruction. The more I study church leadership, the more I disagree with the assumption. Many pastors who would like to, cannot lead their congregations because of a basic lack of sensitivity on the part of the people as to their role as followers.[17]

There is no question about the fact that lack of "followership" is holding back many churches from realizing their potential and accomplishing their mission. As far as the New Testament is concerned, it is not a congregational option. Both I Timothy 5:17-19 and I Thessalonians 5:12-13 give explicit commands to the church concerning honoring and following their leaders.

Accomplishing Change

The foregoing brief summary of some of the New Testament principles of leadership which affect the local church appear in rather vivid contrast to the current concepts of church leadership in the Restoration Movement. While many will have difficulty correlating these striking differences with the problems being experienced within the movement, there is a definite cause and effect relationship. The movement set out to unite Christians in the task of accomplishing the fulfillment of the Great Commission. The leaders of the movement were convinced that the only possible foundation for the essential unity was a united commitment to the Lordship of Christ and to restoring New Testament faith and practice in all things.

---

17. Wagner, p. 107.

We have definitely stopped short of the restoration goal, however, in the area of church leadership. This area we have sought to excuse and retain as our option. Since we live in a democratic culture, we have reserved the right to create for the church a democratic and representative form of government. In so doing, we have undermined the entire endeavor and are now witnessing its slow, but sure, demise. The reason is clear: We have appropriated unto ourselves as the church an authority which we were never given. Any way we may choose to view it, we have challenged the authority of Jesus and refused to allow His Lordship to extend to every area.

Change is urgently needed within the churches if we are to restore the vitality and growth of the movement and achieve its goals. Due to the congregational structure of the movement, however, the need for such change must be recognized and implemented on the local level. Change, though, will be resisted in almost every church. An old man was showing some visitors through the church where he had been a member for many years. "I suppose you have seen a lot of changes over the years," commented one of the visitors. "Yep," was the reply, "and I've been against every one of them!"

What is it that makes change so difficult to achieve? Even in the midst of a society in which the world has become accustomed to almost daily changes, we yet remain resistant to change. Why is change so difficult? Ted Engstrom and Edwin Dayton explain:

> *All change is perceived as loss.* Even when the change is an apparently happy occasion, like marriage, or moving to a new job, there remains the lingering feeling that we have

> left something behind, something which we can never recapture.[18]

This is especially true in terms of the church. There is a tendency to hold on to old forms and comfortable methods, even when they may not be working or accomplishing any purpose. A tremendous amount of rationalization occurs in defending the status quo. Some of this appears so irrational, it is laughable. As one wag recently said, "If God had wanted us to go on the metric system, Jesus would have appointed ten disciples rather than twelve." Nevertheless, change is resisted with such arguments in the church by those who are completely serious in making their objections.

In spite of the fact that the church is supposed to be in the business of change—changing lives and changing the world through those changed lives—the majority of churches fall into the trap of accepting a maintenance orientation. The agenda of the church is designed to keep the folk who are already there happy and comfortable. The notion that programs, facilities or methods should change to accommodate the access of those who are outside the church is usually greeted with a defensive reaction and relegated to at least a secondary status in the church's priorities.

There is no question that many of our current concepts of church leadership are different and that a number of them even exist in direct violation of the principles outlined for church leadership in the New Testament. A key question, though, is: "How much do we really want to restore New Testament Christianity or Christ's mission in our particular church?" If we have become satisfied with our modern substitutes, and we have rationalized enough about them to

18. Ted W. Engstrom and Edwin R. Dayton, "The Anguish of Change," *Christian Leadership Letter*, February, 1982, p. 1.

become comfortable with the obvious challenge they present to Jesus' Lordship over His church, we will do nothing.

When leaders do recognize the need for changes and institute them, they often go about achieving them in the wrong ways. For one thing, they quite often fail to anticipate the anguish which many of the members, along with some of the leaders, will wrestle with as a result. These folk can be expected, in fact, to go through many of the same stages of grief which one experiences with the death of a loved one. This is particularly true if a change is introduced suddenly. In such a case, leaders may find themselves the recipients of the anger and frustration of those affected by the change. Many leaders have misunderstood these reactions and have taken them personally. A common response from leadership is to react in return, rather than responding with understanding and with some attempt to back off and restructure the plan of change. Some leaders have been sacrificed. More than one minister has lost his job as a result of the changes he helped to introduce. Engstrom and Dayton further explain.

> If people are presented with new situations which threaten that to which they have grown pleasantly accustomed, then the discontent will be aimed at removing the cause for the potential change. The amount of resistance to change will be proportional to the threat to perceived vested interests. It is important to understand that resistance may not be against the change agent or even to the program that is being proposed. Both may be *intellectually* perceived as excellent. But however good the program, if it is going to result in what is perceived as changing the way things have always been, it is natural that it will be resisted. . . . The task of the Christian leader then is to introduce change in

a manner that will encourage people on the one hand and not discourage on the other.[19]

Although change is perceived as loss, people are able to make changes. Some changes are made because they are forced on us. We will always resist those. We do not like to be forced to do anything, but we often must deal with such forced changes. Our taxes have gone up, the price of gas has increased, or our house is being condemned to make room for a new freeway. We resent and resist such changes, but we eventually accept them, whether we like them or not. On the other hand, we make other changes because we want to. We will accept, for example, changes which we have become convinced will bring something that is better and more beneficial than that which we have had. If we can move our savings to another type of account, which is also insured, and which pays twice the interest, we will move them. The threat of instability disturbs and frightens us. If the change is presented in such a way, however, to assure us that stability will not be sacrificed, and that by moving to the new we will reap only benefits, we are likely to accept the change.

C. Peter Wagner advises that four steps need to be taken for every major change which is to be made in the church (1) Share your vision; (2) Accumulate feedback; (3) Promote harmony in the body; and (4) Discern the proper timing.[20] This is good advice. Leaders too often share too little of their vision and understanding of God's will for the church with the members and other leaders who will be affected by

19. Engstrom and Dayton, p. 2.
20. Wagner, pp. 196-197.

the changes. Having spent a great deal of time studying and praying about the matter before coming to their decisions, they yet expect others to come to the same conclusions relatively instantaneously upon the basis of a presentation. However carefully prepared that presentation may be, it cannot be expected to automatically eliminate the need for the others to work through some of the same processes themselves before they will be able to accept the validity of the reasons for making any changes.

Church leaders who attempt to make changes in too short a time and with too little opportunity for members to ask questions, or to become accustomed to the idea, will always encounter resistance to the changes which they propose. They will be perceived by the members as attempting to force change upon them, regardless of the real motives of the leaders or the merits of the changes. This is obviously not the way to approach necessary changes in the church. It is imperative that enough lead time be allowed, enough explanation of the reasons for the change be given, enough listing of the benefits to be derived from the change be explained and enough assurances be provided concerning the stability of the church and its leadership.

It is advisable to begin with a small, key group. Make certain the leaders and real decision makers are first sold on the changes, and then let them help sell the others. Give as much opportunity as possible to input and "fine tuning," in order to allow as many people as possible to sense ownership of the agenda. Try to make certain that everyone comes out as a winner from the changes, rather than as the defeated. This is not always possible, but it ought to be the goal in every change. Those who feel defeated will generally leave or will present problems later.

Church leaders will also encounter resistance from those who perceive changes as eroding their control. The fact is that some people have an obsession to control other people, programs and even the whole church. Almost anything can happen—or not happen—in the church as long as they remain in control. The influx of a number of new members into a small congregation, for example, represents a tremendous threat to some leaders who fear that they will lose their control over the church. The institution of a number of new programs, over which a power broker will have no control, is certain to bring a reaction from him, along with an attempt to quash those programs.

This is particularly true in the case of any attempt to eliminate the church board. Even to the average church member, with his cultural background in a democratic society, the church board is viewed as a prudent control on the operation of the church—a sort of system of checks and balances. The idea of doing away with it, even though it is admittedly unscriptural, is always met with fervent resistance; for its demise represents a loss of control.

Herein lies the key issue in church leadership changes: control. Who will be in control? We live in a society with an obsession for controls. We have legislated and regulated to the point that we are hopelessly entangled in a web of our own weaving, but we seem to be convinced that government regulation is the answer to everything. We have certainly not spared the church in our mania to regulate and control. On the other hand, the deregulation of numerous industries in recent years has been viewed with great apprehension; but we have come to learn that our regulations have been destroying those industries and hurting all of us, in many cases.

It is time to do some deregulating in the church. It is time we addressed our fears and questioned our obsession to control. Do we really believe that we have to protect the church by applying the brakes to it? *Are we so convinced that Jesus is incapable of governing and controlling His own body that we must institute and maintain our own system of checks and balances?* Is it really a lack of faith in Him, or is it a personal compulsion we have to be in charge? Facing up to the answers to these questions may be difficult, but they are certainly questions which we will one day have to answer in Judgment if we fail to answer and resolve them now. We will indeed be held accountable for any damages to Christ's body for which we have been responsible.

The High Cost of Leadership

Church leaders are called to be agents of change, rather than preservers of the status quo. Consequently, they will always be the recipients of some form of resistance. This is a fact of church leadership. Leaders are in the business of creating a kind of divine discontent. They are charged with the task of convincing people of their lostness without Christ, their hopelessness without His forgiveness and the necessity of their continuing to grow into His likeness. They are responsible for helping each spiritual infant to see that he will be unable to grow up into Christ-likeness without the nourishment of the Word and the exercise of participation in ministry. They are required to convince fearful Christians that walking by sight is far less productive than learning to walk by faith.

Church leaders are called to continually evaluate the functioning of the church in light of its purpose. They are called to deal with those who would control and manipulate others for their personal benefit. They are called to recognize and refute false teaching. They are called to insist upon the Lordship of Christ being respected throughout the church. They are called to correct, to rebuke and to exhort, as well as to encourage. They are called to a lot of hard work which will not always be appreciated.

Those who must always receive the praise and the approval of their peers have no business in church leadership, nor do those whose course is continually influenced by the complaints of the discontented or the demands of the special interest groups. They will forever be the pawns of others, rather than the servants of Christ. Those whose faith is weak and whose resolve is tentative also need to stay out of church leadership. It will demand more than they have to give.

Church leaders are called to hold a course and to press on toward a goal which has been set by their Leader. They have a glorious opportunity to participate in the accomplishment of the impossible and the conquering of a world for Christ. Theirs is the joy of witnessing transformed lives and divine solutions to insurmountable problems. They who trust in the Lord and are committed to serving Him in leadership live in the realm of His miraculous powers, and yet they must often also deal with the vilest elements of man's character and conduct. Such is the paradox with which church leaders must live.

The price of church leadership can indeed be high. Like Elijah, there will be times when it seems that you stand alone (I Kings 19:10). There will be times when you are falsely accused. There will be many times when you will be unpopular. The Apostle Paul chronicles the cost of leadership for him in II Corinthians 11:23-28. The price of church leadership for Stephen was to be stoned (Acts 7:54-60). Leadership took Jesus to the cross.

The point of all of this is to emphasize that the church will never make the changes it needs to make until there are enough church leaders who are willing to pay the price necessary to make New Testament style leadership happen. Most officers of the church today are content to verbalize about the need to restore New Testament faith and practices in the church, but are unwilling to pay the price to press on to achieve that restoration in the areas of church leadership and church polity. They are content to remain as officers, representing the wishes of their constituents, and hoping that the Lord will somehow never hold them accountable for their apostasy. Very few are willing to risk their popularity or positions by rocking the boat.

There are those, however, who are deeply concerned about the church and the need to restore its proper leadership in order to enable it to realize its potential and to accomplish its mission. They seldom include all of the leaders of any one church, however. These who share this concern need to make this restoration a matter of concentrated prayer and study, including as many of the other leaders and members as possible in the endeavor. It is folly, however, to wait until all of the leaders of a church are convinced and committed before beginning to make the changes. It seldom ever happens. There are too many who now occupy offices and exercise control in the church who will never willingly agree to exchange their positions for New Testament functions expected of church leaders. They have vested interests. Their presence and opposition, however, should not be permitted to outweigh the Lordship of Christ over His church. Those who would be leaders must lead!

Redefining Purpose

Those who would begin to implement the needed changes in church leadership should begin with a redefinition of purpose for their church. All of the existing church leaders, and perhaps all of the congregation, need to be involved in this task. Many will be tempted to by-pass this step, feeling that "everyone already knows the purpose for the church." Those who conclude this are challenged to distribute sheets of blank paper to their leaders and ask them to write a statement of purpose for the church, without benefit of any scripture study. In most cases, the results will be appalling. The truth is, we have lost sight of purpose in most of our churches.

Passages of scripture such as Matthew 28:18-20; Acts 1:8; II Corinthians 5:18-21; Ephesians 4:11-16 and I Peter 2:5, 9 should be studied by all who are involved in the project of developing a statement of purpose for their church. These texts will help to take their definition out of the realm of personal opinion and to build it on a Biblical foundation. Out of their individual and group studies should eventually come a concise, united statement of purpose which is scriptural and can be agreed upon by everyone.

Next, those involved in the project need to list every existing area of ministry of their church. This will include worship, music, evangelism, Christian education, youth, benevolence, missions, etc. The list for every church will vary, but care should be taken that nothing is overlooked. After the list is completed, each area of ministry should be examined in light of the statement of purpose. Does it contribute in any way to the accomplishment of this stated purpose? If it does not now contribute to achieving the purpose, can it be redirected in order to become productive, or should it be eliminated? This kind of evaluation of every program in the church should be done regularly, but it is particularly important at this point in the implementation of changes. Joe Ellis notes:

> The churches that are in trouble are oriented toward preserving human traditions or toward maintaining themselves as institutions, rather than toward accomplishing significant spiritual objectives. People are seeking involvement in meaningful ministry, and they will accept such roles when given adequate preparation and leadership. But it is increasingly difficult to rally support for activities in which people see no point. Much of the current disillusionment with churches grows out of the fact that people perceive much of the activity as pointless.[21]

Finally, the list of areas of ministry needs to be re-examined in light of possible relationships. Rather than having 25 to 50 separate programs, they need to be grouped into 6-10 general areas of ministry; and these areas need to be identified. It will become evident, in most cases, that there are some of these major areas of ministry which have been given very little attention and which have few programs in operation. In churches which have not been growing, for example, the area of evangelism will inevitably be very sparse. This can tell leaders much about the actual present priorities of the church. In contrast to its stated purpose involving both evangelism and edification, most of the existing programs will relate to edification. An inside, or maintenance, orientation of the church is obvious. This is even more dramatically demonstrated by examining the budget allocations or expenditures for each area during the past year. This grouping of

---

21. Ellis, p. 10.

programs into general areas of ministry is also extremely helpful for coordination and goal setting for each of these areas of ministry.

Developing Goals

Every church needs to develop both long-range and short-range goals, along with workable plans for achieving them. As David L. Hocking says:

> Aim at nothing, and you'll hit it every time! We've all heard that from time to time, but its truth sinks into the hearts of very few, unfortunately! Do you know where you're going? Leaders must have a strategy. They must know how to get things done.[22]

Hocking defines a strategy as containing: (1) Objective — that which we have called a statement of purpose; (2) Goals — specific ways in which the achievement of purpose will be measured and accomplished, based on the time, resources and personnel available; (3) Priorities — a determination of which goals need to be tackled first; (4) Planning — the process of assessing available personnel and resources, obstacles to be overcome, determining a course of action and evaluation of the results; and (5) Guidelines — the moral and ethical framework in which the accomplishment of purpose will be pursued.[23]

The sad reality is that a very small minority of churches have taken the time and effort to go through the process of developing any kind of strategy. Most of them just exist from week to week, with the majority of their energies and

---

22. David L. Hocking, *Be a Leader People Follow* (Ventura: Regal Books, 1980), p. 132.
23. Hocking, p. 132.

resources being devoted to simply maintaining existing programs and serving the current membership. They have aimed at nothing, and they are hitting it with regularity as each year goes by. Not a whole lot has changed in the past five years, and not much change is expected in the next five.

These churches have custodians and maintainers caring for them. They lack leaders. Leaders, by their very definition, are going somewhere. They have goals. They have evaluated that which is. They have caught a vision of that which needs to be. They have defined needful, reasonable and reachable goals to help bridge the gap between the present and the possible. They are committed to moving from where they are to where they need to be. They are willing to rise above the comfortable in order to achieve the necessary.

There is a sense of urgency which compels leaders who have comprehended the purpose of the church. Indeed, they cannot be content with inaction. Like the Apostle Paul, they feel an obligation to act, an eagerness to preach and a confidence in the power of God to accomplish His purpose (Rom 1:14-16). "For Christ's love compels us," Paul wrote:

> So from now on we regard no one from a worldly point of view. Though we once regarded Christ in this way, we do so no longer. Therefore, if anyone is in Christ, he is a new creation; the old has gone, the new has come! All this is from God, who reconciled us to Himself through Christ and gave us the ministry of reconciliation: that God was reconciling the world to Himself in Christ, not counting men's sins against them. And He has committed to us the message of reconciliation. We are therefore Christ's ambassadors, as though God were making His appeal through us. We implore you on Christ's behalf, Be reconciled to God. God made Him who had no sin to be sin for us, so that in Him we might become the righteousness of God (II Cor 5:14a, 16-21).

Now if that does not excite and motivate us into developing goals for the church, nothing will! We need to begin by listing all that we are now doing in our church and to categorize these programs into general areas of ministry, as has been suggested. Next we must look at each category of ministry and begin to ask ourselves, "What would Jesus have us accomplish in this area within the next five years—considering our unique situation and the opportunities He has given us?"

Ted W. Engstrom advises us that our goals should always be: (1) Accomplishable — specific actions which we can complete; (2) Reasonable — considering the skills, resources and time available; and (3) Measurable — stating the specific accomplishment and the time required to complete it.[24]

Let us take the area of evangelism, for example. We must begin by assessing our present situation. Where are we now? Where does God want us to be five years from now in this crucial area of ministry? We determine that our church now has 200 active members. We believe that, given our opportunity and responsibility, God would expect us to have 400 within our fellowship five years from now. That represents a net gain of 200 members. Anticipating a certain amount of attrition, however, due to deaths and people who will move away, how many people must we reach for Christ each year in order to net that gain of 200 after five years? We will probably have to add 60 people per year to reach that long-range goal. Our short-range goal for this first year, then, would be to reach 60 people. Assuming that it takes 10 calls to reap one decision, that translates into 600 evangelistic calls

24. Ted W. Engstrom, "Managing More Effectively," *Innovations*, Spring, 1985, p. 10.

which must be made during this year—or approximately 12 calls per week.

We are now getting some identifiable, reasonable and measurable goals. We have just begun, though. How many callers and how many prospects will it take to be able to average 12 calls per week? It suddenly becomes apparent that we need to establish some other goals, or these numbers will never be reached. We may recognize the need to recruit some more evangelistic callers and to schedule a training course for them. Unless we have an unusual number of visitors from the community each Sunday, we may need to set some goals for expanding our exposure and developing additional contacts in the community. We may need to target an area of our community on the map, in which we will set a goal of conducting a convass, or to which we will begin mailing information about the church. Perhaps a goal needs to be set for producing a new church brochure which can be used. Maybe some "bridges" need to be built into the community through the establishment of programs which can meet felt needs, and which will help people to identify our church as one which really cares about them. Should we appoint a committee to explore the need for a Christian preschool or child care center, for example? We may need to set a goal for adding a piece of equipment to the church office, such as a computer, to handle the added volume of records, mail lists, word processing, etc. Another staff member or an additional building may be needed to help minister to the increased number of people.

It is apparent that there is something of an overlap of areas of ministry with some of these goals, but it is important to think through all of the ramifications of the goals we are setting. In Luke 14:28-30 Jesus uses the illustration of a man who had set a goal of building a tower. Jesus pointed out that it was only prudent that he should count the cost involved and plan to be sure he could reach his goal and complete the tower. While He used this example to illustrate the need to count the cost of discipleship, it also reminds us of our need to consider everything which will necessarily be involved in achieving the goals we set for the church. Otherwise they may remain as nothing more than wishful thinking.

Joe S. Ellis brings us another cautioning word in our goal setting for the church:

> Students of church growth have consistently identified additional staff members as essential to keep growth from leveling off or declining. In notable exceptions, however, additional staff has not provided for growth. In these cases the church has very likely employed persons to do its work rather than to equip the church to do the work. Staff members must be seen as equippers of the saints, not as their delegates in ministry. Growing churches also multiply staff by bringing together people whose strengths are different; who supplement, rather than duplicate, one another.[25]

His point is an excellent one! Too many churches set unrealistic goals of adding staff to do the work of ministry for them, rather than calling a specialist to equip them and to coordinate their own efforts in getting the task accomplished and reaching their goals. As we have said before, the church will never be able to hire enough people to do its ministry for the members. Extra staff may be an excellent goal, but only if such staff members are added for the right reasons and with the proper expectations.

---

25. Ellis, p. 60.

Each area of ministry needs to be approached in this way, with five year, four year, three year, two year and one year goals being established and coordinated in as many of these areas as possible. It is vitally important, however, that ample time be allowed for this process to develop a consensus and a commitment among all of the leaders concerning these goals. It will require a great amount of time to develop the first set of 5-year goals. It will be much easier, though, each succeeding year to evaluate and to update those goals. After the goals have been developed, they must then be set down in writing and be shared with the entire congregation. To the degree that leadership is able to secure ownership of the goals by the total fellowship, to that degree the goals will be accomplished.

As mentioned, there must be an annual time set aside to evaluate and to update the 5-year plan. One of the exciting things which will be discovered is that a number of the goals established for the second and third year will have been achieved in the first. Once the goal has been defined, unexpected doors of opportunity will open. Individuals and groups within the church will become excited about reaching a particular goal and will adopt it as their own project. In most cases, not all of the one-year goals will be reached during the first year, but a surprising number will have been reached and exceeded. The excitement generated by the reaching of goals fuels the members and leaders in their resolve to press on to set and to reach others. Consequently, both the goals and their accomplishment need to be advertised as widely as possible.

Formulating a Plan

The setting of goals is absolutely essential for the church, but the formulating of a plan to reach those goals is equally essential. As Ted Engstrom says: "Plans are the vehicles that carry out our goals."[26] After assessing where we are, we must decide how we are going to be able to get from here to wherever we have determined we should be after a year. Perhaps the best method of developing a workable plan, however, is to begin where we want to be, and then to work backwards by steps to where we are. This helps us to assure that we have allowed ample lead time for being able to accomplish each step involved.

First we must identify the method we will use to reach each specific goal. There are many methods which probably could be used and which would work, but we must explore the choices available and select the one which we feel will best meet our needs. Until that method is chosen, we will not be able to get off dead center. Again, it is important that there be an agreement on the method chosen by those who will be charged with achieving the goal. It will not work to attempt a task with a division over the method. Nor will it work to choose a method which is felt to be unworkable or which is opposed by those who must use it.

Secondly we must determine what materials, equipment and other resources may be required to implement the chosen method. It is unfair to expect anyone to do a task with inadequate materials or tools. It is also unfair to expect those assigned a job to have to pay for it out of their own pockets. The reasonable costs involved need to be counted, the necessary amount budgeted, and the funds for supplies be made available as needed. It is poor stewardship to tie up these funds and the workers involved by requiring them to go through unwieldy procedures or endless red tape to be able to secure that which is needed to do the job.

26. Engstrom, p. 10.

Thirdly, we must decide who is best qualified to undertake the leadership of this task. When we are talking about the accomplishment of church goals, we are talking about deacons. Remember? They are the implementers—the people we can put in charge and who can make things happen. If a task will only take one qualified person, why saddle him/her with a committee of five? If it is a really big task like the one in the Jerusalem church that required seven, why appoint four? This is where by-laws and board procedures often get in the way of getting jobs done.

Fourthly, once we have decided who is best qualified, before he or she accepts the responsibility, *it is vitally important that everyone involved understands exactly what is being expected of the person.* Job descriptions can be most helpful in avoiding misunderstandings and hurt feelings! They also help the person involved to focus his/her attention directly on the problem, opportunity or task which has been defined. Be specific, rather than general; and remember to identify the time frame in which the task is expected to be completed.

Fifthly, we must establish accountability. To whom will the person(s) assigned the task be accountable? In other words, who has the ultimate responsibility for seeing that the task is completed or the problem solved? To fail to require accountability is to invite neglect and procrastination, in addition to leaving the person(s) without anyone to come to for advice or help. To fail to define accountability also invites interference and harrassment from critics who are able to hinder the accomplishment of the task. Clear lines of accountability help to assure smooth and efficient functioning of leadership.

Sixthly, we must schedule the phases of the plan. Until something is scheduled on the calendar, it will probably never happen. If we do not schedule sufficient lead time to secure materials, get printing and mailing done, or to allow people to plan to attend events we have scheduled, our plans will be doomed to failure. Plan ahead! Mark dates on the master calendar! Make every possible attempt to be prepared and to avoid conflicts in scheduling.

Adequate planning takes a lot of time, much forethought and a maximum effort in coordination. There is no substitute for it, however. Churches and leaders who insist on "winging it" without sufficient plans will occasionally get lucky, but they will generally live with inferior programs, conflicts of schedules, lack of harmony and a constant mixture of panic and discouragement over never being prepared. Perhaps even worse, their goals will seldom be reached.

Working Your Plan

A strategy is of no value unless there is a consensus and a commitment to carry it out on the part of the leadership. Almost any plan that is worked is better than no plan at all—or even the best plan in the world which exists only on paper. Churches which develop a strategy must hold it. It takes time to see results. It takes time to plant a seed and to grow a tree. Some varieties will grow more rapidly than others, but most require a lot of time, patience, care and some occasional pruning before they become what they are intended to be and begin to produce any quantity of fruit.

Second-guessing is a constant problem with church leadership. There are always those who want to reconsider, un-do, re-do or reverse decisions which have been made. There are occasionally good reasons for this. In most cases, however, such second-guessing is guaranteed to undermine any endeavor. If care has been taken in making the decision in the first place, once that decision has been made, it is generally best to run with it. Those who are continually looking back to where they have been will never be able to keep purpose in view or to see the opportunities ahead. Expressive leadership must hold the course.

Church potlucks usually work out well in the food department, but they can be a disaster in the planning department. Many churches will select a tested and proven plan, but they will want to pick and choose the parts of the plan which they are willing to work. This approach neither works with scripture nor with most other plans. It is amazing how many church leaders are then surprised and become upset when the disjointed remnant of the plan they have chosen will not work for them. A similar approach is often taken with consultants who may be brought in to evaluate the situation and to recommend a plan of action. Churches need to be reminded that all of the parts are required to make almost anything function—including plans.

Indecision is probably the greatest problem church leaders face in adopting and working a plan. With the many how-to books now available, the diversity of opinions among leaders, and the scores of seminars, workshops and conventions which can be attended, there is a tremendous amount of indecision over which is the RIGHT plan. Some churches will actually attempt to institute dozens of these plans over a period of years, trying to find the right plan. Many of the ones they initiate will even be philosophically in conflict with one another. Most of the plans are given an insufficient amount of time and support to succeed, and probably any one of them could succeed if given half a chance.

Some years ago Lowell Brown, noted Christian Educator who was then Minister of Christian Education for the large Van Nuys Baptist Church, was speaking at the Bay Area Sunday School Convention in Southern California. He was asked how many of the teachers and leaders from his church were attending the workshops. He replied, "None. I don't want our people confused with new ideas and plans which work somewhere else. We have a plan which works, and we want our people to know it and to work it." He definitely had a point. Their plan worked. To have introduced in other elements probably would have only weakened the total effectiveness of their system.

A lack of willingness to sacrifice comfortability and control is also a major obstacle to churches' being able to work their plans. A great number of plans have been sabotaged because someone recognized he was losing his control over the church. Other plans have been abandoned simply because they required too many changes on the part of the original members. Joe Ellis says:

> Effective congregations are tough-minded in evaluating their efforts and clear-eyed in deciding what to do. They are more concerned with what is *effective* than what they as individuals may *prefer*. They are marked by a willingness to do whatever is necessary, no matter what the cost. In the lives of the individual members, their constant commitment to God's purpose directs their attitudes, motives, thoughts, concerns, lifestyles, behavior, and temperaments. In congregational concerns, commitment to that purpose is the primary consideration for every ambition, plan, decision, and vote. The degree to which the purpose is being accomplished is never far from the minds of the people.[27]

27. Ellis, p. 22.

Any reasonable plan which is worked will likely bring about the accomplishment of the goal desired, but it will also inevitably bring some other essential changes along with it. It is generally these other changes, which were not fully understood or expected, which produce the flak. Members want growth in one sense, but are unwilling to pay the price it requires. C. Peter Wagner lists the costs of growth for a congregation as: (1) Agreeing to follow growth leadership; (2) Paying the money; (3) Readjusting their fellowship groups; and (4) Opening their leadership circles.[28] These, he suggests, are deemed too high a price to pay by many churches. They would like to have growth, but only if it can come without changing anything. That is "Mission Impossible!" Change is the inevitable, inescapable corollary of any growth. Those who refuse to permit such change as may be essential for the church to accomplish its mission need to prayerfully re-examine both their motives for opposing the changes and their relationship to the Lord. Paul admonishes: "Do not cause anyone to stumble, whether Jews, Greeks or the church of God—even as I try to please everybody in every way. For I am not seeking my own good but the good of many, so that they may be saved. Follow my example, as I follow the example of Christ" (I Cor 10:32—11:1).

Expressive leaders must be willing to hold the chosen course in the face of opposition. Continual teaching and encouragement is required to remind both members and leaders of Christ's purpose for the church and the goals which have been adopted. Every possible attempt needs to be

---

28. Wagner, pp. 63-68.

made to keep the harmony of the church while still pressing on toward the goal. Paul wrote: "Be completely humble and gentle; be patient, bearing with one another in love. Make every effort to keep the unity of the Spirit through the bond of peace" (Eph 4:2-3). The context of that passage, however, does not in any way suggest that leadership should sacrifice purpose or goals for the sake of preserving the harmony. Too many leaders make this mistake. As a result, they exchange the church of Christ for a relatively harmonious private Christian club which has decided to write its own more comfortable agenda.

Finally, working a plan requires a tremendous amount of hard work. Plans never work themselves. They must be worked. Nominal commitment of time and effort to any plan is certain to guarantee its failure. Once a plan has been chosen, every available resource must be committed to its accomplishment, and every leader must be willing to lead the way by doing his part, or no one else can be expected to follow. As we have seen, no church can afford to hire enough staff to do its ministry for it. Neither can any church buy a plan which will accomplish its growth for it. Growth is the natural by-product of effective ministry, and effective ministry is always goal-oriented. Paul sums it up for us:

> Not that I have already obtained all this, or have already been made perfect, but I press on to take hold of that for which Christ Jesus took hold of me. Brothers, I do not consider myself yet to have taken hold of it. But one thing I do: Forgetting what is behind and straining toward what is ahead, I press on toward the goal to win the prize for which God has called me heavenward in Christ Jesus (Phil 3:12-14).

In Summary

We have not yet arrived. There is still a need to press on toward the accomplishment of the goal Christ has set for the church. The Restoration Plea of calling all Christians to a unity for the purpose of accomplishing Christ's mission for his church is still valid. The basis of that proposed unity—the restoration of New Testament faith and practice—is still essential. The greatest frontier left to be conquered by the Restoration Movement is the restoration of New Testament church leadership. Without this, the church is destined to decline and to fail in its quest.

That restoration requires: (1) the recognition of Jesus as Lord of His church; (2) the identification of principles of New Testament church leadership, rather than legalistic patterns; (3) an emphasis upon function in leadership, rather than offices; (4) capable ministers to provide expressive leadership; (5) qualified and functioning elders to work in concert with the pastors in expressive leadership; (6) capable and qualified deacons to serve in implementive leadership; (7) the replacement of church boards; and (8) a willingness to follow and support leadership by the congregation.

All change is resisted because it is perceived as loss. Change, however, is the inevitable companion of accomplishment of purpose, and changes must be made in every church. Ample preparation and time to accomplish changes needs to be planned by leaders, with an attempt to help everyone understand the reasons for the changes and the benefits which will be derived from them. As much as possible, it is desirable for everyone to be able to come out as winners, rather than losers or the defeated, when changes are made.

Both the restoration of New Testament leadership and other changes which need to take place in churches require a rediscovery and re-definition of the purpose for the church. When this is clearly in focus, and when the present program and procedures in effect in any church are compared to that statement of purpose, it becomes clear what goals need to be established and changes need to be made. As many members of the church as possible need to be taken through the process of re-defining the purpose of the church in order to facilitate the changes which will be required.

After enumerating all of the programs operative in a church, these should be categorized by major areas of ministry. Once again, they should be compared with the statement of purpose to recognize areas which are particularly weak, and to see where the majority of resources and effort are being concentrated. Minimum five-year specific goals should be established in each of these major areas of ministry which will be consistent with the accomplishment of Christ's mission and expectations for the church, given its unique situation and opportunities. These should each be stepped backwards to determine the goals which must therefore be reached in the first, second, third and fourth years. All of the possible ramifications of these goals should be considered, with provisions being made for the essential supporting goals necessary to be able to accomplish the primary goals. As in the case of re-defining the purpose, these goals then need to be "owned" by the entire congregation, either by having them participate in their development, or by leadership's work in sharing and selling them to the church. To the degree that these goals are owned by the church, to that degree they will be accomplished. Each year a time must be set aside for evaluation and up-dating of these goals.

No goals are achieved without the development of workable plans, for plans are the vehicles which carry out goals.

Effective planning must involve: (1) Selection of the method to be used to achieve each goal; (2) Determination of the materials, equipment, other resources and cost of the plan, and making these available; (3) Choosing the best qualified implementer(s) for the plan; (4) Defining the job description of the implementer; (5) Establishing the necessary lines of accountability; and (6) Scheduling the phases of the plan.

No plan will work itself. Every plan must be worked by the leaders and the church. Leadership must be united and committed to the plan. Second-guessing must not be permitted to undermine the endeavor. Every part of the plan selected must be worked for it to succeed. Indecision about selection of the right plan must be supplanted with some decision to adopt the best plan available at the time and to run with it. Almost any plan is better than no plan. Once a course is chosen, it must be held by the leaders, even in the face of the inevitable opposition from those who will resist the accompanying changes. Leadership must lead in their commitment to work the plan, whatever that requires of them, or the congregation will never do their part. No one should underestimate the amount of hard work any plan will require to succeed.

No church has arrived, nor has any movement. We must continually press on toward the goal before us, that we might take hold of that for which Christ took hold of us (Phil 3:12). Quo vadis? We press on toward the goal!

Index of Scriptures

(I Corinthians)

II Corinthians

(II Corinthians)

Galatians

Ephesians

Philippians

(Philippians)

Colossians

I Thessalonians

Index of Subjects

D

E

K

L

M

Q

R